Around the Kitchen Table

Around *the* *Kitchen Table*

Métis Aunties' Scholarship

Edited by Laura Forsythe
and Jennifer Markides

UNIVERSITY OF MANITOBA PRESS

Around the Kitchen Table: Métis Aunties' Scholarship

28 27 26 25 24 1 2 3 4 5

University of Manitoba Press
Winnipeg, Manitoba, Canada
Treaty 1 Territory
uofmpress.ca

Cataloguing data available from Library and Archives Canada
ISBN 978-1-77284-073-5 (PAPER)
ISBN 978-1-77284-074-2 (PDF)
ISBN 978-1-77284-075-9 (EPUB)
ISBN 978-1-77284-076-6 (BOUND)

Cover art Nicki Ferland, *Her Roots Go Deep*.
Cover design by Vincent Design
Interior design by Karen Armstrong

Printed in Canada

This book has been published with the help of a grant from the Federation for the Humanities and Social Sciences, through the Awards to Scholarly Publications Program, using funds provided by the Social Sciences and Humanities Research Council of Canada.

Funded by the Government of Canada | Canadä

CONTENTS

FOREWORD

Caroline Tait

Rock Picker

I pick rocks
Rocks of all shapes and sizes
Inviting them to live at the place I call home
Rocks are our grandmothers
Beautiful, ancient, strong and resilient
Rocks speak their own language,
Life of a different nature
Of defiant tender spirits
Whispering the stories of the past
Holding the truths of the land
Rock picking is peaceful work

Three days of rain shaped the foreword for this book. I started the fire, made some tea, crawled under a big blanket, and read the works of my sisters and aunties. The deer came to visit as they do each day, their coats turning grey as winter approaches. The rain played with the snow and finally after three days the sun came out.

Around the Kitchen Table: Métis Aunties' Scholarship is grounded in the love, respect, and determination of Métis women to support one another. Through storytelling, poetry, and Métis methodologies and analyses emerge chapter gifts that tell the stories of generational resilience, recovery, reclaiming, and renewal. As I read, I mused how the voices of Métis women are like the weather, inspired and moved by multiple factors. Some of these bring forth our warmth and generosity while other forces that choose to beat us down are met with fierce resistance. In our resistance Métis women are as forceful as the most powerful hurricane or tornado. We have a collective reputation that is well earned, demands to be respected, and is not to be trifled with. Even though at times we acquiesce, hiding behind academic or "objective" language is not true to our nature; we like to tell it as it is.

The chapters gifted in this edited volume are woven together like the weave of the Métis sash. Beautiful, colourful, and captivating, together recounting the stories of Métis women, our families, and the history of our people. Who knows the Métis people? asks Dr. Emma LaRocque in her chapter, "For the Love of Place—Not Just Any Place." Her question directs the reader's gaze to the everyday life of Métis people, to where we cook, clean, and visit. We are not Indigenous caricatures of the colonial settler imaginary. We are Métis people who do everyday things, who over generations weathered many storms but nevertheless live meaningful and purposeful lives that we are proud of.

For our families, the kitchen table is the place where we discuss and debate, laugh and tease, share our anger and cry our tears. It only makes sense that this is where Métis women find themselves doing research. For Métis researchers, research is visiting and as visitors we show our deepest respect. We bring gifts of tobacco, tea, cloth, honey, and jam. We open up and share our family stories alongside those who share with us. We listen and learn with a good heart. Our gratitude is unquestionable, and our humility is our invitation to return. This is sacred space, not objectified practice.

Kitchen table or sewing circle methodology is, as described by the authors, more than conversation or qualitative research. It is us being us and the formalities of Western research remain in the background, a necessary evil, so to speak, that we hope will not interrupt the natural flow of visiting. The visit involves a journey, kindling new and old relationships with our people, land, and ancestors. Wahkootowin (wahkohtowin), our relationality, is fundamental to the weave of our methodologies and our writing. The gifted chapters reinforce the importance of Wahkootowin as a fundamental Métis ethos from which as children we grew to be respectful, to listen to the old people, to be in and of community, and to stick with one another through whatever adversity comes our way. The kitchen table is the meeting place of our people, where we feel most at home, where we visit about the everyday ups and downs of life. Where our stories are shared.

I remind people that most Métis who subjectively see themselves as being Indigenous did not do so before the Royal Commission on Aboriginal Peoples in the 1990s. I remember first hearing the term Aboriginal when it was used in a community context at the Native Friendship Centre of Montreal (NFCM). At the time I was a university student living in Montreal and a NFCM board member. As calls for community projects rolled out after the release of the Commission's final report, the NFCM and other potential funding recipients adjusted their language to the new term, *Aboriginal*. Up to this point, my identity was solely Métis with an uncomfortable relationship to the term Native. Even though my father spoke about our Cree Métis roots, my family were not First Nations. My mother, a tough settler woman, tirelessly worked with my father for our family, and as such our identity as a family felt seamless in the wake of the everyday challenges of life. We stayed close to home, family, and community and we thrived in ways that are almost unrecognizable in the consumption-driven cash economy of today.

As the term Aboriginal and later Indigenous took hold in government and institutional circles, so did a new hierarchy of Indigenous identity. There are many good things about a shared Indigenous identity; however, in circumstances where governments and other resources are scaled back and access to positions of power and influence curtailed for Indigenous people, Métis people are commonly the first to have their identities challenged and their contributions overlooked. Métis resistance to a pan-Indigenous identity is reflected in the following chapters, with many of the authors pointing out that identity resides in local relational family and community contexts and not in master narratives of trauma and landlessness inappropriately attributed to all Métis people. The intersectionality and complexity of identity are brought forward, as the authors push back against dominating societal narratives of motherhood, gender identity, and perceptions that Métis and other Indigenous people do not belong in urban nor academic spaces.

As with many in Canada, Métis people are angry about the "pretendian" phenomenon, but as is our nature we cannot help but laugh about it too; no one wanted to be us until there were jobs and power! As Dr. Lynn Lavallee describes, the pretendian phenomenon and our society's reaction to it amounts to yet another colonial assault that effectively divides and hurts us all. Despite being a problem inflicted by non-Indigenous actors, pretendian fraud has been laid at the feet of Indigenous people as our collective identities are stolen and our individuals' identities questioned and surveilled and our rights breached. Indigenous communities are divided by the issue; pretendians continue to pretend and academic and government institutions pretend they know how to address the problem. We are truly in a conundrum with no clear road map out.

The work of Métis women has always been about family and community. As we solidify our respective places within present-day society, within our careers, we are positioned to conceive of community within these spaces also. This edited volume is a community of Métis scholars who have, as Dr. Jennifer Markides states in her Introduction, come together "to uncover the beads of our shared histories, address the gaps in the Métis literature, recognize and celebrate our matriarchs, show reverence for our kitchen table pedagogies, and reimagine our relationships with land as a place that is known in our histories and hearts." Working in liminal spaces between our communities and the institutions who employ us, is challenging and demanding work for which we need a community of our kind. Our institutions and even at times our own Métis people take great liberties, some times to our detriment, to define who we are, casting us as the proverbial insider/outsider. The wear and tear of the context in which we seek meaningful careers in service to our people is real, with the deep-seated patriarchy of Western society infiltrating both academic and Métis circles of power and influence. I have yet to meet a female Métis academic who is not pushing a big rock up a hill because she is Métis and a woman. However, what this collection teaches us is that our ancestors, grandmothers, and aunties are strong and resilient, we can speak up with confidence and authority, and we must honour and value our individual and collective truths. We are a community of our own kind.

I began this foreword with a small gift, a poem from an auntie. I link us back to the land, to a relationship that is quiet and serene, where we connect to spirit that is, as described by the authors, not a romanticized version of identity but rather one of ancestral connection and peace. I personally choose to jump in my pickup truck and go rock picking. I seek out the solitude of the land, listening to the sounds that float on the wind, smiling when catching a glimpse of a critter or two going about their everyday life. Rock picking is peaceful work, it is what completes the circle in my everyday busy life, and its purpose and meaning are the gift I return to my sisters and aunties who have gifted these chapters to us.

Around the Kitchen Table

The Work of Métis Women: An Introduction

Jennifer Markides

In this opening, it would be easy to focus on the ways the hegemonic and paternalistic legacies of colonization have occluded the stories of Indigenous Peoples, and in particular Indigenous women, from prominence in life and from the pages of Canadian history for hundreds of years. From our very beginnings in Red River to the days of road allowances, scrip, and beyond, Métis people have been marginalized, displaced, and discounted. Documentation of our people has focused on the stories of men—fur traders, rebels, and leaders—with women assumed to be in the background of our societies. However, we know our stories differently than they have been told. Strong Métis women, inclusive of two-spirit kin, have shaped our communities, culture, and identities with agency.

Perhaps usefully or stubbornly, this introduction serves as a touchstone or route marker for what is ahead and does not include a literature review or standard citations. Instead, the entirety of the book is the source of inspiration and the wellspring of scholarship that has informed these first passages. *Why bend to academic conventions? Rebellious blood flows through these veins.* As a point of process, this opening reflects dwelling with the chapters—listening and learning, gathering, and then listening again until the individual ideas and sensory stimuli fade into an abundantly satisfying cacophonic experience. Like saskatoon berries bursting in your mouth, after having stained your hands. In theory, you should feel the presence of the authors and their stories if you were to reread this setting again at the end. Their voices—ideas, teachings, discoveries, witticisms, inspirations, suggestions, influences, and rich descriptions—mingling, indistinguishable from each other, pleasantly so. A community of Métis thought.

In walking the Red River path, we bring this collection together so that the generations of Métis who come after will have a well-tended trail to travel. For many Métis, the consequences of colonization have included both temporal and physical displacement from identity and community. Fortunately, this has not been the experience of all Métis. Those who have maintained cultural and community connections generously support the reclamation of kinship relations through knowledge sharing. Learning our stories, histories, language, and cultural practices are ways Métis foster individual and collective identities. Teachers come in many forms, including our Métis family and community members, archives, scrip and census documents, cultural artifacts, kokums, Elders, academic aunties, peers, and the land.

While some Métis might still be searching for clues to identity, culture, and belonging, the gathering of our stories and practices is well underway. The Métis intellectuals whose work is shared in this book have researched to uncover the beads of our shared histories, addressed the gaps in Métis literature, recognized and celebrated our matriarchs, shown reverence for our kitchen table pedagogies, and reimagined our relationships with land as a place that is known in our histories and hearts. They have moved beyond the oft-heard narratives of Métis being a displaced people, to a discourse of Métis as relationally situated and deeply rooted. The contributions exemplify Métis scholars' assertions of epistemological self-determination.

Métis have maintained robust relationships to values and ways of being that are distinctly ours. As a matrilineal society, our matriarchs have been the leaders, role models, mentors, mothers, aunties, grandmothers, sisters, and cousins. Many of them have resisted the assimilatory efforts of colonization; relocated geographically but remained steadfast in Métis ways; reclaimed our stolen, lost, and wandering kin in warm embraces of education, responsibility, and love; retained our Michif language in the numerous dialects and variations; maintained strong bonds across religious and other differences; and sewed the sinew that has bound us together in culture and place—beads set with intention—connected in powerful dynamisms with purpose and pride.

Picking up the connective threads, you will find that the Michif language is embedded within many of the chapters in this text. Spelling of words varies across communities but often holds the same or similar meaning, as in the case of the term of Cree origin: *wahkotowin*, *wakotowin*, *wahkohtowin*, *wahkootowin*, which signifies our being in relationship to one another and holds us accountable to our kinship relations. These are not spelling mistakes, and we do not seek to unify the book with common capitalization, hyphenation, italicization, or version of shared words. Like our matriarchs have modelled, we embrace these differences.

Other strands woven through many of the chapters include references to the work of Maria Campbell, Brenda Macdougall, Marilyn Dumont, Gregory Scofield, and Sherry Farrell Racette, to name a few. Some authors reference other contributors to the book, including Emma LaRocque, Vicki Bouvier, and Nicki Ferland. As Laura Forsythe's chapter highlights, being able to cite Métis people when researching Métis-related topics has only recently become possible.

Evidenced throughout the pages that follow, Métis are resilient, resourceful, creative, and courageous. We have been taught to be flexible, hard-working, and supportive of one another. We learn from listening, observing, helping, and doing. With beading, sewing, preparing meals, tending to children, telling stories, and sharing our gifts, there is no time to be idle.

We invite you to join us, from across the homelands, to listen with your heart, body, mind, and spirit—open these channels with senses heightened. Hear the unmistakable heartbeat of the Métis fiddle music and the pounding of moccasins on the wooden floor. Taste the meats, berries, and teas around the kitchen tables. Smell the wood-burning fires, hand-picked medicines drying on rafters overhead or smouldering in healing ceremonies, and the ancient soil being unearthed to reveal a blue bead that will transport you in time and place. See the patchwork of rag rugs and scrap quilts, the colours of the Métis ribbon skirts and ornately beaded moss bags. Witness the stories told through beads purposefully placed in intricate forms as teachings handed down.

Learn alongside Elders, friends, sisters, aunties, and cousins.

This book stands as a testament and tribute to the strength of the Métis/Michif matriarchs who have come before us and is a gift for the future generations we hope to teach, mentor, reclaim, walk alongside, and inspire. May we honour the tireless work of Métis women and take up our places as leaders, educators, mothers, and storytellers who remain committed to upholding our language, culture, place, and sovereignty. Towards a good life.

Part One:

Identity

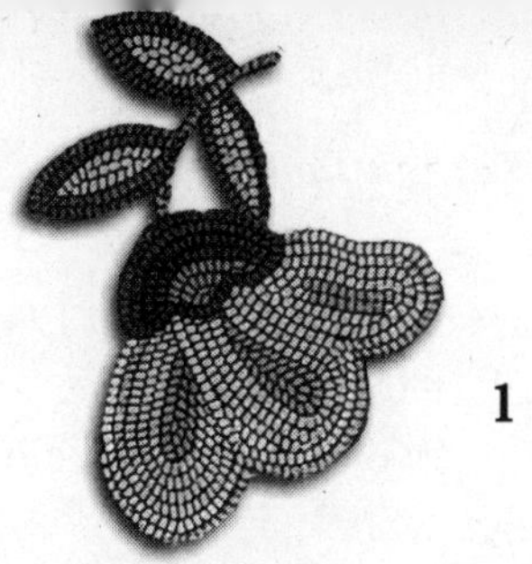

1

Brown Names

Marilyn Dumont

> *Memory is a cemetery*
> *I've visited once or twice, white*
> *ubiquitous and the set aside*
> *Everywhere underfoot*
>
> Charles Wright, "Meditation on Form and Measure"

Ubiquitous walks through me regularly
down streets named Whyte, Grierson, or Jasper
reiterating my absence, I wonder
why this bluff overlooking the North Saskatchewan was envisioned
as brickworks, smokestacks, and glass mills?
When amiskwaciwaskahikan floated in prairie grass
so high, you used a compass to cross it
after a two-month cart ride from Winnipeg
when Karakonti, Calliou, Papaschase, Bobtail, and Atkahkoop gathered on the river flats
long before Oliver, Grierson, or Strathcona—their names barbed-wire reminders

sewn to the Imperial centre, ignore any glimpse of Lapotac,
the fort's hunter flinting chert for deer-hunting arrows
before this city constructed a myth of steel bridges, concrete
stories of "settlement" and "pioneers."

Ubiquitous rarely owns the brown memory of a Métis
great-grandmother, a Cree Iroquois Mohawk Nakoda or
Blackfoot chapan, the Carlton-trail-cart-driving relatives,
the third cousin twice removed in St. Albert, the HBC pay-
master, or the Orkney York boat building side of the family

Ubiquitous knows that exile is space without language to
speak of it

that alienation is a wall only you can see

One Pound One, Big Mountain, Iron Shirt
for Lisette Umfreville

I have crossed this river countless times she thought her unchained self-slipping into updrafts and down turning dreams; name it an itch or an urge; she reached out—her mind in search of a young clerk, his horse returned without him. Who knows what this Métis woman, camped on the tabled- North Saskatchewan River flats, envisioned when the rotund Rowand said, "Tansi" to her fat dowry of horses? He alone went hunting that day the horse reared whipping its backbone into a figure eight, before throwing his Big Mountain—300 lbs—too much for any dumb limb onto the prairie. His leg snapping under the weight of his ambition to rise from good clerk to Czar of the Prairies—where she'd eventually take him—her conveyor belt of relatives delivering pelts right to his front door. Why search for Big Mountain, this Iron Shirt? This foreign man who could out-work 'n swear any man she'd known. What picture of herself did she see in him that day she emerged from her tent to meet his eyes. The days when a fur trade monopoly made both their choices. What seduced her? Him? Or his horse?

Note: One Pound One, Big Mountain, and Iron Shirt were Chief
Factor Rowand's nicknames

Victoria's jig

Victoria Calihoo enters a jigging contest on her hundredth birthday
lining up with girls in stiff crinolines and women with child-rearing legs
she in high-top moccasins, patched dress and hide skinning muscle
take the dance floor
the attention of onlookers converging
on her tiny gray frame alone at the centre
her toes at attention, waiting to spring
to the fiddler's bow, swept along
strumming guitar stitching her feet to strings bending,
the hem of her dress bouncing
onlookers gasping at her feet exacting swift step changes
weightless and nimble she skim-shuffles in the fiddler's trance
her young face shining through her smile, bouncing off the surprised
faces of the child-reading women, the deflated crinolines of girls leaning in disappointment
as Victoria takes first place.

She shone copper

Lizette didn't reflect her husband, Czar of the Prairies
she shone copper in her own image
blue-black hair and cinnamon skin
she gleamed babies through her belly button

a midwife envisioning awasisak in the arms of   babies
Nikawiy, Nimama   mother, mother

nimama
belly cello
bounces circular
rounding

his Fort, your house,
Shining Star—
calculator of beaver pelts and barley
Lac Ste Anne whitefish
North Saskatchewan sturgeon
Pemmican and timid clerks

Lizette a herder of star sisters and horses
a ripe dowry
for a randy Scotsman

her horses windswept
she launches skyward
maneuvers her team of Clydesdales airborne

a teamster winching skyward
proud horse-collars lifting
horseheads straining
fetlocks lofting in their air strides
jingling tack and hooves sculling
the up drafting winds
over the kissaskatchewansipiy   Saskatchewan river

she steers her mother craft south
pulled to her relatives

sweeping over the Grierson Dump
waving to the halfbreeds below
then over the steep banks and swift river
setting down again
striking hooves meeting the ground again near the
Metis squared timbered cabins lining the south bank of Metis Strathcona

Imagines soaring over clerk's heads
passed out, snoring in the bunkhouses
she shows up copper in their dreams

afraid and green they toss in their sleep

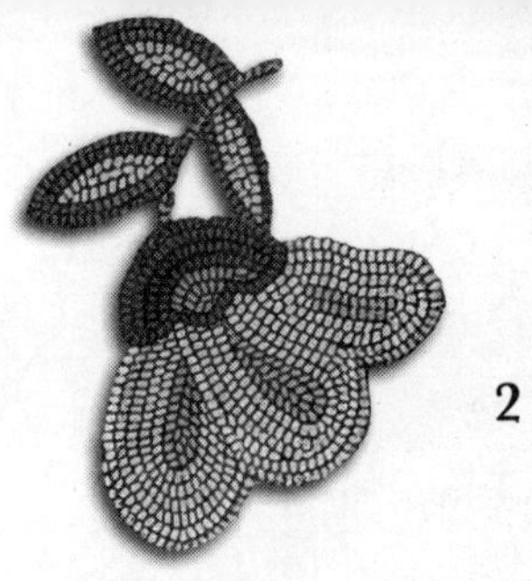

2

We Know Ourselves

Lisa Shepherd

We know who we are. Métis people know ourselves. We can look through a crowd and see each other. When we rendezvous, we share stories about our history, where we come from, and how we connect to each other. We tell about our Ancestors who defended our communities and raised babies under incredibly challenging circumstances.

I say, "my 3x great-grandpa was Cuthbert Grant," and, "My great-great-grandma Grant was a teamster who operated the ferry across the North Saskatchewan River, taking over the business after her husband passed away."

Go to any Métis gathering, and you will hear stories like these. You will hear that we know ourselves. We are enough, and not fractions or percentages. That was a construct meant to disappear us, and I won't even take a sip from that juice. We are whole people with significant and complex histories, living in the here and now, and we continue to contribute to the growth of this country.

I remember when I was teaching jigging to Mrs. Giroux's granddaughter. I asked Mrs. Giroux if she had her citizenship card. She sternly told me, "I don't need a card to tell me who I am. I know who I am." It was her act of defiance against a government that actively worked to assimilate us, and now wants us to carry cards to qualify us as "enough" to be Métis. I remember overhearing her talking to someone about me, and she said, "Lisa knows who she is. She knows our people and where we come from." Coming from Mrs. Giroux, it was the biggest compliment.

Yes. We know who we are. Our identity is intact. It is Canada that is missing its identity. I say this because so many Canadians don't know where the country came from, and they don't know us. I won't get into the history of the Métis and our enormous role in forming Canada as we know it today. There are many Métis historians with storytelling gifts who have written books. There is no shortage of Métis books written by Métis authors. I will say that our Ancestors were there at the beginning of the formation of this country and sacrificed everything for its growth. Yet, when I speak to non-Métis audiences, too many still don't know us. There is no excuse for this lack of reciprocity. It's lazy, and it's convenient.

To my own Métis people, I hope you see yourself in my beadwork, and it stirs you to dig deeper. To go beyond that which you can learn online. There is teaching that comes from standing on the land and spending time with Old Ones, the kêhtê ayak. And not just the one or two Old People whom everyone seeks out, but all the ones in your family and your community, because every single one has a story that paints a part of a bigger picture. They have lived experiences, lifetimes of them, with lessons to help us to better know ourselves. The knowledge they share stays with us for always. We will have it forever, and I hope we carry it and share it responsibly.

There is an attitude that I've been witnessing recently. It comes from the idea that knowledge is meant to be shared. Yes, I believe it is. I also believe, however, that it is to be shared responsibly. I will tell you that every time I have been told by someone that I am "supposed to share" with them, it has come from someone with a sense of entitlement, and I don't believe they will carry it responsibly. We do get to pick and choose whom we share knowledge with. It has always been this way. The Old Ones look for the younger ones whom they see working hard and digging deep within themselves. They entrust them to carry knowledge thoughtfully and authentically.

My nohkôm, Maria Campbell, taught me that, as a beadwork artist, I have a responsibility in how I carry knowledge. A long time ago, her Cheechum and her Old Elder Peter O'Chiese taught her the same thing. Responsibility is one of our foundational teachings. Yet, I hear talk about our rights—land rights, and rights to self-governance—but I don't hear enough talk about our responsibility. We have a responsibility to the land, to the animals, to the plants, to the water, to our families, and to all of creation. We also have a responsibility to the next seven generations in how we carry knowledge so that they still authentically know the culture. I am responsible to my child and future grandchildren, so I take that responsibility seriously.

I don't say this to dissuade anyone from seeking to learn. Not at all. Quite the opposite. I say it to encourage deeper thinking about knowledge's importance so that we gather it respectfully. It is our university. If we just throw it about, or we can buy our way in, without giving it the time, respect, and love that it deserves, then we will risk losing what defines us as a distinct culture and people.

Sometimes I worry that we have moved fast forward into a digital world where information comes too quickly. I suppose it might be a good jumping-off point, but social media is not always safe. People can get hurt there, listening to the opinions of others that they've not vetted. It also makes it possible to gather information in a surface learning way, in which lines are blurred, and that which has always made us distinct becomes pan-Indigenized, appropriated, and even colonized. Perhaps this is because this sort of knowledge harvesting is taking too much from everywhere, instead of stepping gently and with a grateful heart. Perhaps it's because the right place to start searching is from within.

The truth is, all that we need to know is already within us. It's in our DNA. If we listen to the Old People, we will recognize our own stories in theirs. Our stories are a part of us—just as important as our lungs, mind, and heart are to keeping us well. "Knowing" comes to each of us from within, where our inner self safely holds it until we are ready to look at it fully, lovingly, and without judgment.

I'm a beadwork artist. Not a doctor or a lawyer, and certainly not a politician. I do, however, believe beadwork to be healing. It makes us visible. It reclaims our history and culture. It rematriates our story, as well as our path forward. If the beads I stitch down grab your eyes and inspire you to look inward to where your own story lies, I am grateful to the beads. If the thread that connects the beads reaches back in time and helps you, in any small way, to travel to your own knowing, then I am grateful to the thread that connects us like an umbilical cord to our Ancestral knowledge. In any case, I am fulfilled and grateful to do this work.

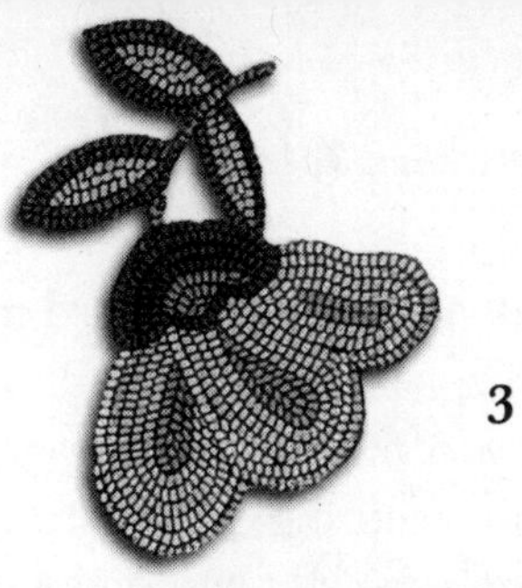

3

Kaa-waakohtoochik: The Ones Who Are Related to Each Other

Vicki Bouvier

Stories that reflect people's worldview, historicity, practices, and mobilizations are profoundly important in solidifying and validating people's identity and self-understandings.[1] Stories can allow people, as individuals and communities, to navigate relationships, with themselves and others, in healthy and nurturing ways. As an urban-dwelling Michif,[2] I have experienced people's ignorance in understanding who I am and find them often perplexed when I explain that I have my own culture, history, and language. This ignorance is connected to the belief that Métis are "just" mixed-blood people; we are misrecognized and seen for not having a historicity that created a distinct, albeit diverse, People.[3] Due to these misconceptions, my own stories have been dismissed or not provided the dedicated space they deserve. This frustration grew, specifically through my undergraduate degree in International Indigenous Studies, where I saw and experienced a large gap in literature and research by Métis people detailing our own histories and experiences.

In 2016, I completed my master's thesis, "Re-storying Métis Spirit: Honouring Lived Experiences," where I came to understand that there are distinct ways in which Métis individuals, born in rural environments, understand their identity through language, kinship, land, racism, and survival. However, as a Michif woman who grew up miles away from my Métis ancestral homeland in the city of Calgary, Alberta, my understandings have developed in ways that differ from my ancestors. Recognizing this differentiation provoked my doctoral research—an inquiry into and with Métis understandings with/in/through the city to understand everyday practices of Métisness. I strived to understand how individuals were practising their Métisness in their everyday lived experiences. My inquiry sought wisdoms, birthed from personal experiences, of other Métis kin, born and raised in the city, to give voice to our practical lifeways that are informed by both our ancestral knowledges and our urban stories.

Trying to understand ourselves in a seemingly new and changing environment—the urban landscape—is particularly important for future generations of Métis to be able to know who they are so they can live well and flourish *as Métis*. I know we have stories; we embody stories, we are the stories, yet we need to continue to gather together and share who we are and how we are interacting with all our relations with/in these environments. Understanding how we are *kaakiihtwaamaan itootamihk waapamishoon aan wiichaytoowuk*[4] with/in cities is crucial to the ever complex and nuanced processes of becoming Métis. I am continually inspired and encouraged each day by the practice of ourselves in relationship(s).

Each moment of the inquiry, I was influenced by the stories, experiences, and energy. The quest for understanding set truthing at the centre, wherein we come to a place of reconciling oneself to ourselves,[5] with hopes that we will continue in such a way as to *miyo pimatisiwin*—live a good life. This work contributes to the growing scholarship of Métis studies while also offering to people, who may connect and be inspired, to "see" the practices in their own lives and to carry those on for future generations. This chapter gives voice to everyday practices that signify Métis people are alive and well—we are here, and we have every right to belong; we have something irreplaceable and vital to contribute to being human.

I am indebted to the co-researchers who created a space in their lives and experiences for me to come to an understanding of Métis experiences in/with/through the city. In the process of the inquiry, moments arrived to greet me where my heart was pierced with an experience, a phrase, or an interaction. In these moments, I was offered a wisdom, a guiding light, to discern a way forward, a direction to orientate myself. This chapter offers the reader wisdoms that were gifted to me during my doctoral inquiry. I will begin by discussing, briefly, the methodology of wisdom seeking and truthing, and then I will offer three wisdoms: the importance of practice, the practice of telling our stories, and understanding ourselves as the ones who are related to each other.

Wisdom Seeking

Wisdom seeking is a process generated from experiential knowledge in pursuit of an understanding, or a wisdom specific to a question(s).[6] The process is governed by Indigenous paradigms specified by language and cultural knowledge that flow from dynamic kinships within a certain locale. Born and raised in Calgary, living in the land of the *niitsitapi* (Blackfoot people), as Michif, I understand that being a good "visitor," a good relative, is to honour the customs and ways of the people on whose land I reside. My wisdom seeking engaged the theories and practices of an oral system, guided by Piikani (Blackfoot) Elder Dr. Reg Crowshoe through smudge and ceremony.

Elder Crowshoe has taught me that, "in an oral model of learning there is always a mandate, or a question, that guides the circle, that guides the purpose of the circle."[7] The inquiry moved through and was held accountable to three questions: How do Métis individuals, born and raised in urban environments, affirm and express their Métis self-understandings in the city? How do our self-understandings situate within a collective? How do they contribute to individual and collective well-being? Being Métis, sadly, has become contested terrain because so many, unbelonging to the cultural milieu, employ it outside its rightful context on too many occasions. In the present study, Métis is an individual who self-identifies as Métis, has grown up knowing they were Métis, and is connected to a historical Métis community, which is held and bound to distinct linguistic, political, socio-economic, and kinship convergences that herald specific lifeways.

Wisdoms that arise from the wisdom-seeking process flow from relationships;[8] they commingle together in the spaces of shared dialogue, and they too, commingle even off the page; they interact and are in relation to one another. Wisdoms help us to understand our experiences, to discern how to *miyo pimatisiwin*—live a good life. Stories are in and of themselves beings; they are their own perspective.[9] Recognizing wisdoms from stories prompts one to see all entities within a circle of universal relationships. In a previous article, I articulate this as "*ni kaakiihtwaamaan itootamihk waapamishoon aan mii wiichaytoowuk* 'I am practice reflected in relationships'. . . [which] means that all my interactions are alive, with beings, and provide understandings within specific contexts."[10] *kaakiihtwaamaan itootamihk waapamishoon aan wiichaytoowuk* (as plural) expresses that we, each of us, are practice reflected in relationships. The contexts in which we practise are cyclical, they spiral from the self, and circle to include the family, community, earth, cosmos, and Creation (Graveline). This circular, relational understanding provides the pattern for placing the wisdoms in symbiotic and connected relationships.

Within my study, we enacted wisdom seeking through an iterative process with six gatherings over the span of six months. The research collective included six Métis folks in addition to me, two Michif Elders, and two Blackfoot Elders. For each gathering, Métis individuals would capture photographs of particular moments of their lived experiences that stood out for them as Métis practice in the city. In unison with the photos, the individuals recorded a video of themselves explaining why that particular moment was captured and how it related to the inquiry. At each gathering, the collective would gather and discuss the photos and videos that were taken over the course of the month as a way of both individual and collective truthing.

aachimooshtowihk: Truthing

An oral system is parallel to a written knowledge system in that both have theories, values, processes, practices, assessments, and ethical commitments in order to understand, generate, renew, and validate knowledge. The differentiation is seen within the worldview that animates each system and gives life to the processes and practices. Within an oral system, the circle is enlivened and protected by smudge; smudge is both a call to convene and a process of knowledge validation. The smudge is our first acknowledgement of ourselves in relationship. Smudge signifies the ethic of "*ikkimmapiiyipitsiin*[11] ['sanctified kindness'] . . . we are obliged to honour the life of all beings."[12] This acknowledgement actuates that entities in the circle are equal and contribute to dynamism of the whole. This ethic is important in wisdom seeking, as it positions relationships as the landscape of understanding.

When asked to interpret the concept of truth from his Piikani perceptive, Elder Crowshoe translated the meaning, "*omanii*—meaning 'real spirit talk' which invokes a sense of responsibility to be truthful."[13]

In asking a Métis Elder, she understood truth from her Michif perspective as "*tapwe*, meaning 'inner truth,' a truth or knowing from within which is connected to your spirit."[14] Through these definitions and teachings from the Elders, "it was clear that truth is a *process* that is connected to spirit. Truth is an ontological process—an enactment in which we live out every day of our lives."[15] The Michif word that can give further contextualization is *aachimooshtowihk,* meaning sharing one's declaration, or truth, with others. *aachimooshtowihk* signals a process of coming together to share one's truth as to inform or direct others; this is truthing.

aachimooshtowihk, is enacted with the smudge. When you are with the smudge, telling your story, there is an individual obligation to be truthful with your word. Additionally, with the smudge, because we are speaking to all of Creation, we are responsible to the words we speak, and they indeed are powerful. It is important to understand that the truthing process is a shared experience—it is inherently collective and relational.[16] The smudge and the collective telling are key in the validation of stories because we need each other to bear witness. As my Métis kin shared their stories with me, and each other, I became part of their story. Thus, they were not only responsible for telling the truth, but I was also responsible for carrying their stories with respect and to discern what I was supposed to learn. I was presented with many wisdoms during my inquiry. However, I offer here only a few that have altered and gifted me with nourishment to better understand becoming Métis.

Wisdom: *Itootamihk* (Practice)

One of the initial wisdoms came from the humbling realization that the basis of my inquiry was disconcerting for some. The word practice mobilized my research question and was the locus of the inquiry. I was naively eager to dive into dialogue with other Métis, also born and raised in the city, to hear about their own practices as Métis. When I first began thinking about and conceptualizing the inquiry, I assumed that individuals who would join the research would, from the onset, have stories to share about their practices. I did not consider that I had been thinking and reflecting on this as part of my research for a few years; therefore, I had pre-emptively been too enthusiastic in my expectations. From the first gathering, I noticed that the research question, and more specifically the term practice, was a source of insecurity for some individuals. As we sat together during the first gathering, sharing our family kinship lines, meeting "new" relatives, I appraised that honing in on our practices may be a new conversation for people. Over the first month of the inquiry, I recognized that not everyone openly practises, is aware that they are practising, or is cognizant of what practices are Métis. Moreover, because we're moving through the systematic impacts of colonization, layered with some being taught it has not been acceptable to be Métis, people were somewhat stumped when I asked them to tell me how they practise their Métisness. Many vocalized that they had not thought about it before, and more specifically, that it was the acute mundane acts of their everyday lives that seemed difficult to pinpoint. Some people had a hard time bringing themselves into the conversation because they were taught, or their ancestors modelled, shame in being Métis. One participant, Patricia, commented that her hesitancy arose from her worry that she might be practising Métisness in the wrong way; this sentiment was affirmed by other kin in our circle. The conversation led to the essentialized notions of Métisness, specifically—the sash and jigging. These enactments are practices of Métisness but are not the only ones. A deeper and nuanced repertoire of how we enact ourselves in spaces and places as to indicate the multi-faceted process of becoming Métis is needed.

Practice, or what Métis Elder Elmer Ghostkeeper may deem as ritual, "is the repeated patterns of Métis behaviour, created by ideas, beliefs, values, feelings, etc., using the aspects of their mind and emotion, in order to make a living."[17] The Michif word for practice is *itootamihk* which I understand to mean "repeatedly doing." This aligns with Elder Ghostkeeper's notion of ritual. What we do day-to-day, how we live our lives, are often implicit, our practices may be invisible to us, or perhaps we have not taken the time to consider *how* we live our lives *as Métis*; the *how* is essential. Understanding who we are is a consistent process of becoming, never static. Becoming Métis is generative, operative, and relational;[18] our attention needs to be attuned to *what is alive in our experiences*. This inquiry became a process of making living experiences explicit, exposing how we move through the world in specific ways and how we are connected to "living lineage."[19] Here, I do not wish to conflate the term practice to induce that anyone can suddenly become Métis through practising a certain cultural ethos. What I am suggesting, as have other Métis scholars,[20] is that our practices are inherently tethered to existing communities, thus we have inherited a "living lineage" that has been continuous through generations. Making practices explicit will help us build our repertoire of the beautiful tapestry of Métis lifeways. Practice needs us to remember where we have come from, what we carry within us, while simultaneously living our own experiences.

The more we understand ourselves as Métis through our practices, the more we can illuminate the aliveness of our experiences, thus provoking a capacity for *miyo pimatisiwin*—a good life. Coming into the inquiry, I already knew that many Métis, in cities, are living good lives, and it's these stories that need to be told! I also knew that I needed to tap into the rhythmic movements of practice that are conjoined with worldview in order to know what *miyo pimatisiwin* requires. The rhythms of our movements, our practices, are much like pulses, wherein there is a frequency over time.[21] Henri Lefebvre, in his theorizing about rhythmanalysis, aligns with Ghostkeeper's ritual in that practices need to be repetitive; they need to be consistent to be "measured."[22] However, "our sensations and perceptions, in fully and continuous appearances, contain repetitive figures, concealing them . . . we contain ourselves by concealing the diversity of our rhythms"; the mundanity of our practices conceals them from being visible; therefore, opportunities to explicate, with others, is crucial to expose the "diversity of our rhythms."[23] Strong and consistent frequencies are needed to ensure that our practices endure and are continuous through generations. At times, the pulse of our practices that carry our cultural knowledge and understanding has been faint, yet not absent; they are still there.

Wisdom: Soul Atrophy—Practising Telling Our Stories

Practising Telling Our Stories

We have been forced by colonizing logics and tactics, sometimes overtly and other times covertly, to put down our knowledge, language, and practices to assimilate into the colonial system.[24] "Putting down" can manifest in different ways for different Métis people and communities. Michif Elder Maria Campbell discussed the act of putting down our stories and our language because of colonial strategies; she stresses that we never did "lose" our language or our stories; we were forced to put them down to serve the colonizers, never to serve ourselves.[25] I have been extremely fortunate to be raised as Michif, to have a connection to

Boggy Creek, Manitoba, and to have relationships within the Calgary Métis community. I understand that many Métis do not have these experiences because their ancestors either chose or were forced to put down who they were for varying reasons. I often hear from fellow Métis that their familial ancestral stories were never told—this is synonymous with putting down or setting down who we are. Unfortunately, at that time, our relatives thought that it *was* serving us. As my Auntie Mary discusses in my master's thesis, she thought in the 1950s that not teaching her children Michif would only benefit them because teaching them hindered their success in society.[26] But now, decades later, she regrets not teaching them. When Maria Campbell spoke about this, I was brought back to my doctoral inquiry, to the stories that my Métis kin shared with me during our gatherings. From the onset, it was strikingly apparent that many of those in our circle, and their families, had put down their stories.

The wisdom, *practising telling our stories*, came to me during the first gathering. As we came together and began getting to know each other, comments reverberated, pointing to the importance of providing a Métis specific place for folks to come together to share stories. I sensed that my Métis kin needed to come into relationship with their own stories and experiences before they could share them. One individual in particular, Bob, was having trouble "finding" the practices in his life. He had reached out to me to see if we could get together for a visit. When together, he shared with me a reflection video; he was articulating the difficulty of seeing the everyday practices because he had to renew his relationship with the past to transpose his own actions. Bob, in sharing with the research collective, discussed that in growing up as a child, he was not taught by his grandmother how to "pay attention" to what constitutes Métis practices. This was felt by the other individuals in the group. Robin Wall Kimmerer provides a mode to be more attentive to our practices: "ceremonies large and small have the power to focus attention to a way of living awake in the world."[27] I learned from Bob, and others, that the stories of our ancestors are crucial to see what is *alive in our experiences*; practices are relational and indicative of our inherited existence.

Kimmerer, in referring to ceremonies, does not imply they are synonymous with those conducted in sacred ways, but more so how Ghostkeeper describes ceremony: "the physical movement of the aspect of the body performed by the Métis in order to make a living."[28] In this way, both Ghostkeeper and Kimmerer are insinuating consistent actions that are bound to worldview that then call for us to notice how we are invoking our worldview daily. Moreover, this affirmed the collectivity and importance of kinship in understanding oneself and our place within community.[29] For us, dwelling in Calgary was of particular importance because the collective dialogue of our daily experiences allowed us to understand that we are not alone and indeed have a kinship circle in the city. One individual spoke of the need to "find" community in Calgary in order to feel a sense of belonging. It takes a collective orientation to determine cultural practices; as individuals, we cannot determine this on our own and in isolation. We needed to come together and begin to talk about our own practical ways in which we express ourselves, while using each other as a mirror to determine what is "like me." At the beginning of the inquiry, I was unaware of the power that such a process could invoke. Not only was I creating a space for us to practise telling our stories, but the act of telling was the sinew that was pulling our small research community together. The telling of our stories became a ceremony, "a vehicle for belonging—to a family, to a people, and to the land."[30]

Soul Atrophy

Explicating our lived practices relied on the method of capturing photographs of everyday moments of practice. Using a photovoice technique[31] allowed us to move through our lifeworld and attune our attention to what practices might be present; as one individual remarked during the inquiry, "photos are the kindling."[32] The belief embedded in this method is that what we are looking for is already present, regardless of whether we can see it or not. The research gatherings each month were the fibrillation we needed to attend to our stories, to ourselves, to each other. For many of the individuals in the inquiry, this was the first time they were sharing their stories—and for some, the first time they had reflected on the stories in such a way as to connect with them to ascertain how their own practices expressed their Métisness. In seeing and feeling this, I began thinking about how putting down our stories has the potential to place us in arrhythmia, in soul atrophy. Soul atrophy is a suitable phrase as it suggests a lack of nourishment, or lack of sustenance to ensure generation of the entity. If stories are all we are, then who are we without our stories?[33] Practising and telling our stories is the nourishment we need to generate our identity, to become Métis. Soul atrophy—and how I understand this from our research collective—is living our lives in such a way that does not align or foster our inherent self and ultimately hinders our capacity to manifest the greatest expression of who we are meant to be. Soul atrophy, living our lives in arrhythmia, causes trauma when you are forced to relinquish who you are, to try to live a life that does not align with your life force.[34] Coming into the circle was somewhat of an electric shock for some people as they came into rhythm with their truest self.

One of my Métis kin, Charmaine, stated during one of our last gatherings, "It's been very spiritual. Seeing everyone's pictures, I can relate, I am enough that way, hearing everyone's stories solidifies that. I'm open to myself, being okay with the past and family, using the city to reconnect, it's not where you are but about spirituality. It's been very spiritual for me in all of this, talking with everyone, I'm open to myself, be okay, felt ashamed before."[35] This work did not intend to focus on healing trauma through sharing our practices, but in telling our stories, healing occurred. Importantly, as articulated previously, because the smudge requires us to be truthful, which enacts *omanii*—"real spirit talk"—and *aachimooshtowihk,* we are connecting to our spirit and expressing what needs to be said, which can be cathartic. Picking up our stories is healing, the telling of our stories, seeing and honouring the Métisness in our everyday practices is an effort to be rhythmic. We desperately need these spaces where it is safe to be ourselves, to explore and have dialogue of becoming Métis, to pick up our stories, and come into relationship with ourselves, our kin, our ancestors—*miyo pimatisiwin*—live a good life.

Wisdom: *Kaa-waakohtoochik:* The Ones Who Are Related to Each Other

Picking up our stories provided a pathway for renewing relationships with ourselves, our kin, our ancestors, and our environments. The renewal of these relationships nurtured a sense of belonging for all of us; this is an important wisdom. As I listened to the stories over six months, and then re-listened to them, the wisdom grew to include the inherent right for each of us to belong to a myriad of relationships. Although we all lived in Calgary at the time of the inquiry, our ancestors and kin came from elsewhere. Our cultural knowledge is tethered to different landscapes; this often causes feelings of disconnectedness. Most of us, at one point or another, felt like we did not belong, whether it be with friends, in our schools, in our cities, or in the world. Because of these feelings, we actively pursued a sense of belonging living in cities, with rivers, other Métis folk, with activities such as beading or sash weaving, or with the food we cook. Coming together solidified and affirmed for us that we do belong. Each of us pulled on the threads of our own practices and, through sharing them, we felt a sense of belonging not only to each other but also to the kinships that envelop us. Through this wisdom, *Kaa-waakohtoochik: The ones who are related to each other* was affirmed. We may be dispersed across the city and have both common and varying practices amongst us, but we know that we are relatives to a larger kinship system beyond ourselves. As each of us calls the city home, we are equally challenged and supported by this environment in becoming Métis.

Cities can be carnivorous places; they can consume us and encourage us to conform and assimilate into mainstream society.[36] Moreover, Métis historicity, specifically, is a story of diaspora caused by colonial violence.[37] Before 1885, and more significantly thereafter, some of our people fled their homes out of fear of being Métis and sought refuge away from our homeland. Particularly for us living in Calgary, we are acutely aware of our displacement. This displacement is felt in knowing we are in other nations' territory, but also that the Métis history in Calgary is only coming into the purview of understanding the city as inclusive of Métis historicity and lifeways. The stories of our research collective are indicative that we have an inherent right to belong, we always have, and we always will. The Métis principle of *wahkohtowin*—being in relationship with a living universe—reifies this. We are *Kaa-waakohtoochik: The ones who are related to each other*.

Conclusion

This inquiry sought wisdoms, birthed from personal experiences, of other Métis kin who were born and raised in the city, to give voice to our practical lifeways that are informed by both our ancestral knowledges and urban experiences. Before we could settle into discussions of our everyday practices, however, we had to position ourselves in a good way with our own stories. Many of us had to orientate ourselves with our kinship in order to see what was alive in our own experiences. Once we were able to do this, we could begin to share our stories with others; the practising of sharing became fundamental. As we practised telling our stories, we could see that we were picking up stories that were once laid down, by ourselves and our kin before us. Picking up our stories and sharing them with each other were the threads that began pulling us into closer relationships, with ourselves, our families, and other beings. Strengthening our relationships with all of Creation affirmed *Kaa-waakohtoochik: The ones who are related to each other*.

Eekoshi. Maarsii.

Notes

1 I am grateful to meestress Souter, Heather Souter, for guiding me in Michif translations.

2 Michif is the language of Métis people; there are different variations based on the respective geographical location. I employ Michif to identify myself. I use both Michif and Métis in this chapter because other kin in my research are not Michif but are Métis.

3 Andersen, "*Métis*."

4 Translated "practice reflected in relationships"; V. Bouvier, "Ni kaakiihtwaamaan itootamihk."

5 L. Maracle, *Memory Serves*.

6 Makokis et al., "iyiniw tapwewin ekwa."

7 Personal communication, 2019. My teachings from Elder Crowshoe have been consistent over the years and have been articulated through smudge.

8 Makokis et al., "iyiniw tapwewin ekwa."

9 V. Bouvier, "kaa-waakohtoochik."

10 V. Bouvier, "Ni kaakiihtwaamaan itootamihk," 35.

11 Blackfoot phrase, taught to me with smudge, by Elder Crowshoe.

12 V. Bouvier, "Truthing," 41.

13 Ibid.

14 Ibid.

15 Ibid.

16 Little Bear, "Jagged Worlds"; L. Maracle, *Memory Serves*.

17 Ghostkeeper, *Spirit Gifting*, 10–11.

18 Brubaker and Cooper, "Beyond 'Identity.'"

19 Gaudry, "Communing," 164.

20 See, e.g., Andersen, "*Métis*."

21 Lefebvre, *Rhythmanalysis*.
22 Lefebvre, *Rhythmanalysis*; Ghostkeeper, *Spirit Gifting*.
23 Lefebvre, *Rhythmanalysis*, 20.
24 Logan, "Settler Colonialism."
25 Campbell, "Michif."
26 V. Bouvier, "Restorying."
27 Kimmerer, *Braiding Sweetgrass*, 36.
28 Ghostkeeper, *Spirit Gifting*, 10.
29 Graveline, *Circle Works*; L. Maracle, *Memory Serves*.
30 Kimmerer, *Braiding Sweetgrass*, 37.
31 Wang and Burris, "Photovoice."
32 V. Bouvier and MacDonald, "Spiritual Exchange."
33 King, *The Truth*.
34 Burley, "Rooster Town"; Duran, *Healing*.
35 Personal communication, 2020.
36 Burley, "Rooster Town"; Campbell, "Michif."
37 Fiola, "Diaspora"; McCall, "Diaspora and Nation."

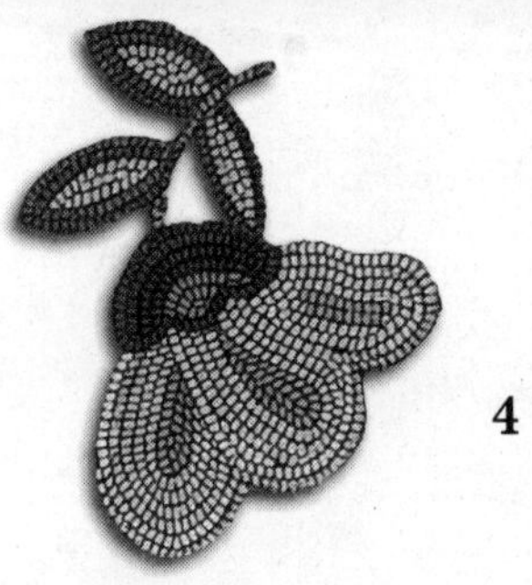

4

The Roots Always Remain:
Reconnecting to Our Communities in the Twenty-First Century

Angie Tucker

A unique tree stood outside my parents' home in St. Francois Xavier, Manitoba. She had purple leaves and pink blossoms as a sapling, but she struggled to live and nearly died. My mother cut her back, sealed the cut ends, and waited. Over the next two weeks, bright green shoots emerged from the ground, and the tree grew back as two distinct entities. One part of her remained a velvety eggplant hue while the other transformed to exhibit fresh-lime green leaves with white fragrant flowers that bloomed in the spring and turned to fruit under the warm summer sun.

This tree, likely insignificant to most, taught me as much about life as any of my human relations. Her memory has become an entity that I return to in my mind to assess if I am physically, emotionally, spiritually, and mentally balanced. She also reminds me that if something seems difficult, or if I feel as though I am failing, a change of course can lead to unlimited and unexpected outcomes. Indigenous peoples have learned from the environment through observation and recognition over many generations.[1] Nature always strives to be in balance, so we do too.[2] As such, the image of this tree continues to be a visual marker for the stages of my life—my youth and maturity, failures and successes, sadness and happiness, past and future. When my mother cut the tree back, we all assumed that the tree would flourish and grow to be the same as she was, yet, although she clearly returned as the same genus, she had regenerated in an entirely unique and unexpected way. She "grafted." Something changed within her growing cycle to alter her experience. This visual representation continued to enter my mind as I considered this chapter's discussion. As a Métis person, the tree that was half-one and half-the-other has not only become a visual representation of the proverbial "half-breed" identity but also demonstrates the reality of defying expectations and accepting new realities. This ever-giving tree continues to come into focus as I consider the complexity and nuances of contemporary indigeneity. But this attachment grows deeper still and demonstrates how locality, knowledge, space, place, and identity are connected. Where this tree once stood is also in the periphery of "home," where my ancestors have lived for many generations. I can place her location and know what is nearby. It is from this place I return to in my memory that I begin my work. I remain grounded in this place but continuously find new pathways that lead me from it. What I am describing is what is called *place-thought*.[3] Place-thought is how many understand the world via physical embodiment. Vanessa Watts describes place-thought as "the non-distinctive space where place and thought can never be separated because they *never* can be."[4] Métis Elders have taught that the land is an extension of our own bodies, and that the land has held the stories of our belonging within it. Therefore, we know that land and identity are deeply intertwined; yet, colonization has perpetually continued to interfere with our ability to maintain our relationships within specific places over time. This interference has, in turn, affected who we are today.

This chapter will argue for a resurgence of Métis belonging that moves beyond the confines of our mixedness and far beyond our placement as historical people. We no longer live in the past, and are a modern and contemporary people with much diversity, complexity, and nuance. For as many Métis people who have grown with the teachings of their ancestors, their language and their communities, there are as many who are struggling to find ways to reconnect to the Métis Nation. We must be respectful of the many decisions that were made as Métis families navigated their own unique political, social, and economic realities within specific locations. These choices were always made in negotiation with a number of factors, and their decisions required making concessions to ensure the health, well-being, and survival of our families. Place, and the experiences within it, therefore shape one's identity and belonging. By using the visual representation and resurgent regrowth of the tree that once stood in St. Francois Xavier, I hope to show that although multi-layered and complex, our relations to place, community, and kin will always be at our core.[5] To return to this foundation honours Métis ways of knowing, makes space for our diversity, and strengthens our Nation.

This chapter will begin with a discussion surrounding the reality that Indigenous peoples have had multiple experiences in the world and that each of us has had complex attachments to our histories, presents, and futures. There have been a number of colonial implications that have led to our present-day realities, and yet many of us continue to categorize ourselves using bureaucratic definitions that have been designed to erase our existence. For Métis and other mixed peoples specifically, the colonial obsession of recognizing one's belonging through categories of ethnicity and blood quantum has not only fractured how we see ourselves but has provided a space for invasive weeds in our Nation. Secondly, I will enter into a conversation about returning to the particular spaces that have shaped who we have become. These places hold our ancestral stories and are the foundation to our connection.

Although our roots push into the earth, many Indigenous peoples have been shaped into colonial topiaries—sheared into shapes of conformity through discriminatory policies and social pressures. Some of us refused to be manipulated, and have taken over the entirety of a garden, while others have become hybridized, transplanted, or weeded from existence. We must refrain from being caught in the thorns of essentialist thinking, and begin to embrace the diversity of our experiences. The presumption that we could remain connected to a pure and unchanged culture from the past is as restrictive as the confines of race. Like the tree in St. Francois Xavier, we do not always come back with the same languages or traditions. We do not always return with all of the stories or knowledge of our ancestors. We must rewrite who we are as a contemporary people while resisting the prescribed models of indigeneity that are still largely controlled, manipulated, and imagined by those outside of our communities.

Aligning ourselves to the static representations of Métis peoples that have been imagined by settler society will not work in our favour. To continue to validate ourselves using these outside categories for recognition only privileges the acts of colonialism that have constrained us. Neither our phenotype nor our culture can be used to define who we must be today. For Métis, this is made more complex since the rhetoric of blood quantum and suggestions of a racial mixedness have monopolized the categories of our inclusion. It is also difficult to define our identity and belonging based on culture—a category that I argue can be as restrictive as the fallacy of race. To fall back on "tradition" and "culture" as inclusion not only negates our ancestors' agency and choices, it also denies that our culture is fluid and adaptable to contemporary life. Our culture has continued to regenerate and change with our experiences.

We also must detach from the historic renderings of ourselves that are no longer possible. Keith Carlson posits, "Since actions and events affect people differently, history has become the arbiter of identity."[6] History continues to define who we are and argues that, at times, we also buy in to these historical narratives. Frits Pannekoek reiterates this in his work "Métis Studies: The Development of a Field and New Directions," that who we are is "too easily confined to the period when we were on the centre stage."[7] We pigeonhole ourselves into compartments of imagined historic authenticity or to famous Métis names—another action that only keeps us in the pages of history books and not a modern, vibrant, and diverse people. I am not implying that there are no Métis people who continue to live in a traditional manner; rather, there are as many (potentially more) who lack these traditions due to reasons both in and beyond their control.[8] What I do hope to impress is that neither is more or less authentic. The diversity of our memories brings together all of the parts to a whole narrative. Furthermore, nobody identifies themselves using only one, single, collective identity,[9] and I argue that Métis are stronger in our diversity. We also must not feel badly that we are not Indigenous enough for the rest of society. Our experiences *are* authentic Indigenous experiences because they are our experience as Indigenous peoples. We have become root-bound in our thinking. For Métis, to return to the land is important. Despite our varying experiences over time, our roots must remain in place as we absorb our knowledges from fibrous systems buried deep in the earth. We must drink up the stories, histories, and memories that continue to be available from the land. But in order to achieve this, we have to confront the reality that colonialism has interrupted these processes.

The base of our knowledges continues to be deeply connected not only with territory, kinship, and identity but more importantly with our human and non-human communities.[10] These factors have continued to remain at our core despite our absence, and continue to be fundamental to how we understand the world and our placement within it. Many Métis people have been transplanted over the years, yet we continue to (and should) find ways to physically or ideologically return to our communities.[11] Our conversations within our communities show us that we are not alone in our struggles. We recognize that we have each adapted and shifted in order to live within an oppressive colonial system and that we have continued to be restrained and conformed by its processes. But these realities do not invalidate who we are. Our multitude of experiences has only reshaped us into an entity that may be less expected. I argue that at its most simplified and historic base, the dispossession of our homelands, the shift of economic activity to industrialization, the division of our communities, racism, and the recreation of our spaces into settler territories under colonial law have generationally affected us. Our fundamental relationship with the land and the loss of teachings within specific places that hold the protocols for our belonging have been lost, twisted, and gnarled. By forcing supremacy over our traditional spaces and the knowledge contained within them, colonialism has been responsible for separating us.

Imperialistic worldview has forced many generations of Métis to move from their once strong collectives to individualistic realities. Our connections and our roots once extended over great distances across the prairies. Colonizers not only desired to obtain the land, but they knew that to remove our relationships with animate and inanimate relations, places, medicines, and our ceremonies would destroy our root systems.[12] Furthermore, "non-Indigenous history colonized and abstracted the relationships between humans and land, animals, time, stars, and the sun."[13] The colonial worldview was like a disease impressed upon us in order to negate our systems of knowledge. How we once understood place is now overshadowed by Lockean definitions of territories and bordering, private property, and improvement.[14] Colonization resulted in the restructuring of our ancestors into bands or groups within specific places. Yet these boundaries that have been created are artificial and arbitrary. I argue these spaces were only invented to compartmentalize how we understand ourselves using non-Indigenous worldviews[15] and to contain and confine all aspects of our lives.[16] Therefore, even today, there continues to be the notion that in order for Indigenous peoples to claim an authentic identity, we must continue to be fixed to specific places that exist in the present. This is clearly incorrect. Indigenous peoples have not always been fixed to specific places (especially to the places that they are in now), nor can all of us fit into the neat descriptions of specific bands or tribes within a multinational landscape. Both categories of identity and locale have been generated within a colonial system in order to assert control over Indigenous bodies.

Indigenous peoples are more broadly understood as a rural and remote people, but over time, a large number of Indigenous peoples have migrated from rural to urban spaces.[17] This is a reality for Métis people. The 2021 Census found that over 80 percent of Métis live in larger city centres.[18] Despite the misconception that we were "rejecting our traditional cultures and wished to assimilate if we moved to cities,"[19] Indigenous peoples experienced mobility due to their adaptation to new situations such as marriage, intellectual aims, access to appropriate services, or labour and economic opportunities.[20] Métis did not always intend to turn away from who they were, yet assimilation would be the most devastating by-product of this movement. Today 30 percent of all Indigenous peoples in cities are second and third generations who have never lived anywhere else.[21] Our movement into urban spaces also may not have been by our own doing; rather, our parents and grandparents made these decisions for us in previous lifetimes based on their own independent experiences. But this movement from rural to urban areas has presented a problem for Métis peoples. We are often not recognized as authentic versions of ourselves within the twenty-first-century city, and become less recognizable to a non-Indigenous audience.[22] The reality is that cities are built upon traditional Indigenous lands,[23] and many Métis people continued to live within spaces where cities would be built. My family, specifically, sat on plots close to modern-day Portage Avenue and Main Street at the Forks and in the Point Douglas area of Winnipeg as early as 1824. Both Hallet Street and Spence Street are named after them.

Places shape who you are and who you will become.[24] But often these places are subject to varying expectations, policies, and guidelines, and are places of power, belonging, and non-belonging. The soil that we grow from is not always ideal, yet we find ways to adapt. Furthermore, the spaces that our families occupied were not always static, nor were they always familiar. Although some Métis families continued to live on farms or other plots of land, many were also removed from their original territories through the scrip system or by encroaching settlers. Many of our ancestors were pushed onto road allowances along the water and roadways.

The colonial understanding of land differed from how Métis people may have once known and interacted with their territories. Métis knowledge was "vernacular, local, and was keyed to common features of a *local* ecosystem."[25] Métis historically engaged in "oral geography,"[26] and related to the land using stories and songs about the specific territories that they once shaped and occupied. Landmarks and geographical knowledge, oral tradition, and sharing were fundamental to Métis people's sense of self and their intimate connection to other human and non-human entities. It is to our detriment to privilege the colonial framework of space and land because it erases the reality that land is far more than physical space—specific places carry our specific histories and our specific knowledges.[27] This is further problematized because mainstream society often conflates physical placement with race. If the colonized mind is unable to recognize people apart from being from specific places (countries, territories), they then resort to determining inclusion and authenticity based on blood quantum. Blood quantification is a bureaucratic practice intended to categorize humans. Métis continue to be quantified by the outside using bizarre calculations of belonging that even date back to one Indigenous relative 400 years ago. But Métis is not just mixed. If that were so, all Indigenous peoples would be Métis. We are all mixed. Purity of race is a fabrication that was invented by racial scientists to validate their supremacy over others. Métis are a unique group with specific definitions of selfhood and language who were historically restricted from their physical landscapes and diverse kinship systems within a specific place during a specific time.[28] Much like Cree, Saulteaux, Haida, or Soto, Métis are their own people. Despite this, our identification continues to be couched in policy and social understanding of "mixed-blooded" backgrounds rather than by the ways in which we are capable of defining *ourselves*. The Métis are a complex group that is historically, geographically, and genealogically bound.[29] Regardless, Métis people continue to be authenticated through some fictitious variety of blood calculation. This is not an Indigenous practice. Métis is not a race. Métis is not quantifiable by blood. If pure is authentic, and racially mixed is lesser, how does this colonial rhetoric shape how we have continued to relate to the world? My grandmother responded to this by denying her inclusion in the Métis Nation. Maybe she no longer felt a sense of belonging. Maybe she no longer recognized herself as Métis. Rather than embrace community, her parents fabricated a false white genealogical record. Her family continued to live in poverty and under the scrutiny of local non-Indigenous neighbours, and yet they strived to fit in with settler society—pushing their indigeneity under the rug with their feet as they jigged. My grandmother denied her Métis roots as she turned her dough for bannock and drinking tea at the kitchen table with her cousins, and turned a blind eye to the history books with their family names—Spence, Parenteau, Hallett, Fidler, Foulds. This was not an uncommon practice. Maria Campbell claims that Métis, including herself, were ashamed of their background and that due to this shame, "half-breeds turned away from each other, which is just what the government wanted."[30] Like Maria Campbell, Métis poet Marilyn Dumont feels judged by settlers, and chose to deny her indigeneity as well.[31] Métis academic and activist Howard Adams feels inferior to settlers and recognizes that denial is actually a result of colonialism and racism.[32] This is a reality that we must confront and accept.

Brenda Macdougall discusses that our ability to understand who Métis are is limited by our resistance to hear the stories that our families have left us.[33] We lack stories of our own history from our own perspectives. We lack the stories about our changing worldviews and the dismantling of our social structures.[34] We neglect to understand how mobility and generational decision-making have affected our selfhood. We do not always know where we belong but must realize where and from whom we come *from*. Storytelling can be a form of resistance.[35] Stories are generative, and I think about how the tree in my memory regenerated to be thick and lush despite her rough beginnings and unique circumstance. Through stories and reconnecting to our communities and landscapes, we can flourish too. The tree began to heal, and in her place, two bright green shoots and one purple sprang from the ground. Although the tree began as one variety, she returned as another. It produced an alternate version of what was expected.

Therefore, we can be the producers of our own indigeneity that goes beyond "authentic," "traditional," or expected narratives—indigeneity that is inclusive of our diversity.[36] Our multiple narratives are what provide the storyline for contemporary indigeneity.

If anything is taken away from this chapter, we must return to the place where the rich nutrients feed the soil, which in turn feeds us. We must return to these spaces of belonging in order to belong. Cardinal and Hildebrandt stress the importance of *miskasowin*; that is, a Cree action for finding a sense of origin and belonging in order to heal.[37] *Miskasowin* is found within origin stories and with the land. But *miskasowin* and *wahkohtowin* (kinship and relationality) also lead us to our collective realities and straight into the inner ring of our communities. Kinship is our obligation,[38] and thus "we must learn, listen to and repeat stories, but also, continue to tell those stories,"[39] as difficult as they may be. A tree never does well when it is planted alone—especially those that bear fruit and that feed other entities. As such, trees should be planted in groups because they look to each other for strength and cross-pollination, and to warn each other about possible threats. Trees communicate.[40] Although the tree that once stood proudly in St. Francois Xavier would flourish and return each year to provide safety for the returning robins, shade for the *wapos* in spring, and a home for chirping squirrels, she eventually succumbed during a brutal winter that only Manitoba could provide.

If we return to the notion of place-thought and reconnect to spaces even in our memory, we have what we need in order to thrive and to rebuild our sovereign communities. It is from this soil that we can grow new forests. Our seeds continue to sprout, and our attachments to our home, family, and community continue to be imprinted upon us. We recognize that we are not Métis alone. Like trees, we know that we are stronger together.[41] Places are transformative and can continue to be sites of healing and health.[42] Like the tree that I will always continue to return to in my imagination, we all grow new (and sometimes unexpected) shoots.

Notes

1 Kimmerer, *Braiding Sweetgrass*.
2 Bastien, *Blackfoot Ways*, 36.
3 Watts, "Indigenous Place-Thought."
4 Ibid., 21.
5 Tough, "*As Their*"; Innes, *Elder Brother*; Peters and Andersen, *Indigenous in the City*; Andersen, "Urban Aboriginality."
6 Carlson, *The Power of Place*, 277.
7 Pannekoek, "Métis Studies," 116.
8 Peters, Stock, and Werner, *Rooster Town*.
9 Carlson, *The Power of Place*.
10 Kermoal and Altamirano-Jiménez, *Living on the Land*; Watts, "Indigenous Place-Thought."
11 Bastien, *Blackfoot Ways*; Innes, *Elder Brother*; Macdougall, *One of the Family*.
12 Belanger, "Breaching."
13 Bastien, *Blackfoot Ways*, 31.
14 Locke, *Two Treatises*.
15 Tough, "*As Their*"; Kimmerer, *Braiding Sweetgrass*.
16 W.A. Wilson, *Remember This!*; Daschuk, *Clearing the Plains*; Innes, *Elder Brother*.
17 Campbell, *Halfbreed* (1973 ed.); Adams, *Prison of Grass* (1989 ed.); Dumont, *A Really Good*; Ramirez, *Native Hubs*; Andersen, "Urban Aboriginality."
18 Statistics Canada, "The Daily."
19 Norris, Clatworthy, and Peters, "The Urbanization," 29.
20 Tough, "*As Their*."
21 Andersen, "Urban Aboriginality," 46.
22 Hokowhitu, "Producing Indigeneity"; Peters and Andersen, *Indigenous in the City*.
23 Dorries et al., *Settler City Limits*.
24 Campbell, *Halfbreed* (1973 ed.); Adams, *Prison of Grass* (1989 ed.); Dumont, *A Really Good*; Hungry Wolf, *The Ways*; Bastien, *Blackfoot Ways*; W.A. Wilson, *Remember This!*; Ramirez, *Native Hubs*; Thrush, *Native Seattle*; Macdougall, *One of the Family*.
25 J.C. Scott, *Seeing Like a State*, 311–12.
26 Rivard, "Le Fond," 144.
27 Tough, "*As Their*"; Innes, *Elder Brother*.
28 Andersen, "Urban Aboriginality."
29 Ibid.
30 Campbell, *Halfbreed* (1973 ed.), 47.
31 Dumont, *A Really Good*, 30.
32 Adams, *Prison of Grass* (1989 ed.), 9.
33 Macdougall, "Speaking of Métis."
34 Ibid., 49.
35 Jobin, "Double Consciousness."
36 Hokowhitu, "Producing Indigeneity."
37 Cardinal and Hildebrandt, *Treaty Elders*.

38 W.A. Wilson, *Remember This!*; Macdougall, *One of the Family*; Innes, *Elder Brother*.
39 W.A. Wilson, *Remember This!*, 93.
40 Kimmerer, *Braiding Sweetgrass*.
41 Ibid., 15.
42 Horn-Miller, "Distortion and Healing."

5

For the Love of Place—Not Just Any Place: Selected Metis Writings

Emma LaRocque

This essay has an express purpose of exuding orality, raising awareness about Metis love of land, or of landedness. As such, I am approaching the discussion more from a literary and creative perspective. I am, of course, aware that any mention of the Metis can bring up any number of issues from pretty much any number of disciplines. I will not try to address these multi-faceted issues, which can involve historical, constitutional, social, and ethnographic questions. My discussion here is obviously quite exploratory, and I have taken some poetic liberties with style and organization.

While the displacement and dispossession of the Red River Metis is more or less a well-known historical fact within academia (and, to a lesser extent, in the wider community), ironically, rarely is the theme of place associated with the Metis. By *place*, I mean more than geographical location or mapping, though all that is included; by *place*, I mean more like attachment, rootedness, groundedness, and materiality. Familial-ity. Home. Homelands. A particular and unique land area in this country where we carry out body- and home-stitching everydayness. A place where we live. And go to work from. Or in. A place where we come to know the ways and voices of family and neighbours. A place where we become familiar with pots and pans, woodpiles and water pails. Or computers and iPods. A garden we tend. Blueberry meadows we work or rest in, meadows bathed in sunlight streaming through poplars and birch. A place where we dream. Yes, there was the Red

River, and that was and is a place. To be sure, a very significant place. But Red River has been so overpoliticized that we can barely recognize it as a real place where real people practised their everyday ways of life and livelihoods. What did Riel eat?

Let me put this matter of place in another way. People in western Canada, and especially Manitoba, know about the Red River Metis. Or should. Everyone knows that Riel defended Metis interests and died for the Metis cause. And everyone knows the prairie Metis (or a handful of them) took a sort of last stand at Batoche, put up a good fight but lost.[1]

And everyone knows the other Canadian story—the sanitized school story— the pioneer version of how the *coureurs de bois*, or the voyageurs in early fur-trade times, sang and joshed their way up and down the St. Lawrence, portaging their way into the interior. Strapping, jovial "halfbreed" men who seemed to be forever paddling.

Another theme of halfbreed wanderings is to be found in Norma Bailey's "Daughters of the Country" series produced by the National Film Board. In the third film, titled *Places Not Our Own*, there is a scene where a Metis family is travelling by horse and wagon. It is sometime during the Depression. It is somewhere in the Prairies. Here the Metis are the prairie gypsies—apparently homeless and with no specific place to go.[2] And where did Morag's Metis lover in Margaret Laurence's *The Diviners* live? Where does he come from? Where does he go? Like an apparition, he fades in and out of Morag's life.[3] Whether the Metis are presented as portaging minstrels, prairie gypsies, or inconstant lovers, popular culture has romanticized and perpetuated the myth of Metis as roaming transients with little or no sense of rootedness to homes and lands, to homelands.[4]

Yet everyone knows the Metis fiddler. Or the Metis fighter. And the Metis martyr. But who knows the people? Who knows where they played their fiddles? Who really knows why they fought, or why they sacrificed their lives? Who knows who the Metis are and what they love and hold dear? Who knows where they have lived—or where they live now? Who knows how they felt or how they feel now about being displaced, then replaced? And today—where are their places? How do they live in those places? What do they feel about these places? Or that one place?

Of course, I am not going to answer these questions or issues. I raise them poetically rather than ethnographically. Here I only have time to offer vignettes of thoughts from several Metis writers and to highlight those facets and issues that often get neglected in film, literature, and other popular productions, but even in critical discussions. Generally, critical attention to Metis writers focuses on socio-economic and identity issues.[5] Here I take three well-known Metis—Maria Campbell, Marilyn Dumont, and Greg Scofield—who clearly express their profound attachments to home and landedness. I turn first to Maria Campbell, who in *Halfbreed* (1973) offers considerable cultural information tracing Metis life from the Metis Resistance era of the late 1800s to her own era of the 1950s–1970s from which she wrote the memoir. Maria Campbell is of Cree/Scottish Metis Nation ancestry from Saskatchewan. Her parents raised her and her siblings with Metis material culture as well as Metis values. It is not incidental that Maria begins her facts of biography with this: "I should tell you about our home now before I go any further."[6] She then proceeds to describe their "two-roomed large hewed log house," detailing their homemade tables and chairs, beds and hay-filled canvas mattresses, the hammock that babies swung from, the huge black wood stove in the kitchen, the medicines and herbs that hung on the walls, the wide planks of floors scoured evenly white with lye soap, and so forth. I am sure it was with tears of love that she reminisced: "The kitchen and living room were combined into one of the most beautiful rooms I have ever known."[7] Clearly, these tangible everyday objects remain a cultural palate of warm memory and strong attachment from which Maria Campbell has written and lived.

In a very short non-fiction piece called "The Gift,"[8] Alberta Metis writer Marilyn Dumont writes about watching her father revisit and linger over a beloved spot of land he had long ago lost. This land, located in northeastern Alberta, had been given to him as a wedding gift by his father—but he and his wife (Marilyn's parents) were unable to keep it due to the Depression in the 1930s. Many years later, Marilyn and her aging father climb up a hill to see—and to say a final goodbye to—this place. Before leaving this ancestral high ground, Marilyn watched with pain as her father "tucked some blades of grass and twigs into his wallet." She describes her own reaction: "My thoughts raced. I wanted to take something too. Something to say I'd been here. My eyes searched in the grass. A light flickered. I picked up a brown piece of glass. The heavy broken bottom of a jug. I didn't know what I'd do with it. It didn't matter; I gripped it against me."[9] This fact-based story is another very moving testament to Metis attachment to place, in this case, a parcel of land. Not just any land. But a very site-specific, family-significant, and much-loved place. It is excruciatingly difficult to lose places we love. As Marilyn Dumont puts it: "Who knows what it's like to leave, to give up a piece of land? If you do, it might haunt you forever, follow you til you come back."[10]

Many Metis—not all, but altogether too many—have been forced in some way or other to leave their special places. In this sense, there is some truth to the image of the Metis as prairie gypsies, but this should be seen as a consequence of displacement—not as a cultural or individual trait to be romanticized. The sad fact is that many Metis cannot come back to their places of origin due to urban and industrial encroachments, or outright dispossession by either federal or provincial laws and actions. But even this reality does not erase the Metis love of home, kin, or community. Some have had to adopt symbolic places that hold great significance. One such place is Batoche. In his autobiography *Thunder Through My Veins* (1999), Metis poet Gregory Scofield titles one chapter "Pekewe, Pekewe" ("Come Home, Come Home" in Cree). He had come home to Saskatchewan, to the Prairies, to what he calls his roots. After a very long and troubled and confused youth, Gregory had finally discovered Batoche—on one hand, a historic place of sacrifice, loss, and pain, but for him, a new place of peace and belonging. A place, a people, a culture that he could identify as his very own.[11] These prairie writers, each work reflecting a different period of time, nonetheless experienced some form of uprootedness in their personal and community lives—yet each is deeply rooted to particular histories, places, geographies, and families. To be sure, there are many differences between these writers (age, gender, experience, and genre among them), yet one constant stands out—a strong identification with placeness. Landedness for the Metis remains an unbroken bond.

My father used to say we are nothing without land. Rarely did my gentle father make such categorical pronouncements. He was born in northeastern Alberta at the turn of the twentieth century, his roots coming directly through the Red River Metis of the 1870s–1890s. Bapa was a hard-working man forced by colonial history to raise his family in a road allowance section of land he never got to own. "We are nothing without land." It took me some time to realize the full profundity of his statement. He was not just talking about legal ownership of property—although land and resource rights remain an unfinished business for the Metis, certainly for the Red River Metis. My father (and mother), who never had the means to own property, had a philosophy and praxis about land far greater than capitalist notions of land as a real estate commodity. Metis writers reflect and express what Metis peoples know and feel—that they are deeply, ancestrally, Indigenously, and fundamentally rooted to their lands and families. To my Metis parents, land represented identity, culture, self-sufficiency, and independence. Landedness also meant family, home life, kin, and community. Landedness is purposeful; it gives meaning to language and life.

For all our efforts to explain our identity and our epistemic worldviews in relation to land and place, stereotypes and ignorance about the Metis persist. I come back to the beginning. I have just spoken to the well-known and perhaps worn-out old stereotypes. Earlier in my research, I had been struck by the portrayals of Metis as alienated loners who insert into Native or white lives without context or belonging. Like Billy Jack in the movie *Billy Jack.* Sometimes they were romanticized like Morag's lover in *The Diviners*. Often they were demonized. Historians and novelists presented Metis as volatile males splintered between the chasms of civilization and savagery.[12] These should be old stereotypes, yet have these rather classic images changed? I am not so sure. I have noticed that some Native American writers and academics make no distinction between individuals who are half-white/half-Indian and those Metis Nation peoples of western Canada who formed a distinct ethnic culture and community.[13] The more recent post-colonial emphasis on hybridity or border-crossing, useful concepts in some contexts, can serve to further obscure Metis national identity and culture and, in turn, Metis land and resource entitlements.[14] But even in Canada, we still have films, poems, stories and books, titles, and academic treatments that tend to focus on Metis homelessness, identity crises, marginalization, or an in-betweenness. Of course, there is some sad truth to these images. The Red River Metis did lose their beloved lands in the Red River, and about 83 percent of this population were forced to relocate, and many could not find a new place or new homelands.[15] If they did, they would face other dragons, such as the "scrip" that the federal government gave as poor compensation for Metis claims, the Gatling gun at Batoche, provincial confiscations of traplines through

Natural Resource laws, or the oil sands in northeastern Alberta. To name but a few. And notwithstanding the somewhat recent *Powley* Supreme Court decision of 2003 that recognized specific Metis harvesting rights,[16] neither the provincial nor federal governments are anywhere near fulfilling the Canadian constitution—that is, of actualizing Metis land and resource rights as Indigenous peoples. But despite all these historic pressures, Metis managed to stay together and even to develop strong communities in central and northern parts of the prairie provinces, many along road allowances. The Metis Nation story is a remarkable feat of survival and cultural tenacity. For despite all the succession of losses and obstacles, there are thousands of Metis Nation families and individuals across western Canada who live lives quite similar to those of "ordinary Canadians." That is, they have homes—maybe even "homelands"—and culturally cohesive and functioning family lives with meaningful occupations. Without in any way seeking to minimize those Metis who have suffered much personal and cultural dislocation, some of us Metis have had to say "hey—not all of us were stolen or fostered, not all of us suffered identity crises (even despite huge obstacles) and not all of us had to look for homes and places." Historians and literary critics now need to refocus and enlarge their portrayals and treatment of Metis peoples, issues, and themes. I say this to draw attention to our rootedness and integrated identity as Metis Nation peoples. To our love of our lands.

Love of land does not depend on property ownership (though that certainly should be a right that Metis have). My family still owns no lands. But long before the province of Alberta was established, long before Confederation was arranged, my paternal and maternal Plains and Woodlands Cree/Metis ancestors filled these lands by use and love of the land. Like other Red River Metis Nation peoples of their generation, my parents knew every nook and cranny of lands stretching hundreds of miles within their areas. My brothers—along with others of our generation and their children—still know, occupy and use these lands. Metis scholars, writers, and poets like Maria Campbell, Marilyn Dumont, and Greg Scofield carry the nooks and crannies in their hearts. As do I. I end with Marilyn Dumont's poem "not just a platform for my dance":

This land is not
just a place to set my house my car my fence

This land is not
just a plót to bury my dead my seed

This land is
my tongue my eyes my mouth

This headstrong grass and relenting willow
these flat-footed fields and applauding leaves
these frank winds and electric sky

are my prayer
they are my medicine
and they become my song

this land is not just a platform for my dance[17]

Notes

1 I am referring to the Northwest Metis Resistance at the Battle of Batoche in 1885 where some 250 Metis men fought some 900 Canadian Militia troops. The Metis took a last stand to protect their lands against imperial forces. See Hildebrandt, "The Battle"; and Barron and Waldram, *1885 and After*.

2 Mazur, *Places Not Our Own*.

3 Laurence, *The Diviners*.

4 I am not suggesting that we confine any Indigenous group, including the Red River Metis, to the sort of rootedness that freezes them to the past which would keep them "in their place" so that colonizers can gaze or segregate them. For an interesting discussion on the uses and abuses of notions of "roots," see Eigenbrod, *Travelling Knowledges*, especially the chapter on "The Rhetoric of Mobility."

5 See, e.g., Damm, "Dispelling and Telling." For a more post-colonial reading see Hoy, *How Should?*

6 Campbell, *Halfbreed* (1973 ed.), 16.

7 Ibid., 17.

8 Dumont, "The Gift."

9 Ibid., 46.

10 Ibid., 44.

11 Scofield, *Thunder*.

12 LaRocque, "The Metis in English Canadian Literature."

13 Native American writer and academic Elizabeth Cook-Lynn takes a very troubling view of "Métis" as halfbreed individuals who threaten Native "tribal" identity. There is no mention or appreciation of the Red River Metis as Indigenous with Indigenous identity; see Cook-Lynn, *Why I Can't*. See also Harrison, *Métis: People Between*.

14 For further explorations of these issues, see LaRocque, "Native Identity"; LaRocque, "Reflections on Cultural Continuity"; LaRocque, *When the Other*.

15 See Sawchuk et al., *Metis Land Rights;* Government of Canada, *Report of the Royal Commission,* Volume 4, Chapter 5 on "Metis Perspectives"; and Sprague, "Asserting Canadian Authority."

16 *R. v. Powley*. Also see the decision in *Manitoba Métis Federation v. Canada*.

17 Dumont, *A Really Good*, 46.

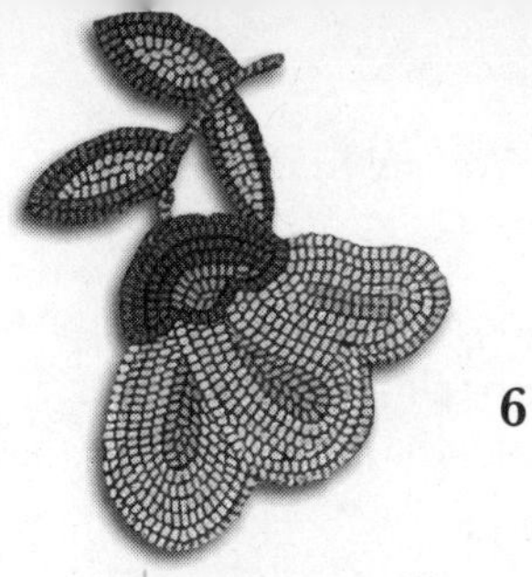

6

Coming Home through Métis Research

Allyson Stevenson

Throughout my life, there have been women who came alongside me at critical moments and taught me lessons necessary for my growth as a Métis woman and scholar.[1] This chapter honours the Métis women whose caring work in community, in the academy, and in social relationships are rebuilding communities through nurturing connections to home.[2] Their emotional labour, in addition to their professional and scholarly work, builds the next generation of scholars and community members. For many disconnected Métis, our connections to our ancestors are often found through archival research, and often when seeking out genealogical connections for Métis citizenship.[3] In other cases, they emerge from a desire to make sense of gaps, silences, and missing stories. My experiences of coming home through Métis research also speak to the conditions where I, as a disconnected Métis youth, was able to gain access to Métis histories, literatures, artwork, Elders and ceremonies, and a community. The possibilities for Métis research, grounded in Métis worldview, enable us to put the pieces of our shattered lives and histories back together.[4]

My personal narrative articulates some of my formative experiences as an academic and as a Métis woman, while also illustrating some of the ways that Métis women's scholarly writing and community-building activities work together to form a core of Métis Studies today.[5] Métis Studies, as a developing field of inquiry, is grounded in the storying of our histories as a people whose lives are inflected by histories of resistance, colonial erasure, and a commitment to rebuilding our communities wherever we find ourselves.[6] In telling our own stories, or storying our own lives, we can connect ourselves not only to a scholarly tradition but also to a people who write ourselves back into the present. Our ethical commitment to positioning ourselves, our influences, and our experiences enables others with whom we work to know us not only as scholars but also as members of families and communities. My reflection also emerges from a feminist commitment to unmasking the illusion of the individual scholar unconnected to place or community, while also situating narratives of "coming home" as a core area of consideration in Métis Studies literatures and frameworks.

Coming home through Métis research was, for me, a personal experience, but I believe it has a larger significance to Métis Studies. Métis scholar and artist Gregory Scofield recounts his experience returning to Batoche in *Thrown My Veins: Memories of a Métis Childhood* in his chapter "Pekwew, Pekewe" ("Come Home, Come Home"). Scofield recalls his first encounter with Métis culture and history at Back to Batoche Days, where he finally experienced a sense of belonging.[7] I would not have seen my work from this perspective until I began to engage more deeply in Métis research from a Métis perspective and Indigenous Studies more broadly.[8] Coming home through research is being able to claim your identity as a Métis person, ground yourself in a Métis worldview, understand where you belong in your family web of relations, identify the lands around you as the homeland, and, finally, connect to the broader community to help to rebuild lost relationships.[9] As an adoptee, this sense of connection, belonging, and, most importantly, sense of home was something I was searching for. My academic work on Métis history, the Sixties Scoop, and, finally, family connection has brought me home.

As I have said elsewhere, various government policies, such as the criminal mismanagement of the scrip system, road allowance dispersals, and the Sixties Scoop, have severed connections to Métis historical consciousness, as well as kinship connections. Historical erasure and misrecognition have additionally contributed to intellectual and cultural confusion about who Métis people are more broadly, despite the recent flourishing of Métis research and artistic production.[10] Métis Studies has an important role in offering a decolonized intellectual space for reconsidering our histories utilizing our own methodologies and theoretical approaches.[11]

As Métis scholars have illustrated, storytelling and visiting constitute important methods for Métis scholars undertaking Métis-specific research.[12] Likewise, Métis women's social and familial relationships with each other can be considered a foundational element of being Métis, as illustrated by the work of Dr. Brenda Macdougall and Dr. Sherry Farrell Racette.[13] In highlighting my own relationships with strong Métis women, I want to voice resilience, relationality, and the spiritual world of Métisness that brings meaning and connection to my work, carving a space for vulnerability. Anishinaabe writer Maya Ode'Amik Chacaby articulates the profound importance of home for contemporary Indigenous peoples:

> So what is really missing? A place to come home to. Home is my language and the privilege of subjective agency as well as the necessary resources to find my sense of self in something other than what I have been subsumed by. This includes an unsettling of what we consider being human and having rights. Home is a network of Clan and kinship ties that allow safe passage through multiple spatial and conceptual territorialities; this is the definition of Anishinaabe Nationhood. Home is a social environment where Anishinaabe leadership, gender, life-cycle, and Clan responsibilities are imbued in everyday interactions. Home is the economic infrastructure to fulfill those responsibilities; this is our true measure of wealth. Home is ceremony, upliftment, and rites of passage through every life stage. Home is being celebrated, mentored, welcomed, and wanted. Home is my bundle.[14]

The absence of home, our longing for home, and its "missingness" in our lives for those who have experienced "life" outside our families and communities is not a problem of place or location but rather the disconnection of a set of knowledges grounded in Indigenous sociality and disruption to collective histories and connections to storied territories. Being home, then, is the recuperating of these knowledges, gaining a sense of ancestral embeddedness, and being restored to a web of relationality where your role as a future ancestor is present and directs actions. As a Métis woman who, at different stages of my life, was searching for my lost kinship connections and also a way to understand the experience of exile, there were two important junctures in my journey when Métis women came alongside me to teach me important values that have sustained me, and brought me into the circle of Métis women and community. Two stories illustrate these turning points that changed my life trajectory. I would not be where I am without them. There are also many other strong Métis women who are incredible sources of inspiration, support, and sisterhood work that reflect the women-centred family systems of Métis peoples.[15]

When I Was Gifted with My First Sash

Métis women have been at the forefront of engaging at the community level and at the academic level to preserve Métis culture and history while also building community organizations and educational spaces for our worldview to be passed on to the future generations.[16] People like myself, who have been separated from family and culture, have come to rely on these elder aunties whose work has enabled us to have spaces to come home to.

Much of the building of urban Indigenous organizations and community work in the 1960s and 1970s was undertaken by Indigenous women. In cities and towns across Turtle Island, Indigenous women worked to create political, cultural, and women's organizations to address the growing needs of urban Indigenous families.[17] Métis-specific organizations likewise grew in this time. As Métis scholar Cheryl Troupe argues, "Over time, the role of [A]boriginal women in urban organizations has evolved from working behind the scenes, to leading organizations, asserting their political will and creating organizations to meet their own needs."[18] Métis women created organizations, such as the ones in Saskatoon that Troupe examines, but also in smaller prairie cities, such as the Marguerite Riel Centre in Melfort, Saskatchewan.

In 1998, when I married and returned to the community of my biological Métis family, I sought out the local urban Aboriginal organization in the small prairie city of Melfort, Saskatchewan. The Canadian Métis Heritage Corporation and the Marguerite Riel Centre, named for the wife of Louis Riel, were operated by the late executive director Debbie Edin. This is a personal example of the importance of such organizations and the way in which they can bring those who have been removed back into the circle of the Métis community.

In my new home, married and finding a way to become a community member in rural Saskatchewan after living in larger centres, I was welcomed by the director Debbie Edin who, in the Métis way, was related to my mother-in-law. As Fidler descendants, they both were part of a large and extended Métis family. I was included in this extended family through my marriage, and also, as a Métis person (with Fidler ancestors also), welcomed and given a role. As an adoptee, without a very clear understanding of what it meant to be a Métis woman, connecting with the Centre and being mentored by Debbie was and is one of the most pivotal experiences in my journey coming home. To be accepted by the Métis community, given a role and responsibility, and a place to learn about our culture and history in a Métis environment provided a grounding in my culture that enables me to now walk with pride. Through my work in the Centre in editing residential school survivor stories, planning and helping to put on cultural events, creating programming for the community, and reaching out to community partners, the day-to-day activities for the community enabled me to see how our labour is part of a larger effort to rebuild our lost connections and continue building our nations that have been impacted by settler colonial efforts to erase our presence.

Debbie Edin was a vibrant, beautiful, deeply engaged Métis mother and grandmother who was taken from the world all too soon. Her vision for the Centre was to create a dynamic space for Métis culture to flourish, while also providing critically needed programming for families impacted by the intergenerational traumas of colonization, whether Métis, First Nations, or non-status. While I was a young mother, undertaking my Master's studies in history from the University of Saskatchewan, Debbie was an auntie who not only employed me but was there to teach me about the importance of community and how to participate in cultural protocols, and gifted me with a sash, while also teaching me about the obligations that the sash would demand. This is an obligation I continue to reflect on, and which, in part, I am fulfilling through this contribution. The strong Métis women in my life, like my "auntie" Debbie, put me on the path that I am now on today. She passed away in 2010.

Showing Indigenous Care

Strong Métis women building up others in the community is one critical aspect of how we decolonize and ensure that the next generation is taught the responsibilities and obligations of being a Métis community member. Our community includes the academic community more broadly, and strong Métis women have been instrumental in bringing us into this community as well. Senior Métis women academics faced a much more hostile institutional environment than we do, and as those who broke trail, we are very indebted to their strength, perseverance, and determination to endure.[19] Métis Studies has been deeply enriched by the critical contributions of scholars such as Sherry Farrell Racette and Emma LaRocque as the foremothers of the current discipline. Without the critical interventions of these Métis women scholars in the areas of decolonial representations and women's artistic production, our discipline would be deeply impoverished.

Because my own training was in the discipline of Canadian history, by scholars who were non-Indigenous, I often sought out Indigenous scholars on my own. The work of Maria Campbell and Howard Adams resonated with me deeply because they engaged with the racism and economic exploitation of First Nations and Métis people on a deeply relational level.[20] While profoundly important, the traditional discipline of history has been challenged by Indigenous scholars for its reliance on documentary sources while failing to account for its complicity in the colonial project of dispossession.[21] In 2007, I was accepted to a doctoral program at the University of Saskatchewan in the Department of History. I was planning to undertake research into the transracial adoption of Aboriginal children in non-Aboriginal homes. Before entering the graduate program in September, I attended Congress, which happened to be held that year on the University of Saskatchewan campus.

At the Canadian Historical Association annual meeting, I attended the "Women's History as Public History" roundtable, where I sought to familiarize myself with women's history, one of my upcoming comprehensive fields of study. I first encountered Dr. Sherry Farrell Racette as she gave her presentation, "Don't Get me Started! Absence, Tokenism, and Missed Opportunities? Aboriginal Women and Public History in Canada." She spoke of the importance of photos and visual images of the care given to Indigenous children. By drawing our attention to the carefully braided hair, tiny but beautifully crafted moccasins, and detailed finely rendered clothing, we were invited to consider the love and devotion that had been shown by the child's mother or grandmother. Dr. Farrell Racette's artist's eye translated for the audience the significance of the beadwork and the time and skill that went into dressing the child. As I listened to her speak, I connected the work I was about to undertake on the Sixties Scoop to the harm that I imagined would come as children were removed from families and communities, and the erasure of mothers and grandmothers. Her words and her presence in the room as one of the only Indigenous women historians I had encountered reflected the caring work of Indigenous women academics—she demonstrated the importance of showing care in our work and seeing care in the past.[22]

Dr. Farrell Racette is a prolific artist, scholar, and strong Métis woman. I had the deep honour to work with her at the University of Regina, my first academic position. Her work has had a profound influence on me, and she had contributed greatly to the preservation of Métis culture and art in Canada. Her knowledge of Métis beadwork, art forms, history, and women's experiences is woven together in such a way that Métis women's strength, courage, and centrality to the nation are always evident.[23] Her work speaks to the deep connections between women's roles working, creating, caring, and holding families together through the hard times after 1885. As the flower beadwork people, women's artistic production has been a fundamental element in the emergence of the Métis people as a distinct people. Scholarship that explores Métis women's labour and art, caring work, and strength remains central to Métis Studies, but frequently is unacknowledged.

Dr. Farrell Racette's talk encouraging scholars to situate children in the centre of research had a profound impact on me as I started my own research on the Sixties Scoop. Despite my being an adoptee, my research was not intended to be a personal account or involve survivor experiences. Even as I approached my research on transracial adoption from the perspective of a policy history, I remained mindful that my work was primarily about Indigenous children—First Nations and Métis—who had been removed from families and communities, and also remained mindful of the families that were impacted. Inspired by Dr. Farrell Racette's work that centred women and children, my research sought to examine what I came to understand as the Sixties

Scoop from the perspective of Indigenous kinship and resistance. The experiences of Métis communities and families in the twentieth century has rarely been documented, and this work sought to explore the origins of Indigenous child removals in twentieth-century Saskatchewan.

The impact of the removals of First Nations and Métis children from families and communities is part of the larger continuum of colonial processes. As I became more deeply engaged in Indigenous decolonial research methods, I came to see the necessity of situating my own experiences of adoption in this larger colonial process. Again, it was strong Métis women who pressed me to engage in my own story. Dr. Tara Turner and Dr. Cheryl Troupe were instrumental in demonstrating the importance of our own family stories.[24] As a result of their encouragement, I undertook an extensive genealogical reconstruction of my Métis family tree, locating scrip documents from both Manitoba and Saskatchewan, as well as homestead records, and my great-grandfather's WW I and WW II military records. While many Métis families share stories of their Métis culture and past, as an adoptee, I was disconnected from these stories. For me, coming home through Métis research revealed my own deep connections to the land on which I now live, my ancestors, as well as our family experiences of diaspora and resettlement and reconnection.

In reflecting on my journey as a Métis woman academic, I see it as a series of steps in a journey that has led me close to home. While the year 2020 and the pandemic have brought many stressful, challenging, and life-altering events to the fore, this time was also when I published my first monograph, *Intimate Integration*, and began a position as the Gabriel Dumont Chair in Métis Studies at the University of Saskatchewan. These professional accomplishments would not have been possible without the support of mentors and "aunties." In the years that followed the completion of my PhD, visiting across Turtle Island for my post-doctoral research on Indigenous women's activism brought me into the home of Dr. Kim Anderson. Invited to participate in a decolonial public history performance by Dr. Kim Anderson, Dr. Lianne Leddy, and Dr. Brittany Luby at the University of Guelph, we dressed in the clothing of our grannies to inscribe Indigenous women's presence onto the nation-state. I donned a replica of my great-great-great-great-grandmother Nancy Bremner Fidler's (d. 1886) severe black ribbon skirt in an act of collective transgressive resistance through embodying my ancestral Métis grandmother.[25] The research necessary to enact my grandmother's presence at Confederation was another opportunity to come home. Strong Métis women's stories illustrate the importance to the nation of women who build connections, inspire younger generations, and keep alive the stories and values of sharing, culture, and strength. These women, in addition to many others, have been instrumental in my journey as a Métis woman academic. They also reveal, I would argue, the importance of the community, art, and women's experiences to Métis Studies in ways that have yet to be adequately recognized. Kim Anderson states in the concluding paragraphs of *Life Stages and Native Women*, "Rebuilding the circle in whatever context we find ourselves in is a work in progress, and we must be creative to find means of reinstating the position of women, connecting with all our relations and picking up those pieces that were scattered because of colonial interference."[26] Moving forward, within Métis Studies, it is imperative that Métis women's voices are amplified, and complex gendered experiences attended to meaningfully, while considering the full range of Métis embodied and interconnected positionalities.

Notes

1 It is an honour and a privilege to be included in such an important collection alongside these inspiring Métis women who have contributed to the field of Métis Studies. I am very grateful to editors Laura Forsythe and Jennifer Markides for inviting me to contribute to this important collection. Maarsi.

2 Scofield, *I Knew*.

3 Adese, "'R' Is for Métis."

4 Maria Campbell uses the metaphor of a shattered puzzle to illustrate the impact of colonization on Indigenous kinship; see K. Anderson, *Life Stages*; Jesse Thistle draws on Campbell's metaphor of the puzzle in "The Puzzle."

5 K. Anderson, *A Recognition of Being* (2000 ed.); Troupe, "Métis Women"; Flaminio, Gaudet, and Dorion, "Métis Women Gathering"; Gaudet and Caron-Bourbonnais, "It's in Our Blood"; Iseke and Desmoulins, "The Life and Work."

6 Campbell, *Halfbreed* (2019 ed.); Adams, *Prison of Grass* (1975 ed.); Thistle, *From the Ashes*; Thistle, "The Puzzle"; Teillet, *The North-West*; LaRocque, *Defeathering*; LaRocque, *When the Other*; Oster and Lizee, *Stories*.

7 Scofield, *Thunder*, 166–67; I consider the very successful personal story of Jesse Thistle as also suitable for inclusion in this form of narrative; see Thistle, *From the Ashes*.

8 For those interested in Métis scholars reflecting on academic and personal connections to Métis research, see Lischke and McNab, *The Long Journey*.

9 For the importance of returning to community and families after disruptions due to the child welfare system among Métis peoples, see Carrière and Richardson, *Calling*.

10 Andersen, "*Métis*" discusses the racialization of the Métis people and the ongoing misrecognition of the Métis people as mixed.

11 Macdougall, *One of the Family*; Macdougall, Podruchny, and St-Onge, *Contours*; Gaudry, "Insurgent."

12 K. Anderson, *Life Stages*; Troupe, "Mapping"; Flaminio, ""Kiyokewin"; Gaudet, "Keeoukaywin."

13 Macdougall, *One of the Family*; Farrell Racette, "Sewing for a Living."

14 Chacaby, "(The Missing Chapter)."

15 Brown, "Woman as Centre"; Dorion, "Opikinawasowin."

16 See, e.g., in Alberta, Iseke and Desmoulins, "The Life and Work," and in Saskatchewan, Troupe, "Métis Women."

17 In Saskatchewan, see Stevenson and Troupe, "From Kitchen Tables"; Valaskakis, Stout, and Guimond, *Restoring the Balance*; Howard-Bobiwash, "Women's Class Strategies"; Janovicek, "'Assisting Our Own'"; Krouse and Howard, *Keeping*; S. Maracle, "The Eagle"; Mihesuah, *Indigenous American Women*; George, "'If I Didn't.'"

18 Troupe, "Métis Women," 131.

19 LaRocque, "The Colonization."

20 Campbell, *Halfbreed* (1973 ed.); Adams, *Prison of Grass* (1989 ed.); Adams, *A Tortured People*.

21 Miller and Riding In, *Native Historians*.

22 Farrell Racette, "Showing Care."

23 Robertson and Farrell Racette, *Clearing a Path*; Farrell Racette, "Sewing for a Living"; Farrell Racette, "Looking."

24 At that time, Dr. Tara Turner was the Health Director of the MN-S; Cheryl Troupe also worked at the MN-S. I was working with the MN-S for my research on the Sixties Scoop.

25 K. Anderson, "Kika'ige Historical Society."

26 K. Anderson, *Life Stages*, 178.

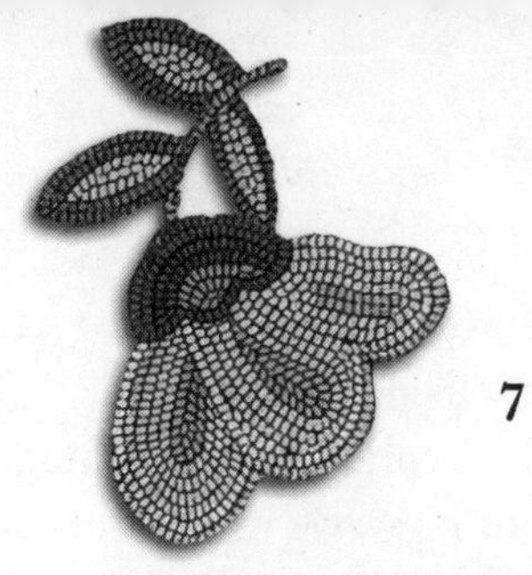

7

Valuing Métis Identity in the Prairies through a "5 R" Lens:

Our Digital Storytelling Journey

Amanda LaVallee and Chelsea Gabel

Introduction

The field of Métis Studies has focused on Métis issues primarily undertaken by historians, ethno-historians, and political scientists examining issues relating to what "Métis" means and who the Métis people are,[1] and most recently, who the Métis people are not.[2] Currently, there is a severe underrepresentation of Métis in academic research and a lack of adequate, accurate, and accessible information about Métis health and well-being that is community-based and participatory.[3] There is, therefore, a strong need for research in Métis communities from a Métis perspective. Little is known about how current Métis generations perceive one another and their respective roles and identities. Our research addresses this gap in knowledge by engaging with Métis academics and community members to discuss their experiences and address barriers and enablers that influence their ability to communicate, understand, and engage with each other. Our work is timely given the current questions surrounding the contentious nature of Métis identity in Canada. This includes the increase in numbers of individuals claiming Métis status, how Métis see themselves, and how their understandings are prescribed by others, including the state. Our research uses the digital storytelling method to bring Métis people together to share their stories of strength, perseverance, and reclamation of Métis identity. This research also shows the potential for digital technology to support teaching and learning from Indigenous perspectives.

Our contribution to this special collection dedicated to Métis women in the academy is threefold. First, we assess the benefits and overall strengths of the digital storytelling method. Specifically, we discuss what is involved in digital storytelling research and its importance, including the inherent trade-offs and distinctive contributions to knowledge digital storytelling presents. Our second aim is to describe the digital storytelling process, focusing on the four-day workshop. Here, we discuss the specific steps of the workshop, from writing the story to recording it, and then creating a short video out of it. Finally, we conclude this chapter by focusing on our own workshop experience and how this kind of storytelling can contribute to the identity of an individual or a community. While the digital storytelling workshop is an individual process in that each individual creates their own story, it is also a strongly collective process—our team was invested in the importance of each other's story and the significance of the stories as a collection. We describe this experience from a culturally relevant research paradigm, i.e., a paradigm that comes from a relational, respectful, reciprocal, and responsible perspective.

In this chapter, we have relied upon our individual and collective understandings as Métis women, and our experiences with participating in a community-engaged research method. Importantly, we want to make it clear that our Métis experiences are grounded in the Prairie provinces and are specific to Red River Métis peoples. Therefore, our stories, views, and perspectives come from that standpoint. We are determined to create a research space for Red River Métis knowledge, experience, and expertise to be utilized and valued.

Digital Storytelling: Strengths and Benefits

In the last decade, digital storytelling has continued to grow as an international movement[4] and, importantly, as a rigorous research method in its own right. Digital storytelling is an arts-based research method in which participants create short stories to document their understandings of the research questions. Originally codified by the Centre for Digital Storytelling, now known as the Storycentre,[5] digital stories are "3 to 5 minute visual narratives that synthesize images, video, audio recordings of voice and music, and text to create compelling accounts of experience."[6] Digital storytelling is a powerful participatory, digital, short-film technique that enables individuals to a) assess community strengths and concerns, b) communicate community ideas to researchers and policymakers, c) put the power of filmmaking into the hands of community members, d) promote critical dialogue and knowledge about issues through group discussion of digital stories, e) facilitate power-sharing by having the participant rather than the researcher determine the subject and meaning of the digital story, f) facilitate a richer understanding of the issues being studied, and g) help individuals reflect on and recognize their own perspectives on issues facing their communities. Indigenous digital storytelling incorporates Indigenous theories "associated with proactive measures for addressing change and reflective of our [Indigenous] ways of knowing, being and doing, and built on strategic skills in community."[7] Digital storytelling is an ideal approach for research with Indigenous communities because it fosters trust, gives community members ownership over research data, and shifts the balance of power to community members; it is consistent with a community-engaged research paradigm.

Since its inception in 1998, the San Francisco Center for Digital Media moved to Berkeley and became the Center for Digital Storytelling, and in 2015, the organization became, simply, StoryCenter (https://www.storycenter.org). StoryCenter has run in-person and online public workshops for academics, individuals, communities, and organizations with a mission of finding a story that they want or need to tell, helping them define that story in the form of a solidly written script. It is important to note that INDIGITAL is the Indigenous arm of StoryCenter Canada and is led by the first author of this book chapter. For many storytellers, including the authors of this chapter, this process of clarification has proven to be a transformative experience.[8] Choctaw-Haida scholar Carolyn Kenny suggests that "stories are a creative act of leadership through which we manifest our solidarity and strengthen our people to take their next step in encouraging good and healthy lives."[9] Digital storytelling was used by our research team to visually and emotionally show how *we*, as Red River Métis people, thrive and flourish because we are connected to our families, our communities, and our land.

A Culturally Relevant Research Method

There are a number of influential Indigenous scholars who have encouraged our understanding of engaging in Indigenous research.[10] They attest to the rootedness of Indigenous culture in Indigenous research, and have taught us as Métis researchers that research on and with Indigenous peoples must be carried out in a culturally appropriate and relevant manner. Research methods must take into consideration Indigenous worldviews that are inclusive of family and community life, cultural traditions, contemporary practices, and artistic expressions.

Storytelling is a central focus of Indigenous epistemologies and research methods.[11] Storytelling is used to define Métis people culturally, ideologically, and individually. Stories teach facts and provide lessons about ourselves, our culture, and ways of viewing the world.[12] The digital storytelling process recognizes elements of storytelling, including the oral tradition, the writing process, and the power of visuals.[13] Métis scholar Cora Weber-Pillwax writes that research "is within the context of a real person doing real research in a real community." She notes that "the most serious consideration for me as a researcher is the assurance that I will uphold the personal responsibility that goes along with carrying out a research project that I have decided to work within."[14] Through the use of the digital storytelling method, we were able to create a meaningful narrative in our understanding of our identity. Our stories allowed us to connect our past, present, as well as a future for our children. Thus, creating digital stories helped to reinforce our Métis identity and how it is connected to the place, land, community, and spirituality. The process of sharing photos and telling our own stories was relevant to us. Respect required that we listen intently to the stories, experiences, and ideas of others throughout the workshop.

Storytelling nurtures relationships and the sharing of Indigenous knowledge and culture.[15] Who we are as Métis women is anchored in our histories, and knowing these histories provides us with strength and resilience. Being Métis and sharing our stories define our people and our nation and help us to understand our identities through telling stories of what we know, how we think, and what we feel. Our stories preserve our culture and pass on our cultural knowledge to our children, keeping our identities alive.

For our research team, in order to fully understand and learn about the digital storytelling method, we chose to engage in the process ourselves. We wanted to understand how this method could be in alignment with Métis health and well-being research that is relational, relevant, reciprocal, respectful, and responsible. Indigenous researchers include and situate themselves in their methodologies. This includes the researcher's location, memory, motive, and search for congruency. Indigenous worldviews and principles are actualized by Indigenous researchers who are consciously connected to their roots and have continued channels of support. Central tendencies of Indigenous research come from the self and from understanding the self in relation to the whole. Therefore, for this book chapter we engaged in critical reflexivity as part of a three-day digital storytelling workshop where we created our own digital stories as they relate to Métis identity, health, and our overall well-being. As such, throughout this chapter, we take the readers on a storytelling journey about our understanding of the digital storytelling method as well as how we have grown from these experiences. We engage in a reflexive practice to explore issues of power and positionality and to make the role and assumptions we have as Métis researchers more explicit.[16] A reflexive practice allowed us to think about what we did, how it worked or did not work, and, subsequently, what we would do differently when we engage in our research project with Métis community members. Reflexive practice as analysis was well suited to the evaluation of our engagement with the digital storytelling method, and it aligned with our positionality as both Métis community members and researchers.

The 4 Rs were first used and applied to framing First Nations higher education by Verna Kirkness and Ray Barnhardt in 1991.[17] Since then, many Indigenous researchers have applied the 4 Rs in creating meaningful research, including a 5th R of relationships or relationality.[18] In the remainder of this chapter. we contextualize our experiences and understanding of the digital storytelling method using the 4 Rs of respect, relevance, reciprocity, and responsibility[19] with the inclusion of a 5th R, relationships/relationality, as a reflective tool.

A Relational Method

A researcher's worldview influences self as a researcher, the research process, choice of methodology, and implementing such methodology. One's worldview has the ability to ground research theory, motivations, purpose, and process.[20] Shawn Wilson draws on relationality as an Indigenous worldview to describe the interconnections between family, community, and all extended human and non-human relations. Within an Indigenous worldview, relationships are considered vital because they allow for the transfer of knowledge between individuals and generations.[21] Relationships provide people with a critical sense of belonging, being valued, with a network of historical linkages and social support.[22]

The storytelling process at StoryCenter is described as a journey, and thus they prefer to use the metaphor of "Steps," rather than "Elements," because it more practically guides storytellers along the path of creating a meaningful digital story.[23] As the first of seven steps of the workshop, the story circle began with each participant sharing a story (we called this *owning our insights*). Within the circle, each participant had the opportunity to talk but also listen intently. We listened to each other's stories and provided feedback on specifics within each story that resonated with us. Step two, *owning our emotions,* helped participants to consider what parts of our stories that we spoke passionately about as well as the aspects of our story that had the most impact on those listening. Many stories shared were of past, present, and future hopes, and aspirations and motivations. These stories were embedded in people's identities and worldviews that centred on their family, community, and nation. The story circle provided a space for relationships to develop. According to Neal McLeod, "narrative reciprocity is central to oral cultures . . . the flow of information helps to cement social relationships."[24] This process provided the relational foundation we needed to ground us moving forward. From the feedback, step three involved writing a 250-word script that would be read and recorded for inclusion into the digital format (we called this *finding the moment*).

Reflecting on our experiences on the first day, we can see how they allowed us to form real relationships with each other as a research team as well as with the rest of the workshop members. Being relational for us was about living in relation to others and the recognition of the interconnectedness of our lives, and our stories. As participants in the workshop, we were engaged, grounded, honest, compassionate, and humble. We always sought opportunities to engage with our stories and those around us. We shared about ourselves, demonstrating our willingness to trust. We asked questions and listened attentively to exemplify that we genuinely care about people's stories and experiences. We communicated openly and spoke with those around us to see how they were doing throughout the workshop. We continually had the opportunity to speak up when we misunderstood specific directions. As participants, we invited others to be part of our process by asking questions as well as accepting feedback and help when needed. We shared the space, meals, and our stories, photos, and chosen sounds and music.

Building relationships is the groundwork that must be laid before initiating research. The digital storytelling method works well in creating and maintaining relational ties. Shawn Wilson suggests that as Indigenous researchers, we must transcend assuming an Indigenous perspective on non-Indigenous research paradigms and understand that methodologies used within research must come from a fundamental belief that knowledge is relational.[25] As Thomas King states, "all my relations" is at first a reminder of who we are and of our relationship with both our family and our relatives.[26]

A Respectful Method

Respect is about honouring where we come from: our cultures, traditions, and ourselves. It is the driving force of our communities because it impacts all of our life experiences, including our relationships, health, and work.[27] Respect is based on creating relationships grounded in connection, communication, honesty, and trust.[28] Being respectful means showing that we value other people's perspectives, time, and space. Listening to what others have to say validates them, which conveys respect. When we affirm someone, we are providing evidence that they matter, are valued and worthy of respect.

Respect was demonstrated in numerous forms, such as introducing people at the workshop, listening and observing, and allowing others to share about themselves, their families, and experiences. Workshop participants helped each other edit stories, choose pictures, and learn the technology and software. This also speaks to the relationships we built with each other throughout the workshop, as well as the respect we had for each other. For us, the process was just as important as the end product. All of the workshop participants helped to create our digital stories—it was our relationship with others at the workshop that allowed us to share what we shared. Smith states, "Respect is a reciprocal, shared, and constantly interchanging principle which is expressed through all aspects of social conduct."[29] It was the digital storytelling process that helped us to connect with our story and pictures of ourselves, the land, family, and our children. We were in a respectful space to explore what was worth remembering.

A Reciprocal Method

Reciprocity dictates that both the researcher and the participant mutually benefit from such engagement because participants share their time, knowledge, and experiences to aid the researcher in achieving the purpose of the study.[30] Reciprocity reflects an Indigenous relational worldview and the understanding that we must honour our relationships with the land, people, and all things.[31]

On the second day of the workshop, all participants continued to work on their scripts and began step four, which involved selecting images that conveyed the story we wanted to tell (*seeing our story).* From here, we continued on to step five, *hearing our story*, and began to write out and record our digital story voice-over—choosing music or ambient sound to create depth. One by one, each participant went into the sound room and recorded *our story*. This part of the workshop was where the group supported each other and helped edit each other's story. Step six, *assembling our story*, included learning how to use digital editing software to structure and integrate all the elements from the previous steps. Throughout this process, we drank coffee and shared food, discussing our stories and images. The images we used to tell parts of our story connected us with our identity and how our identity is rooted in a place connected to the people around us. Revisiting photos allowed us to remember our past. For us, this included picking fruit, berries, and mushrooms, followed by making jam, jellies, and preserves. It also included visiting our aunties, uncles, cousins, grandparents, extended family, and friends—attending kitchen parties where we would eat, play cards, jig, fiddle, play music, sing, storytell, and story listen. By sharing our stories and photos, we also shared our emotions. Sharing the intimate details of our memories attached to the photos often elicited sadness, sorrow, and anger, but at times they also provided us with a deep sense of connection, pride, and joy. Within an Indigenous research paradigm, reciprocity is an interchange between individuals to connect them in a ceremony of giving and receiving, listening and talking, teaching and learning.[32] Storytelling and story listening are examples of reciprocity within the digital storytelling workshop. As a research team, it was an opportunity to understand each other, which allowed us to recognize our shared collective stories as Red River Métis people and academics. Stories remind us of respect, perseverance, and the promise we have with ourselves, families, communities, and spirituality.

A Responsible Method

Responsibility is a commitment that we dedicate ourselves to our family, community, and nation. Responsibility is empowerment and is fostered through active engagement and participation in the digital storytelling workshop and method.

On the third and final day of the workshop, participants completed their digital stories and continued to help those who needed assistance. Step seven, *sharing your story,* involved showcasing our digital stories to the entire group, where they were projected on a screen for all to watch. We had a sense of responsibility within our group to share in the emotions of completing our digital stories. As Métis community members and academics, relationality is a social, moral, and ethical contract that we are bound to that stems from our philosophical stance. We felt responsible for the physical, mental, emotional, and spiritual well-being of our workshop members. Watching and listening to the digital stories required us to maintain an active presence, empathy, and openness to hear and see each other's stories. When we actively listened, we validated the storyteller, our attention affirmed that they, and their experiences, mattered. Wilson states, "The responsibility to ensure respectful and reciprocal relationships becomes the axiology of the person who is making these connections."[33]

Our Vulnerability

As Métis community members and academics, we understand that telling our stories with individuals whom we may not have much rapport with can be very vulnerable. Sharing personal stories may be more frightening to some than to others, and this depends upon their personal histories, cultural backgrounds, and personality traits.

Moreover, feelings of shame are a risk for many individuals, especially if they were raised in a shame-based culture. A story can be tragic or happy, possibly both. Regardless, as researchers and participants, we will always bring our own emotional baggage and biases while storytelling and story listening. As researchers, we must be prepared to advise participants, to deepen their self-awareness, to understand how they are reacting to their own story and others, as well as reminding them to remain present and impartial throughout the workshop setting. As researchers, we must do what we can to provide an environment where participants have the opportunity to connect with each other, building relationships so that feelings of vulnerability are reduced. We must caution that not all stories will evoke such emotions. However, given our history and present-day experiences (discrimination, racism, and sexism to name a few) as Métis peoples, we must be mindful of possibly triggering stories within the digital storytelling workshop. For example, sharing our Métis identity, health, and well-being is personal. We may feel a sense of being exposed when we share our intimate feelings about ourselves and our children. When we share our digital stories with friends, colleagues, and family, we may feel an immediate fear of judgment and shame attached to our identity. These are attached to feelings of not being "Métis" enough because Métis identity is under public scrutiny, as it is being debated by scholars across Canada. Many of us do our best to compartmentalize our identity in different aspects of our lives. But, compartmentalization creates isolation—we isolate ourselves. As such, we often do not feel supported or connected with other Métis researchers. But, our awareness of the impact that judgment and shame have on us, and on others, gives us a reason to change this negative internal and external narrative, and pursue the research we are doing. Perhaps our sharing will help others find the courage to delve into their own stories.

Conclusion

Our personal digital stories on Métis health and well-being are embedded in the relationship with ourselves, family, community, culture, spirituality, and with the land. We have learned that doing community-engaged research has the potential to expand, stretch, and teach the researchers, collaborators, partners, and community members involved. This demanded vulnerability from each of us. However, it also allowed us to learn about our roles as researchers as well as Métis community members within our research relationship.

So how do we enrich Métis research outside of the archives and bring it into contemporary space? As Métis women, we know that our Indigenous knowledge is based in oral traditions. Oral traditions form the foundation of our Indigenous families and communities, connecting speaker and listener in a communal experience and uniting past and present in memory. Story is one of the main methods of traditional Indigenous learning and teaching. Stories enable holistic learning. They meld values, concepts, protocol, practices, and facts into a narrative. As well, art has always been an integral part of the preservation and expression of our culture. Therefore connecting stories with art such as music, photos, drawings, and paintings is a relational, reciprocal, respectful, and relevant method for us to use within our research about Métis identity. Digital storytelling has the potential to connect with our families, ancestors, children, and even who we are as Métis people.

Community-engaged research and the digital storytelling process has the ability to showcase who we are as Métis people and provides us with an important platform. We must remember that Indigenous ways of being, doing, and knowing is not one of living in the past, but continually adapting to the now and considers the impact of all actions in the seven generations to come.

Our research team developed our own digital stories that documented our understandings of identity, culture, health, and well-being. With the elements of audio, photos, video, art, text, and music, our individual digital stories share topics of racism, poverty, and isolation, as well as our relational ties to people, community, and the land.

Notes

1 Voth, "Her Majesty's Justice"; Gaudry, "Métis in Canada"; Gaudry, "The Métisization of Canada"; Andersen, "*Métis*"; Macdougall, *One of the Family*; Campbell, *Halfbreed* (1973 ed.).

2 Gaudry and Leroux, "White Settler."

3 Métis Centre of the National Aboriginal Health Organization, "Paucity."

4 Lambert and Hessler, *Digital Storytelling: Capturing Lives.*

5 Lambert, *Digital Storytelling Cookbook.*

6 Gubrium, "Digital Storytelling," 186.
7 Leclair and Warren, "Portals," 4.
8 Lambert, *Digital Storytelling Cookbook.*
9 Kenny, *Leadership*, 1.
10 L.T. Smith, *Decolonizing Methodologies*; S. Wilson, *Research Is Ceremony*; Kovach, *Indigenous Methodologies.*
11 A. LaVallee, "Converging Methods."
12 Barkwell, Dorion, and Préfontaine, *Métis Legacy.*
13 Gubrium, "Digital Storytelling," 186.
14 Weber-Pillwax, "Indigenous Researchers," 79–80.
15 Poitras Pratt and Daniels, "Metis Remembrances."
16 Guillemin and Gillam, "Ethics."
17 Kirkness and Barnhardt, "First Nations."
18 A. LaVallee, "Converging Methods"; A. LaVallee, Troupe, and Turner, "Negotiating"; Henry, Tait, and STR8 UP, "Creating."
19 Kirkness and Barnhardt, "First Nations."
20 Absolon, *Kaandossiwin.*
21 S. Wilson, *Research Is Ceremony.*
22 Hart, "Indigenous Worldviews"; S. Wilson, *Research Is Ceremony*; K. Anderson, *A Recognition* (2000 ed.).
23 Lambert, *Digital Storytelling Cookbook.*
24 McLeod, "Exploring," 25.
25 S. Wilson, *Research Is Ceremony.*
26 King, "Introduction," ix.
27 S. Wilson, *Research Is Ceremony.*
28 A. LaVallee, Troupe, and Turner, "Negotiating."
29 L.T. Smith, *Decolonizing Methodologies*, 120.
30 A. LaVallee, "Converging Methods"; A. LaVallee, Troupe, and Turner, "Negotiating."
31 S. Wilson, *Research Is Ceremony*; Kovach, *Indigenous Methodologies.*
32 Absolon, *Kaandossiwin*; A. LaVallee, "Converging Methods."
33 S. Wilson, *Research Is Ceremony*, 79.

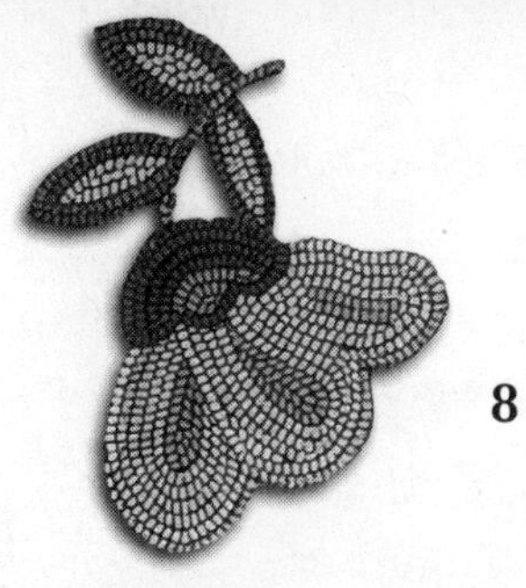

8

Prenatal/Postpartum Ceremonies and Parenting as Michif Self-Determination

Chantal Fiola

Historically, some Michif[1] in the Red River region (and beyond) participated in pipe ceremonies, sweat lodges, Midewiwin,[2] Sundance,[3] and prenatal/postpartum ceremonies.[4] Colonization tried to dispossess Michif and First Nations from our spiritualities, genders, and sexualities, among other things; the consequences have been widespread, including disconnection from ceremonies,[5] the stereotype that all Métis are Christian, and the oppression of Two-Spirit (2S) people.[6] Fortunately, our resilience also takes many forms, including Michif (and First Nations) people increasingly returning to ceremony, and Two-Spirit people reclaiming our power and place in communities.

My research seeks to contribute to the resurgence of Michif spirituality as inclusive of ceremonies[7] and to empower Michif and 2S people.[8] As a Two-Spirit Michif person who participates in ceremonies, I try to model these efforts in my personal, scholarly, and spiritual life. By becoming Midewiwin and a Sundancer, marrying my wife in a *wiidiigewin* ("union of souls") ceremony, becoming mothers together, and parenting in ceremony, we exercise our self-determination. In this chapter, I highlight wisdom from Michif (Métis), Anishinaabeg (Saulteaux/Ojibwe), and Nêhiyawak (Cree)[9] Elders and mothers/scholars regarding prenatal/postpartum ceremonies and parenting.[10] I also share the personal experiences, challenges, and joys that my 2S Michif family has experienced on our journey of spiritual and ceremonial reconnection. I hope to encourage other 2S families and inspire further resurgence of Michif spirituality as sovereignty.

Building a Life of Ceremony Together

My wife, Nicki,[11] and I are Michif; our ancestors established the historic Michif communities of Lorette and St. Laurent, respectively, in the early nineteenth century. We are founding members of the Two-Spirit Michif Local dedicated to serving 2SLGBTQ+ Michif citizens in the Manitoba Métis Federation (MMF)—a first in Métis Nation governance. We were raised Catholic but reconnected to ceremonies before we met. We are committed to Michif ways of knowing, being, and ceremony in relation with our Michif, Anishinaabeg, and Nêhiyawak ancestors and relatives. We face challenges as 2S Michif women in a same-sex family, but experience privilege as cisgender, white coded, educated, and employed in academia.

Nicki and I began our respective journeys of spiritual reconnection ten and sixteen years ago. I initiated into the Three Fires Midewiwin Lodge in 2011 but had been attending Mide and non-Mide ceremonies prior. I was adopted by the late *Mizhaakwanagiizhikbaa* (Charlie Nelson, Chief of the Minweyweyigaan Midewiwin Lodge); he conducted my Midewiwin adoption, clan confirmation, and naming ceremony, witnessed by community. I am called *Zaagaate Kwe* (Sunrays Shining through the Clouds Woman) and belong to the *biizhew doodem* (lynx clan).[12] I put down alcohol and drugs (fifteen years ago) and continue to frequently participate in *asemaa* (tobacco) and *nibi* (water) ceremonies as part of my Mide commitment. In 2016, I began my Sundance journey with the Blacksmith Sundance Family; my wife is a Sundancer with the Nokomis Lodge. We also participate in ceremonies with our 2S community, including sweat lodges conducted by our 2S/trans Michif Elders.

We had our Midewiwin wiidiigewin wedding ceremony on Nicki's family's land in their Michif community (Lorette), conducted by our friend Ron Indian-Mandamin, an Anishinaabe 2S Mide Chief from Shoal Lake First Nation. We prepared for a year: offering our asemaa, harvesting birchbark, participating in sweats and a cedar brushing, preparing a feast and spirit dish, and listening to scroll and grandmother waterdrum teachings confirming that 2S people have always existed.[13]

Our 2S and trans Michif Elders, Barbara Bruce and Charlotte Nolin, respectively, also helped us prepare, including harvesting a bird of prey, making birchbark bowls, and assisting during the wiidiigewin. Elder Bruce, who comes from my mother's Michif community (St. Laurent), was our officiant. Mothers play an instrumental role in the wiidiigewin, helping us build and dress the arch we were wed under, witnessing our cedar brushing, listening to the teachings, and walking us down the aisle (we included our fathers). Our wiidiigewin reconnected our loving families to these beautiful ceremonies.[14]

Beginning Our 2S Michif Family

Navigating assisted reproduction is extra challenging as a 2S Métis couple; again, we turned to ceremony. We Sundanced to find our donor, petitioned the spirit that would choose us as parents, and prayed for a healthy pregnancy, delivery, and baby. We decided I would carry first since I am older. We selected an anonymous Indigenous "Open ID" donor.[15]

We conceived on our third try; five months later, the World Health Organization declared COVID-19 a global pandemic. When I worry about our baby growing up during these troubled times, I find comfort in our spiritual knowledge. Cree/Trinidadian writer (and my Sundance relative) Tasha Spillett-Sumner reminds us that, according to our teachings: "It's children who chose their parents and use their own agency to come into the world. What incredibly courageous and hopeful babies we have. They have seen the days ahead and have still chosen to step forward. These spirits are surely the medicine that the world needs now."[16] So, I strengthen my resolve to help create a healthier future for my child and all our relations.

Nicki and I sought Indigenous teachings about pregnancy, birth, delivery, and parenting. The early days of COVID-19 prevented us from offering asemaa to our teachers, but we remained connected to our support network, and writings by Indigenous mothers/parents and educators, via technology. Mohawk midwife and women's health activist Katsi Cook links Indigenous teachings to exercising self-determination, explaining that mothers[17] are their babies' first environment: "When a woman is pregnant, the fetus grows and develops through her experiences. The baby sees through her eyes, hears through her ears—everything the mother experiences, her growing and developing fetus experiences. . . . This is true even after we're born. . . . She is not just incubating a fetus; she herself can be incubated, supported by, a culture that stretches back hundreds of years and is alive around her now. That's why we reference our teachings in order to affect our capacity for self-determination, sovereignty and freedom in all of the areas of our lives."[18] Cree/Métis scholar Kim Anderson reiterates, "These protocols or practices were based on the understanding that whatever the pregnant mother took in would be ingested by the baby. This applied to what she ate or drank, as well as to what she saw, heard, or experienced." Consequently, "personal discipline was crucial because everything a woman thinks about and feels would go to the baby."[19] I ate healthier (thanks to my wife's wonderful cooking!) and stopped watching true crime shows. I tried to be gentle with myself and my thoughts, though I sometimes struggled with prenatal/postpartum anger (an effect of hormones lesser known than prenatal/postpartum depression). My wife, asemaa, nibi, and smudging ceremonies helped me regain balance.

Before the first COVID lockdowns began, we secured a midwife team. According to Anderson, "midwives carried authority into the 1950s until hospital or doctor-assisted births began to take over in Native communities."[20] We hoped for an Indigenous midwife, but none were practising in our city; this is not uncommon due to impacts of colonization.[21] Our three midwives were white settler women; we especially connected with the queer midwife who is married with children—she attended our baby's birth.

We also began the adoption process while pregnant. In Manitoba, both our names would appear on our child's birth certificate; however, Nicki would not legally be considered a parent. The expensive and time-consuming process was finalized six months postpartum. One month prior, a Manitoba judge ruled that the Family Maintenance Act's definition of *parent* was unconstitutional: "Under current legislation, couples who have children through assisted reproduction aren't considered legal parents of their child if they have no biological connection, meaning couples have to go through costly court orders or adoption processes to be declared the legal parent *of their own child*."[22] The Family Maintenance Act will be updated to protect non-biological parents, for example, during separation or divorce. Nonetheless, our adoption lawyer[23] helped us finalize the adoption since other legislation (e.g., the Wills Act) still defines *parent/family* unconstitutionally. Nicki is just as much our child's mother as I am; her rights must be protected, including in the event of my death.

We prepared our birth plan, hoping to deliver at the birth centre with our midwife, and without medical intervention/drugs (except nitrous oxide/laughing gas). We packed our bundle, including medicines, asemaa and *mushkodaywushk* (sage), our smudge bundle, our *migizii miigwan* (eagle feather from our wiidiigewin), items for a "feet touch the earth" ceremony, and affirmation posters Nicki made for me. When the time came, she texted our 2S Elders (at their request), letting them know we were in labour so they could begin a prayer circle for us.

Our plan changed after two days of painful contractions; I was admitted into the Women's Hospital. I laboured in the birthing tub with lights dimmed, our wedding playlist sounding softly, holding hands with my wife as I breathed in the nitrous oxide—I felt peaceful and connected to my ancestors, my wife, and our baby. Later, complications arose; I agreed to a transfer of care from our midwife to a surgeon, accepted an epidural, and was told I needed an emergency C-section. The meds made my teeth chatter and upper body shake uncontrollably; my arms needed to be restrained. Nicki and our midwife comforted me, massaging my aching jaw.

After seventy-four hours of contractions, our beautiful, healthy daughter made her appearance at 3:39 a.m. I wept in relief and gratitude when Mireille sounded her powerful voice; my shaking stopped when she was placed on my chest. Our midwife stayed to advocate for our wishes (e.g., keeping my placenta, and skin-to-skin time) and to help establish breastfeeding. We learned that while we laboured, our 2S/trans Elders held a prayer circle with twenty community members who made offerings, smudged, smoked pipes, sang, and drummed (in their own homes due to COVID-19) to guide our spirit baby's entrance into this physical realm, and for our little family's health.

Reconnecting to Postpartum Ceremonies

Indigenous people, including Michif people, recognize that birth itself is a sacred ceremony, and that other ceremonies involving the placenta and umbilical cord occur postpartum.[24] Discussing Métis, Cree, and Anishinaabe birthing ceremonies, Anderson notes that "Care for newborns included customs that began with the treatment of their placentas and umbilical cords. These practices were considered vital in terms of protecting babies and ensuring they had long, healthy, and productive lives. A placenta was not something to be disposed of or left lying around, it held a life force and needed to be disposed of properly. . . . [For example, one could] bury them in specific locations to help with the work the child could expect to do in his or her lifetime."[25] According to Anderson, "Umbilical cords signified connections that were made between the child and his or her relations"; one teaching is "that the umbilical cord and the placenta should be buried under the roots of a young tree with an offering of tobacco."[26] Likewise, Lawrence Barkwell, Darren Préfontaine (Métis), and Anne Carrière-Acco (Métis) explain that "Many Metis families still follow the First Nations' post-partum practice of taking the baby's placenta and burying it at the base of a young tree (usually cedar). If the birth occurs in winter, the placenta is kept frozen until spring and then the ritual is performed. Once the umbilical cord separates, this is placed in the branches of a tree for boys, and in the crotch of a tree or buried on a small rise for girls."[27] My wife and I wanted to honour our daughter through these customs and ceremonies, seeking blessings for her good, long, healthy life, and connecting her to our traditional territory and relatives.

We had a placenta burial ceremony on Nicki's mother's land in their Michif community (Lorette—where we had our wiidiigewin). My mother-in-law joined us (wearing masks due to COVID-19) in a small ceremony involving the selection of a young tree, smudging with mushkodaywushk, offering asemaa, a feast, and a spirit dish. Nicki, Mireille, and I also drove to my mother's Michif community (St. Laurent) for an umbilical cord ceremony on my uncle's treed acreage; he dug the hole and left us a small wooden table. We laid out our bundle items, cleansed them and ourselves with mushkodaywushk, and made offerings of asemaa. We buried our daughter's umbilical cord, wrapped in red cloth, and did the same for our niece's cord, who was born eight months prior. Our prayers recognized that we are spiritual beings living a physical existence and that our bodies will eventually return to the earth.[28] We petitioned for them to have good, long, healthy lives, and to remain connected to the land of their Michif ancestors, communities, and relatives.

Another Indigenous practice my wife and I reclaimed for our family is the *tikinaagan* ("cradleboard"). Tikinaagans were widely used by

Algonquian peoples across North America, up to the mid-twentieth century, to carry their babies.[29] Made from a wooden board, footrest, bow and a rawhide/fabric covering, the baby is placed inside (often in a moss bag) and laced up. Tikinaagans are often built by parents or relatives and sometimes passed down intergenerationally.[30] Anishinaabe mother and scholar Andrea Landry explains, "This provides a balance of kinship—everyone plays a part in ultimately providing security and comfort, and a space for observance and learning for the baby."[31] Anderson notes that sometimes the tikinaagan would have a dream-catcher on it: "a hoop made of willow or the small branches of other softwood trees, and a spider net made of sinew . . . to catch bad dreams and allow only good dreams to come through to the baby."[32] A tiki-naagan can be carried on one's back using a strap around the chest or forehead and propped up (against a tree, for example) so the child can be socialized (learn as they watch their parents and community members work and interact).[33] We obtained a tikinaagan made by my Midewiwin relatives (Hilda Atkinson and Barb Smith) through a fundraiser, and our 2S Michif friend David Heinrichs beaded the covering in Métis-style floral beadwork—it is a stunning work of art and craftmanship illustrating our love for Mireille.[34] I envisioned baby-wearing with the tikinaagan while engaging in activities on the land; unfortunately, we rarely left our home during the first couple of years to protect our daughter from COVID-19. Moreover, we wanted to have a "walking out" ceremony, which occurs once the child takes their first steps—it is the first time their feet touch the earth.[35] Anderson explains that this strengthens the relationship between baby and land and teaches children the importance of community responsibility. Family and community would gather to celebrate the transition into toddler years and "bring gifts and wishes that pertain to the child's future, as he or she 'walks out' in that direction. These things are placed into a bundle that they carry as they walk around the circle of friends and family. They are thus literally and figuratively equipped to move into the life stages that are to come."[36] However, since we were unsure of how long the pandemic lockdowns would prevent us from physically gathering with our loved ones, we decided upon a "feet touch the earth" ceremony shortly after birth.

According to Three Fires Midewiwin teachings, and Anishinaabe-Métis scholar Aimée Craft,[37] who works extensively with Anishinaabeg

Elders in Treaty Three territory, a "feet touch the earth" ceremony happens at birth, or soon thereafter. Historically, a birthing lodge was built, and upon delivery, the midwife would touch the baby to the earth before placing them upon their mother. Contemporarily, this practice has been modified, for example, with parents bringing a baking pan of earth into the birth centre.[38] Nicki and I passed asemaa to my cousin for earth from St. Laurent, to Nicki's parents for earth from Lorette, and to my parents for earth from Ste. Geneviève, where I was raised. We held this ceremony in our home (in Winnipeg) a few days postpartum.

Two weeks shy of Mireille's first birthday, we held a walking out ceremony for her. Besides her feet touching the dirt in the baking pan shortly after birth, we had honoured the tradition of carrying her and not letting her touch the land until she learned to walk (indoors). At that time, Nicki and I invited our sisters (still cautious of COVID-19) to a small ceremony in Henteleff Park (where my late maternal grandfather, Robert Normand, had worked the land in his younger days). There—on land my family has an intergenerational relationship with—Mireille took her first steps upon the earth. Each of these ceremonies (placenta, umbilical cord, "feet touch the earth," "walking out") reiterates the importance of our relationship with land, our (Michif) communities, and all our relations.

Childrearing as Ceremony

My wife and I are committed to a resurgence of Indigenous birthing and childrearing practices and ceremonies to promote self-determination and Michif sovereignty; this requires unlearning and healing from colonial traumas. Colonization has deeply impacted Indigenous birthing, parenting, community cohesion, and women's (and 2S) sovereignty. Anishinaabe mother and scholar Leanne Simpson explains:

> When colonialism hijacked our pregnancies and birth, it also stole our power and our sovereignty as Indigenous women. . . . It made us feel powerless and afraid of our most important and powerful ceremony—the one where we have the honour of carrying another spirit-being inside the water in our bodies. It made us afraid of ourselves. It made us question our body's knowledge and our Grandmothers' and aunties' knowledge, and our ability to bring forth new

> life. . . . The western medicalization of birth replaced our ceremony. Bottles and substandard formula took the place of nursing, detachment supplanted attachment, and mothering was replaced by the physical, psychological, sexual, and spiritual abuse of the residential school system. By undermining our most sacred and powerful ceremony and our most sacred responsibilities as mothers, our colonizers thought they could achieve the destruction of our nations.[39]

Anderson elaborates upon these themes:

> White doctors, who were "experts" on birth, replaced our midwives and displaced our confidence in our bodies, our reliance on our traditional knowledge, and our trust in our clans, our spirit-helpers, and our ancestors. Our midwives, aunties, and grandmothers were not allowed in delivery rooms, and neither were our medicines, our singing, our drumming, and our birthing knowledge. We were strapped flat on our backs on hospital beds, not allowed to use our knowledge of birthing which told us which positions to use, ways of minimizing pain, and ways of birthing naturally and safely. . . . We were told that for the safety of our babies we needed medical intervention and to rely on the western medical system; to do anything else, we were told, would be irresponsible.[40]

Yet, colonization failed, and Indigenous birthing and parenting persist. Landry insists that colonialism has motherhood and parenting all wrong and could never take away our intergenerational childrearing and kinship practices, asserting that "our babies will never cater to the colonizer, their systems, or their standards of what a 'good child' is."[41]

Anderson interviewed Michif, Nêhiyawak, and Anishinaabeg Elders about the resilience and persistence of Indigenous approaches to birth and parenting (including ceremonies) and found "an unmistakable reverence for life that defined many of their cultural norms and practices."[42] In her interview, Michif Elder Maria Campbell recalled a naming ceremony for a baby in her Michif community, illustrating that "communities carried on with their ceremonies in a modified manner despite the government's oppression of traditional ways."[43]

Understanding the precariousness of new life, utmost care was taken during pregnancy, infancy, and toddlerhood, and involved parents, family, and community to "ensure that the newest members learned to trust and depend on the world they had entered."[44] Similarly, Simpson writes about the "strong attachment to children, nurtured in those first seven years, and including things like long-term breastfeeding, on cue feeding rather than on schedule feeding, co-sleeping, baby-wearing, and gentle, positive, non-violent guidance, discussion, and empathy."[45] The Elders interviewed by Anderson agreed that "infants enjoyed a sense of comfort and security through swaddling and being in close contact with their mothers" and were never alone.[46]

Practices like bedsharing, co-sleeping (room sharing), baby wearing, use of swings, and prolonged breastfeeding were common among Indigenous nations.[47] Landry affirms: "No, our babies will not sleep alone as they have been sleeping beside us, on us, and between us, for generations before the colonizer told us what was 'right.' No, our babies will not 'cry it out,' as they are designed to cry in order to get their needs met through us."[48] Nicki and I researched sleeping practices (Indigenous and western, including with our midwives and family doctor); our decisions to bedshare, and later co-sleep, were supported. We shared a bed with our baby for her first six months of life—until she began to locomote and hog the bed!

Anderson notes that Indigenous children were breastfed until age two (to five), but "conflicting values that had begun to creep in with the mainstream movement towards bottle-feeding in the 1950s" pressured women into bottle-feeding.[49] Moreover, residential/day schools disrupted the generational knowledge and community support required for breastfeeding.[50] Black and Indigenous people of colour (BIPOC) have the lowest rates of initiation and duration of breast/chestfeeding;[51] formula was deliberately marketed towards these communities "as a symbol of 'good parenting' and 'upward mobility.'"[52] Maria Campbell remembers the public health nurse coming to her Michif community and telling mothers that breastfeeding is "unhealthy," and pushing them to give their babies cow's milk.[53]

BIPOC and queer parents are reclaiming breast/chestfeeding. Countering colonial pressure, Landry declares that Indigenous "aunties and mothers (and even kokums) have been co-nursing our babies longer than colonialism has even existed."[54] My wife and I were committed to exclusively breastfeeding despite struggling for months, which contributed to my postpartum anger.[55] We visited a lactation consultant, pediatric surgeon, and pediatric osteopath,[56] and finally, breastfeeding became enjoyable for both of us. Nicki bottle-fed our baby once or twice daily (since I began also pumping early on). I nursed until Mireille decided to stop around fourteen months but continued to pump for another two months before switching to dairy.

Two-Spirit Michif Family: Kinship and Ceremony

It is important to my wife and me that we raise our child(ren) according to Michif ways of knowing and being, including ceremony, in relation with our Michif, Midewiwin, Sundance, and Two-Spirit communities. We have learned that Mireille also belongs to biizhew doodem (through me), and offered asemaa to learn her spirit name. Ron accepted our asemaa again and conducted her beautiful naming ceremony during the first ever (to all our knowledge) 2S Sundance in late August 2023 surrounded by her relatives and loved ones.

Michif mother and Cree language instructor Chelsea Vowel reminds us that missionaries, teachers, civil servants, residential schools, and the child welfare system either misspelled, translated, or imposed foreign names upon Indigenous people in a systematic attempt to erase our cultures, languages, and identities. Even today, Canadian provinces forbid characters from non-English alphabets or require having a surname.[57] Indigenous people are reclaiming the practice of spirit-naming using Indigenous languages. Naming ceremonies can range from casual events to formal ceremonies involving family, community, a feast, and a giveaway. Anderson recalls that in Plains Cree communities, female Elders were often called upon to name girls, establishing a lifelong relationship resembling that of grandparent/grandchild, calling each other *nikweme*.[58] Vowel fasted for her children's spirit names and ensured they are spelled correctly in standardized Cree so her descendants can be sure of them. She asserts: "These lands formed *nêhiyawêwin* (Cree), and when we speak our language, even if it's just our names, the land hears us. The political doesn't get much more personal than speaking the names of my children every day."[59] Nicki and I try to speak to Mireille in Michif often; we speak French with her daily.[60]

As we got used to life during the pandemic and babies finally became eligible for the vaccine, we cautiously started venturing further outside of our home. Each summer, my wife and I have brought Mireille to our respective Sundances so she could meet her Sundance families and learn about the Sundance way of life. Most recently, I finally brought her to a Midewiwin ceremony: six Midewiwin lodges from across North America gathered to visit and feast seven very old Midewiwin birchbark scrolls (brought from storage by the Glenbow Museum in Alberta to Winnipeg at the request of Mizhaakwanagiizhikbaa and others); Mireille got to meet her Midewiwin family, look upon the ancient scrolls, and participate in several Mide ceremonies, including dancing in a children's honour song. We look forward to bringing her to more ceremonies, including a berry fast[61] and full moon ceremonies.

The importance of community in reclaiming Indigenous ways of life and ceremony cannot be overstated. Anderson asserts that the health of the baby was connected to the health of the community, and that "connections between the baby, family, community, the natural world, and the spirit world were ensured through . . . ceremonies."[62] Community remained central amidst pandemic isolation. Unable to participate in (Indigenous) Land Back and Black Lives Matter demonstrations, Spillett-Sumner realized that "parenting in a time of protest doesn't mean you're sitting on the sidelines. . . . You breastfeed the revolution. . . . The frontlines are wherever our bodies are, and some of our bodies are at home, raising the revolution."[63] She reminds us that it takes a village to raise a child, even during a pandemic, and that respecting parents' boundaries to protect their babies is an act of love.[64] Our daughter's birth brought together her communities in ceremony: the prayer circle during labour begun by our 2S/trans Elders; my masked mother-in-law and the placenta ceremony; my uncle preparing his land for the umbilical cord ceremony; our parents and my cousin who brought us earth for the "feet touch the earth" ceremony; our Mide and Michif relatives crafting our tikinaagan; our sisters who participated in Mireille's "walking out" ceremony. Even in a pandemic, our relatives, and the land itself, showed Mireille she is loved.

Indigenous Parenting an Ceremony as Sovereignty

Reclaiming the sacred work of Indigenous motherhood/parenting and the resurgence of prenatal/postpartum ceremonies are examples of Indigenous self-determination and sovereignty. Being a mother/parent, fostering, adopting, and nurturing the next generation, fulfills *mino-bimaadiziwin* (a good path in life) and requires reclaiming our responsibilities as aunties, grandmothers, teachers, visionaries, and carriers of culture.[65] According to Simpson, self-determination begins in the womb and is linked to the sovereignty of Indigenous nations: "Reclaiming Indigenous traditions of pregnancy, birth, and mothering will enable our children to lead our resurgence as Indigenous Peoples, to rise up and rebel against colonialism in all its forms, to dream independence, to dance to nationhood."[66]

My wife and I are doing our best to raise our daughter with self-determination according to Michif ways of knowing and being, grounded in kinship. Reclaiming ceremonies surrounding pregnancy, birth, parenting, and rites of passage ensure our daughter will grow up securely in her identity as Michif, in her Michif family, culture, and nation, and in relationship with our Sundance, Midewiwin, and Two-Spirit communities. Landry asserts that "our babies will grow up firm in their kinships and strong in who they are and where they come from. Based on raising them as best as we can with the teachings, morals, and principles, of our nations and teachings. . . . Because this is [I]ndigenous parenthood. And it is a force to be reckoned with."[67] Parenting in these ways offers a path back to the ceremonies of our ancestors that makes space for other (Two-Spirit) Michif (families) to do the same, as well as a path forward for our future babies. Together, we actualize Michif sovereignty, and remain accountable to all our relations, including the land.

Notes

1 The term *Michif* was used before *Métis* became common in the 1980s and is being reclaimed contemporarily; see Fiola, *Returning to Ceremony.* It is also the name of our language.

2 The Midewiwin is an ancestral, spiritual way of life involving various ceremonies practised among the Anishinaabeg and other Indigenous nations; see Benton-Banai, *The Mishomis Book.*

3 Held in summer, Sundance is a ceremony wherein adherents sacrifice water, food, and comfort while dancing and praying in an arbor for days; see Robinson, "The Sundance Ceremony."

4 Spaulding, "Métis Receive"; Barkwell, Préfontaine, and Carrière-Acco, "Metis Spirituality"; Vrooman, "Many Eagle"; Thompson, *Red Sun.*

5 Pettipas, *Severing the Ties.*

6 Two-Spirit (2S) is an umbrella term recalling Indigenous nation-specific conceptions of gender and sexuality, including those on the lesbian, gay, bisexual, transgender, queer (LGBTQ) spectrum, and non-binary folks; see A. Wilson, "N'tacimowin inna nah'"; Brayboy, "Two-Spirits"; Fiola, "Naawenangweyaabeg."

7 Fiola, *Rekindling*; Fiola, *Returning to Ceremony*.

8 Fiola and Ruprai, "Two-Spirit"; Fiola, "Naawenangweyaabeg"; Fiola and McLeod, "Two-Spirit Resistance."

9 These three nations share much in common, including across kinship, culture, linguistics, and spirituality; see Barkwell, Préfontaine, and Carrière-Acco, "Metis Spirituality"; Vrooman, "Many Eagle"; Innes, *Elder Brother*; Fiola, *Rekindling*; Fiola, *Returning to Ceremony*.

10 Simpson, "Birthing"; K. Anderson, *Life Stages*; Landry, "Why I Carried."

11 Nicki also authored a chapter in this book, and her beautiful textile art appears on the cover and features our daughter as a baby in her tikinaagan (cradleboard).

12 Nicki also came to learn her name and clan, but those are not my stories to share.

13 Fiola, "Naawenangweyaabeg."

14 To view photographs from our wiidiigewin (and from other family ceremonies described below), see Fiola, *Returning to Ceremony*.

15 Children can contact Open ID donors once they reach their eighteenth birthday.

16 Spillett-Sumner, "Pandemic Parenthood."

17 Cook, "Women Are." Literature on pregnancy and parenting (and their ceremonies) is often cisnormative and heteronormative—not everyone who gives birth identifies as female or a mother, nor do they all have cismale husbands who identify as fathers. Anishinaabe scholar and mother Renée Bédard also clarifies that "the Anishinaabe ideology of mothering and motherhood is not dependant on whether, as individuals, we produce children biologically. Women can be mothers in different ways, such as aunties, grannies or even through adoption" and fostering ("An Anishinaabe-kwe," 66).

18 Cook, "Women Are."

19 K. Anderson, *Life Stages*, 44.

20 Ibid., 40.

21 Simpson, "Birthing."

22 Blunt, "Manitoba Judge" (emphasis added).

23 She is also a married lesbian with children; like our midwife, she shared professional and personal insights with us.

24 Barkwell, Préfontaine, and Carrière-Acco, "Metis Spirituality"; K. Anderson, *Life Stages*; Fiola, *Returning to Ceremony*.

25 K. Anderson, *Life Stages*, 50.

26 Ibid., 51–52.

27 Barkwell, Préfontaine, and Carrière-Acco, "Metis Spirituality," 196.

28 Benton-Banai, *The Mishomis Book*.

29 Oberholtzer, "'A Womb'"; K. Anderson, *Life Stages*.

30 Oberholtzer, "'A Womb'"; Landry, "Why I Carried."

31 Landry, "Why I Carried."

32 K. Anderson, *Life Stages*, 59.

33 Oberholtzer, "'A Womb'"; K. Anderson, *Life Stages*; Landry, "Why I Carried."
34 Oberholtzer, "'A Womb.'" See also the book cover to this volume.
35 Oberholtzer, "'A Womb.'"
36 K. Anderson, *Life Stages*, 63.
37 Craft, "We Are Born."
38 Ibid.
39 Simpson, "Birthing," 28.
40 K. Anderson, *Life Stages*, 28.
41 Landry, "Colonialism."
42 K. Anderson, *Life Stages*, 39.
43 Ibid., 55.
44 Ibid., 63.
45 Simpson, "Birthing," 27; see also K. Anderson, *Life Stages*, 58.
46 K. Anderson, *Life Stages*, 58.
47 Landry, "Colonialism."
48 Ibid.
49 K. Anderson, *Life Stages*, 61.
50 Santilli, "Here's How."
51 The lactation consultant profession has also been heteronormative and cisnormative since its establishment in 1985—"LGBTQ+ parents may not identify as a 'mother' or 'father,' may have a partner who's also lactating, or may not be able to bodyfeed at all"; *chest/bodyfeeding* are more inclusive terms (Santilii, "Here's How").
52 Santilli, "Here's How."
53 K. Anderson, *Life Stages*, 61.
54 Landry, "Colonialism."
55 Breast/chestfeeding is not always possible or desirable; bottles, formula, and combo-feeding are also effective.
56 These were all white women who were supportive of our 2S Michif family. However, nearly 75 percent of lactation consultants are white women, and many are not well versed in the historical inequities that queer BIPOC parents face (Santilli, "Here's How").
57 Vowel, "Giving My Children."
58 K. Anderson, *Life Stages*, 54.
59 Vowel, "Giving My Children."
60 These languages (and Anishinaabemowin and Nêhiyawawin) were spoken by our ancestors.
61 Bédard, "An Anishinaabe-kwe."
62 K. Anderson, *Life Stages*, 63.
63 Spillett-Sumner, "Raising the Revolution."
64 Spillett-Sumner, "Pandemic Parenthood."
65 Bédard, "An Anishinaabe-kwe"; Simpson, "Birthing," 29.
66 Simpson, "Birthing," 32.
67 Landry, "Colonialism."

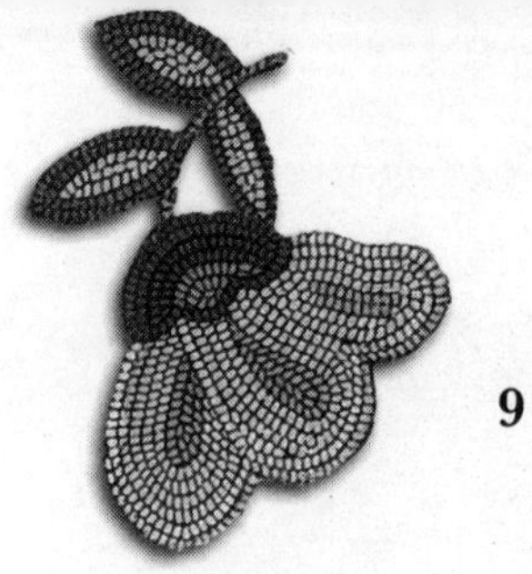

9

Medicine Women

Jennifer Adese

My contribution is a departure from my usual kind of writing. Academic writing could only carry me so far. What appears below is a poem—a single poem—honouring some of the Métis women who have shaped and continue to shape my being in this world and the gifts that they have given me and so many others. They are some of the women who have welcomed me home, who have worked to heal me, and who helped me find my place in the world as a Métis woman. The poem is part grief and gratitude, as each of these women have passed on to be reunited with our ancestors.

Marge

I heard your voice behind me, smoky and rich
cadence rising as the rickety school bus carried us
along the gravel road to the conference
your laughter cracked with joy
the way sun breaks through clouds after a rainstorm
a woman
who knew that Laughter is medicine

Rose

I saw you reach, arms outstretched
to welcome me as your cousin
your smile widened from across the meeting room
like our grandmother in the sky,
beaming eyes reflecting the essence of the stars
a woman
who knew that Family is medicine

Auntie Helen

I smelled your bannock, baking
wafting over the suitcase of family photos
kids from the rez would come hungry to your door,
asking "Kokum do you have some bannock?"
I was hungry, too, so you said to call you kokum
a woman
who knew that Love is medicine

Shelley

I tasted the peanut butter squares, chewy
like that time in Athabasca with your branch
family reconnected, you laughed at me, asking,
"Cousin, who wears ballet flats to a farm?" and
"Who kisses a farm dog on the head?"
a woman
who knew Humility is medicine

Grandma

I tenderly caressed your hair, silvered strands
fingers sliding as if time through an hourglass
that would far too soon run out. I broke.
your frail body hurled sandbags,
stemming the flood with a whisper, "Don't cry"
a woman
who knew that Grandmothers are medicine

10

Lii Michif

Lisa Shepherd

I want you to see the movement of the lines and hear in them the sound of the fiddle and the muffled horse-cantered step sound of the moccasins on the wood floor. I want you to know the connection of this to the buffalo runner horses and the fiddler on the prairie plains, practising for the great buffalo hunt, and to realize that this is where the RCMP got the idea for their Musical Ride.

I want you to see the blue of the ribbons and to know they go with the tan leathery wrinkles of my grandmother's face and her striking blue eyes that would stop you in your tracks. With her full, aproned belly that cradled many babies lovingly, the Blue Eyed Grandmother brought life from spirit through water and to this world. She had skillful hands that pulled the thread through fabric and beads, outfitting the entire big family out of necessity. After her husband passed, she drove the team for the trading company, steadying the horse on the ferry that pulled away too soon, she in the cart, bobbing along on the North Saskatchewan River.

I want you to see this mask that, rather than hiding my face, exposes my identity, and wonder about the stories that Great Auntie Mary told me, in trade for a bucket of Kentucky Fried Chicken. Years later, whenever I pass a KFC, it's my heart that smells those spices first. Auntie kept our stories, and in her ninety-plus years, she was still quick as a whip and could recall all the birthdates and death dates and all the life between the two. Those stories are for me, and my family, and if you are dear to me, I might share a few.

I share these stories through my beadwork and hope they inspire you to embrace your own authentic personal stories.

Lisa Sheperd, *Lii Michif,* 2021. *Lii Michif* was commissioned by Museum Natur und Mensch, Germany. Materials: velveteen, glass beads, ribbon, cotton lining, tin cones, and hand-tied tassels. Photo credit: In View Images.

Christi Belcourt, *Water Has No Flag*, 2006. Courtesy of the artist.

11

Water Has No Flag

Christi Belcourt

Water has no flag
Water knows no race

The earth's belly grew
of sun and moon
and stars
until her waters broke
and all of creation
took its first breath
crying out "glorious is life" into the four directions

And for a million moons
and a million cycles around the sun
she danced,
birthing beings as miraculous as the stars,
while the sun and moon
danced like jewels
on the surface of her seas
and all of creation sang in unison "glorious is life"

For a million moons
and a million cycles around the sun,
all drank from the shores of her veins,
all whose bones returned to her flesh
all who come from her
all here now
carrying within them all who ever was
and all who will ever be.

Our mother
whose waters broke on that first day and made song possible.
We sing now for you
To you
For you
Drumming to your heartbeat
with nothing left to give but our bones and flesh as an offering
so that we too can drink in life from the shores of your veins
for another million moons
and another million cycles around the sun

Christi Belcourt, *I Envy Their Freedom,* 2020. Courtesy of the artist.

Christi Belcourt, *Man Forgets to Follow the Paths of the Animals and Begins to Fall from Earth*, 2018. Courtesy of the artist.

Christi Belcourt, *Little Grandma*, 2006. Courtesy of the artist.

Christi Belcourt, *The Night Shift*, 2023. Courtesy of the artist.

Part Two:

Women in the Academy

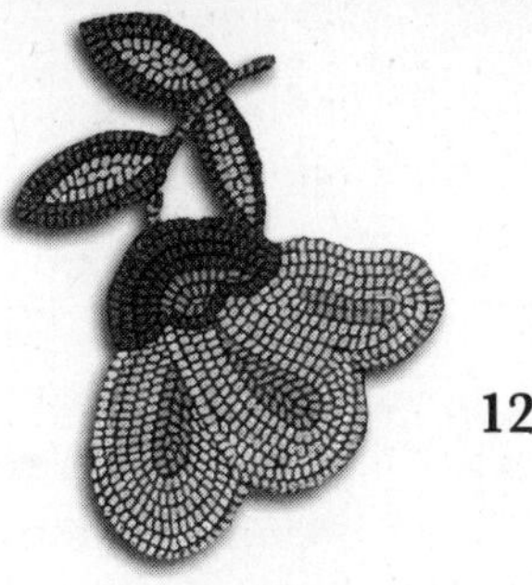

12

Métis Women's Contributions to the Academy despite Colonial Patriarchy

Laura Forsythe

Following the model of Métis scholars like Emma LaRocque,[1] Janice Acoose,[2] and Jennifer Adese and Zoe Todd,[3] a Métis introduction begins this paper. I am Michif/Métis from the Red River Settlement, and I grew up in the heart of the Métis Homeland, like the generations of women before me. My maternal great-grandmother Nora Berard was born in Rooster Town on land known as Lot 31, owned by my ancestor Jean Baptiste Berard, and my lineage includes Joseph Huppe, who fought in the Victory of Frog Plain. My maternal great-great-grandmother, Sarah Morin, came to Rooster Town from Turtle Mountains.

My family has been in Winnipeg Region[4] since the inception of the Métis Nation, with our women serving as equal contributors to the pursuit of nation building and the strength of our communities. Following the First World War, Sarah Morin carried the family and was everything to everyone, including over fifteen children, after pleurisy took my great-great-grandfather, Peter Berard. My maternal great-grandmother ran a farm and wrangled cowboys while raising a family of nine. Like the Métis women who surrounded them, they were "nurturers and protectors of the nation"[5] and their families.

I firmly believe that Métis women are equal contributors to the community and our Nation, including academia. Elder Myra Laramee and Métis scholar Emma LaRocque have similar sentiments, saying that "their fathers were feminists."[6] Métis men never questioned the respect Métis women deserved or the regard for the work they did in our communities.[7] Through an exploration of the roles of Métis women in the community throughout history, a discussion of the continued role of women as influencers beyond gender-implied norms forms the basis for the current reality in Métis Studies. A brief note of the patriarchal structure of academic institutions and the gendered approach to lifting up individual Métis scholars that is devoid of the reality of scholarly contributions is presented.

Historical Roles of Métis Women in Our History

Métis nationhood and communities are built on the foundational principles of Indigenous societies, which are matrilineal.[8] Adese and Todd[9] insist that Métisness pushes back against colonial notions of binary truths of male and female roles, which is confirmed by Maria Campbell's[10] description of the role her own great-grandmother played as head of the community and her demonstration that women who took on these roles were respected and revered. Métis women were instrumental in the buffalo hunts, the top economic driver of the Métis Nation.[11] Campbell recalls her childhood and the impression Métis women in her community made about the importance of working hard: "I do not remember any of them ever sitting around, and if they did sit, they were beading."[12] Diane Payment refers to Métis women as "*une femme en vaut deux* (strong like two women),"[13] as women were the backbone of the society. Métis women were heads of the family but also integral in child rearing, managing the home, and acting as traditional healers, breadwinners, midwives, hunters, translators, cultural material producers, and political strategists.[14]

Due to their tenacity, Payment proposes "work, work, and more work" as the motto for Métis women. Parity or a disregard for gendered colonial norms is seen through much of the literature, which shows women's equality within the Métis community. LaRocque comments that "my mother enjoyed working outside alongside my dad," adding that "my mom was free to trap and do other so-called masculine tasks."[15] Politics from a Eurocentric or colonial view is male-dominated. Within the kinship networks and the Métis Nation as a whole, women made decisions as their mothers had before them. Women are foundational to early and contemporary Métis society and thus to our identity.[16] Through storytelling, Métis women have intergenerationally taught

Métis history to their communities, including traditional knowledge, community history, ancestor biographies, and our ways of life.[17]

Due to the ongoing presence of empowered women throughout the Métis Nation who defy colonial gendered approaches to all aspects of Métis identity, it is not surprising that these colonial norms do not overwhelm Métis Studies. Indeed, the grandmothers of Métis Studies often worked at the kitchen table. In a performance at the Sâkêwêwak Storytellers Festival on 3 February 2017, Sherry Farrell Racette spoke to this space not as a women's domain but as a space of action, a work surface for creating that is shared by men, women, and children. As Métis women within Métis Studies, we are "taking research places in those spaces inspired by grandmother teachers like Maria Campbell,"[18] and we have been doing so since 1953.

The Blinders of Patriarchy in the Academy

The acknowledgement of the contribution by Métis women over the past seventy years to academia and our understanding of who we are has been challenged and undermined by the patriarchy of the academic institution. Those elevated and celebrated by the academy prior to 1980 were the beneficiaries of a system structurally fraught with gender politics. The institution allowed inequalities to persist, willfully supporting divisive, masculine, and elitist tendencies built on competition, target orientation, and individualism.[19] Joanne Lampert states that "universities are knowledge production sites that authorize particular knowledges at the same time they purport to be spaces where knowledge is tested,"[20] and most of the literature produced is by non-Métis who studied Indigenous people as othered. The absence of any discussion of racism towards the Métis and the focus on the sexism with which academic institutions are rife reveal a male-dominated culture with a set of values that both define and maintain gender roles well into the twenty-first century.

However, a comment is needed regarding the distinction between 1) the academy built on misogyny, patriarchy, and sexism and 2) the subfield of Métis Studies built on inclusion and gender parity. Métis Studies has not actively denied, obscured, or delegitimized the work of either Métis or non-Métis women. The subfield is not predicated on systemic gender discrimination and has never embraced the pervasive nature of inequality, as Manulani Meyer has accused academia as a whole of enabling.[21] Chris Andersen,[22] a prominent scholar in the field, agrees in his foundational work *"Métis": Race, Recognition, and the Struggle for Indigenous Peoplehood.* While the scope of the present study precludes in-depth discussion of the motives of this inclusion, there is this recent admission from a male Métis scholar: "cuz we'd get slapped if we didn't."[23] Due to the Métis perception of women built on equality and inclusiveness and the academic suppression and avoidance of the Métis, genuine contributions by women are unthinkable.

The Whiteness of Sources

The following is a brief discussion of the contributions of both White men and women to the disciplines of history, political science, and anthropology. The subfield of Métis Studies relies to a certain degree on these works, but since its inception, it has exhibited high-quality research and an engagement with truths free of bigotry and racist vitriol towards the Métis community created by Métis women.

White Men

The violence to which readers are subjected today by being expected to read the racist blathering of colonial historians (due to their work within the archives researching racist and sexist documentation about the Métis) is appalling. The biased rhetoric and blatantly racist statements found in most historical work prior to 1990 by White scholars cannot be addressed in full detail, given word limit constraints. However, the commentary of Frits Pannekoek, in a review of Métis Studies, notes that it is "best to look at more recent literature"[24] when considering the quality of research done by Marcel Giraud, George Stanley, and William Lewis, due to those authors' reinforcement of stereotypes. Darren Préfontaine states that Métis academics have had to overcome long-held racist interpretations of their community.[25] Jean Teillet asserts that historical records created by White sources are biased and flawed, chronicling the various infractions committed by White male scholars.[26] According to Teillet, Marcel Giraud questions Métis morality, Thomas Flanagan calls Métis morally repugnant, Alexander Begg refers to the Métis as being wild, and George Stanley claims the Métis are "thoughtless and improvident, unrestrained in their desires, restless, clannish and vain."[27] These racist views become even more problematic when one realizes that their research long underpinned the very understanding of who is—and is not—Métis. After all, they are acclaimed historians and political scientists whose careers were built on their exploration of the Métis.

White Women

Following years of feminist rallying in the second movement during the 1970s and 1980s, the landscape of typically male-dominated fields associated with Métis Studies began to change. White women began to take up prominent roles in history, anthropology, and political science, as is shown by the increasing number of White women researching and publishing as Métis theorists in the canon of both Indigenous Studies and its Métis Studies subfield. Victoria Haskins charges White women with an inability to forcefully speak against colonization as historians,[28] while Lampert defends the White hegemony of the university, which pushes back on the neoliberal feminism that allows White women to be in the university.[29] During this period, much groundbreaking research was conducted on the Métis, although the validity of each stance cannot be addressed due to space constraints. Nevertheless, a brief examination of their sources and citations will be undertaken to question the depth of the transformation actually afforded by this influx of female academics.

Beyond the problem of repeated reliance on White males' historical work discussed above, another issue emerges. Reviewing the citations used by Jacqueline Peterson,[30] Peterson and Jennifer Brown,[31] Nicole St-Onge,[32] Sylvia Van Kirk,[33] Irene Spry,[34] and Brown[35] leads to a shocking revelation. These writers incestuously cite one another's work yet neglect to include work from Métis scholars, especially Métis women. Van Kirk's *Many Tender Ties* does cite *Halfbreed*; however, her volume is the exception, and a work explicitly on women that cites only one Indigenous woman is hardly reassuring. Indeed, her White counterparts, such as Brown,[36] St-Onge,[37] Carolyn Podruchny and St-Onge,[38] and Evelyn Peters, Matthew Stock, and Adrian Werner[39] all cite Van Kirk. Understandably, *Many Tender Ties* holds a place within the histography of Métis Studies that does not diminish the value of these works; they too, fail to cite any Métis women. The trend continues with this particular set of women; they only cite one another's work to support their theories of the origins of the Métis Nation, Métis identity, and a history devoid of any Métis voices. Aileen Moreton-Robinson states that "white feminist academics who advocate anti-racist practice unconsciously and consciously exercise their race privilege,"[40] as seen through these academics' choice of citation.

St-Onge[41] cites only two Métis women's work: Campbell's *Halfbreed* and an article written by Heather Devine,[42] despite the decades of work that women in Métis Studies have produced; almost a decade later, St-Onge was a co-editor of a volume that only cites Brenda Macdougall once in St-Onge's chapter. *Métis Politics and Governance in Canada*[43] exemplifies the work needed to ensure Métis women scholars' work and voices are heard throughout scholarship. Allies and their work to lift consciousness of Métis existence past, present, and future is needed but only following the model of Kelly Saunders and Janique Dubois in terms of Métis women scholars' inclusion.

Métis Women

As a subfield of Indigenous Studies, Métis Studies is based on Indigenous fundamentals of supporting matriarchs and empowering women. Métis women as academics and their contributions have been heralded throughout the community and the discipline of Indigenous Studies. The issue from the 1950s through the 1990s was that the broader academy did not recognize their work. In the past thirty years, however, a shift has resulted in numerous faculty hires, research chair appointments, and accolades bestowed on Métis women. Many of the incredible Métis scholars whose work has been present in the academy for over four decades are found in this book.

Grandmothers of Métis Studies

Through a chronicle of grandmothers of Métis Studies—Victoria Callihoo, Dorothy Chartrand, Anne Anderson-Irvine, Maria Campbell, Emma LaRocque, and Audreen Hourie—we see the exemplary contributions that each has made to Métis Studies while supporting the work of countless disciplines with their research, starting in the 1950s.

Victoria Anne (Belcourt) Callihoo

It is fitting to begin our discussion of the grandmothers of Métis Studies with the actual maternal grandmother of a contemporary Métis scholar, Jennifer Adese.[44] Victoria Callihoo, born in 1861, lived to be 105 years old and left behind 241 descendants at the time of her death.[45] She was born in Lac St. Anne as the granddaughter of Fort Edmonton's chief factor John Rowand, and the dramatic life of Granny Callihoo is well documented by scholars like Lawrence Barkwell,[46] Campbell,[47] Nathalie Kermoal,[48] Grant MacEwan,[49] and Cora J. Voyageur.[50] However, being the subject of research is not the only way in which Victoria Callihoo contributed to the literature of Métis Studies. Callihoo published three historical articles in the *Alberta Historical Review* between 1953 and 1960.[51] All three have been widely cited and were written before Native or Métis Studies had come into existence. These first accounts sparked interest in the work this historian could share with the academy, leading to the publication of numerous others in the following decades.

Anne (Gairdner) Anderson-Irvine

Born on a river lot farm east of St. Albert in 1906 of the Callihoo and Gairdner families, Anne Anderson-Irvine spent her early adult life as a nurse and teacher. She did not write her first book until the age of sixty-four;[52] the monograph is based on oral tradition and opens a window onto the contributions of Métis to the St. Albert community. Despite her late start, Anderson-Irvine would author ninety-three works on Métis history and the Cree language, creating a Cree dictionary and accompanying it with audio records and a curriculum while championing the teaching of Indigenous languages at both the K–12 and post-secondary levels in Alberta. Anderson-Irvine developed the Dr. Anne Anderson Native Heritage and Cultural Centre.[53]

Anderson-Irvine received the Aboriginal Achievement Award (1975), Order of Canada (1975), and an honorary doctorate from the University of Alberta; a park in Edmonton with a bronze buffalo sculpture is named for her. The extensive catalogue of her work speaks to the contribution of Métis women academics throughout the twentieth century, just as the Métis Studies subfield was coming into being.

Dorothy Josephine (Bellerose) Chartrand

A descendant of Cuthbert Grant through her great-grandmother, Dorothy Chartrand was born in 1918 in St. Albert. Chartrand shared her story as a Métis woman in the World War II Canadian Women's Army Corps from 1939 to 1945. She is featured in two documentary films.[54] Much like Callihoo, her life has been chronicled in academic work.[55]

Beyond her contributions to Métis Studies, however, Chartrand was also a historian, educator, storyteller, genealogist, community historian, and author of biographies. Her first-hand accounts yield a deep understanding and have often been the basis of subsequent research.[56] Chartrand spent over twenty-five years in archival work, sifting through church records, baptismal records, Hudson's Bay Company servant records, and census data to provide as detailed an account of her family's experience as possible. Again, before the inception of departments of Native Studies and the creation of the Métis Studies subfield, Dorothy Chartrand used both a historiographical and ethnohistorical approach to her Métis community during the fur trade era.

Maria Campbell

Born on the trapline in northern Saskatchewan in 1940 to the Campbell and Dubuque families, Maria Campbell is a grandmother to Métis Studies as a journalist, playwright, filmmaker, academic, and author of fiction, children's literature, and non-fiction. Her academic work covers research topics like the road allowance, governance, cultural practices, Louis Riel, oral history, Indigenous medicine, missing and murdered Indigenous women, and Métis history.

Campbell's compassion and drive stem from her lived experiences as a residential school survivor and her involvement in sex work, which resulted in the establishment of the first halfway house in Edmonton for women.[57] Her commitment to her community can also be seen in actions such as being the National Grandmother for Walking with Our Sisters.

Campbell has always championed women. Préfontaine calls her "the first author to address the hard issues surrounding the life and times of Métis women."[58] Her pathbreaking *Halfbreed* (1973), which challenges stereotypes, has since been cited in works by hundreds of scholars and is the basis of works by Peter Allen,[59] Julie Cairnie,[60] Brendan Edwards,[61] Kristina Fagan et al.,[62] Shawna Ferris,[63] Jodi Lundgren,[64] and Deanna Reder and Alix Shield.[65] *Halfbreed* appears in curricula in women's and gender studies, Canadian literature, Métis literature, and Indigenous Studies classes throughout Turtle Island.

Campbell's work extends well beyond *Halfbreed*. Another work heralded as a novelty in academia was *Stories of the Road Allowance* (1995), "which cultural producers and other colonizers of Aboriginal oral culture have failed to do."[66] Campbell cites all the Elders who shared their stories, prompting later scholars and even institutions to follow suit.

During her time in the academy, Campbell has received five honorary degrees, the Vanier Award (1979), Native Council of Canada (1979), the Order of the Sash from the Métis Nation of Saskatchewan (1985), the Gabriel Dumont Medal of Merit (1992), a National Aboriginal Achievement Award (1996), induction into the Saskatchewan Theatre Hall of Fame (2000), the Canada Council for the Arts Molson Prize (2004), the Saskatchewan Order of Merit (2006), the Order of Canada (2008), and the Pierre Elliott Trudeau Foundation Fellowship (2012).

As a grandmother of Métis Studies, Campbell has worked tirelessly for over five decades, paving the way for Métis women and Métis writers while broadening the possibilities for Métis Studies as a discipline. The high regard in which she is held shows that it is unimaginable that Métis women have been hindered by a gendered approach in the discipline. Indeed, Campbell is revered because of her lived experience not just as a Métis but as a Métis woman.

Emma LaRocque

Emma LaRocque was born in 1949 into a Cree-speaking Métis family in northeastern Alberta. For over forty years, LaRocque has been an academic dynamo at the University of Manitoba, furthering Métis Studies in myriad ways. Her first publication, *Defeathering the Indian*, assessed the situation of Indigenous interpretations in classrooms in the 1970s. The text could, in many respects, be republished to describe the post-secondary climate in the 2020s.

LaRocque's work through the 1980s spoke to Indigenous literature and Métis identity.[67] In the following decade, she branched out and began to write about racism, violence in the community, and the colonization of women scholars.[68] By the 2000s, LaRocque had been researching for twenty-five years and continues to expand her repertoire, tackling Indigenous epistemology, feminism, and—returning to concepts explored in her earlier research—identity, stereotypes, and resistance.[69] In the last decade, she has continued to produce rich pieces, contributing to Métis and Indigenous Studies with her reflections on resistance writing and teaching, which were included in *The Oxford Handbook of Canadian Literature*.[70]

LaRocque and her contributions to the academy offer powerful support to who we as Métis are through our being and through surviving the colonial experience. Like Maria Campbell, LaRocque continues to teach, research, and contribute to our overall understanding of the Métis experience. She is another example of a Métis woman who, despite the patriarchy, has thrived in the academy.

Audreen Hourie

Born in 1943 in Grand Marais, Manitoba, of the Hourie and Orvis lineages, Audreen Hourie played an integral role as a historian for the Manitoba Métis Federation (MMF) in the development of countless resources used throughout Métis Studies; she published with the Gabriel Dumont Institute and was a founding board member of Pemmican Publications, serving as its managing editor from 2000 to 2004. Hourie's contribution to Métis Studies is profound.

At the MMF, Hourie worked in various capacities for over twenty-five years, including as a historian on the Manitoba Métis Federation land claim court case.[71] With her passion for preserving Métis culture and history, Hourie co-edited *Métis Legacy II: Michif Culture, Heritage, and Folkways*,[72] which explores topics ranging from bush lore to contemporary Métis existence through the use of archives, interviews with Elders, and a Métis Studies literature review. This groundbreaking two-part collection was heralded as the first systematic account of the Métis worldview, providing readers with a rich sense of what it is to be Michif.

The Gabriel Dumont Institute Virtual Museum of Métis History and Culture hosts countless articles authored or co-authored by Hourie, ranging from the Michif language, storytelling, housing, clothing, traditional medicines, games, music, dance, spirituality, superstitions, and buffalo hunting. Hourie's work since the 1970s has influenced governmental decisions, and her academic production has secured her a position as a grandmother of Métis Studies.

Other Grandmothers

Due to length constraints, an in-depth account of the contributions of other grandmothers of Métis Studies, such as Louise Erdrich, Rita Flamand, Mary Guilbault, Myra Laramee, Lee Maracle, Beatrice Culleton Mosionier, and Grace Zoldy, cannot be included. However, their contributions over the last six decades have been vast and helped set the tone for future generations of Métis women.

Conclusion

Acoose states that powerful voices can be heard over the influence of "white Christian Canadian patriarchy."[73] The body of work by Métis women in Métis Studies is a testament not only to their resilience and tenacity but also to their birthright. Métis women have been adaptive, cunning, and essential in supporting their communities throughout history, and those skills have long extended to the academy.[74] The work of Métis women transforms public consciousness and understanding.[75] Throughout history, Métis women have served as influencers outside of colonial gender-implied norms and have provided a basis to the subfield. By highlighting the work of Métis women scholars—the grandmothers, and the generations that follow them—and their contributions to this book demonstrates that, while the academy struggles with a gendered approach that has long been supported by patriarchy, the subfield of Métis Studies has consistently supported the women who have contributed so much to its advancement.

Notes

1 LaRocque, *Defeathering the Indian*; LaRocque, "Foreword."

2 Acoose, *Iskwewak*.

3 Adese and Todd, "Mediating Métis Identity."

4 The Manitoba Métis Federation Winnipeg Region borders are coterminous with the City of Winnipeg.

5 Campbell, "Foreword," xxiii.

6 As quoted in K. Anderson, *A Recognition*, 96.

7 K. Anderson, *A Recognition*.

8 K. Anderson, Campbell, and Belcourt, *Keetsahnak*.

9 Adese and Todd, "Mediating Métis Identity."

10 Campbell, "Foreword."

11 Brown, *Strangers in Blood*; Callihoo, "Early Life"; Macdougall and St-Onge, "Rooted in Mobility"; Saunders and Dubois, *Métis Politics*; Shore, *Threads in the Sash*.

12 Campbell, "Foreword," xxiii.

13 Payment, "Une femme," 265.

14 K. Anderson, *Life Stages*; K. Anderson et al., "What Can"; Campbell, "Foreword"; Farrell Racette, "Kitchen Table Theory"; Macdougall, *One of the Family*; Payment, "Une femme."

15 LaRocque, "Métis and Feminist," 60.

16 K. Anderson, Campbell, and Belcourt, *Keetsahnak*; Saunders and Dubois, *Métis Politics*.

17 A. Anderson, "Affirmations"; Campbell, "Foreword"; Préfontaine, "Métis Writers."

18 K. Anderson, Campbell, and Belcourt, *Keetsahnak*, 124.

19 Parsons and Priola, "Agents."

20 Lampert, "The Alabaster Academy," 2.

21 Meyer, "The War."

22 Andersen, "*Métis.*"

23 Personal communication, 21 August 2020.

24 Pannekoek, "Métis Studies," 111.

25 Préfontaine, "Métis Writers."

26 Teillet, *The North-West*.

27 Ibid., xvii.

28 Haskins, "Beyond Complicity."

29 Lampert, "The Alabaster Academy."

30 Peterson, "Red River Redux."

31 Peterson and Brown, *The New Peoples*.

32 St-Onge, *Saint-Laurent, Manitoba*.

33 Van Kirk, *Many Tender Ties*.

34 Spry, "The Métis and Mixed Bloods."

35 Brown, *Strangers in Blood*.

36 Ibid.

37 St-Onge, *Saint-Laurent, Manitoba*.

38 Podruchny and St-Onge, "Scuttling."

39 Peters, Stock, and Werner, *Rooster Town*.

40 Moreton-Robinson, *Talkin' up*, 127.

41 St-Onge, *Saint-Laurent, Manitoba*.

42 Devine, "Les Desjarlais."

43 Saunders and Dubois, *Métis Politics*.

44 Adese and Todd, "Mediating Métis Identity."

45 MacEwan, *Mighty Women*.

46 Barkwell, "Victoria Anne (Belcourt) Callihoo."

47 Campbell, "Foreword."

48 Kermoal, "Métis Women's."

49 MacEwan, *Mighty Women*.

50 Voyageur, *My Heroes*.

51 Callihoo, "Early Life"; Callihoo, "Iroquois"; Callihoo, "Our Buffalo."

52 A. Anderson, *The First Métis*.

53 Préfontaine, "Métis Writers."

54 Iseke-Barnes, "Grandmothers of the Métis Nation."
55 Iseke, "Indigenous Digital Storytelling in Video"; Iseke, "Indigenous Storytelling"; Iseke-Barnes, "Grandmothers of the Métis Nation"; Iseke and Moore, "Community-Based."
56 Iseke-Barnes, "Grandmothers of the Métis Nation."
57 Barkwell, "Maria Campbell"; Ruest, "A Pictorial."
58 Préfontaine, "Métis Writers," 2.
59 Allen, *Geneish*.
60 Cairnie, "Writing."
61 Edwards, "Maria Campbell's *Halfbreed*."
62 Fagan et al., "Reading the Reception."
63 Ferris, "Working."
64 Lundgren, "Being."
65 Reder and Shield, "'I Write This.'"
66 Préfontaine, "Métis Writers," 2.
67 LaRocque, "Three Conventional Approaches"; LaRocque, "Conversations."
68 LaRocque, "The Uniform"; LaRocque, "Racism Runs through"; LaRocque, "Violence in Aboriginal Communities"; LaRocque, "The Colonization."
69 LaRocque, "From the Land"; LaRocque, "Métis and Feminist"; LaRocque, "Native Identity"; LaRocque, "When the 'Wild West'"; LaRocque, *When the Other*.
70 LaRocque, "Contemporary Metis Literature."
71 Barkwell, "Audreen Hourie."
72 Barkwell, Dorion, and Hourie, *Métis Legacy II*.
73 Acoose, *Iskwewak*, 13.
74 K. Anderson, *A Recognition*.
75 Kearns, "(Re)claiming."

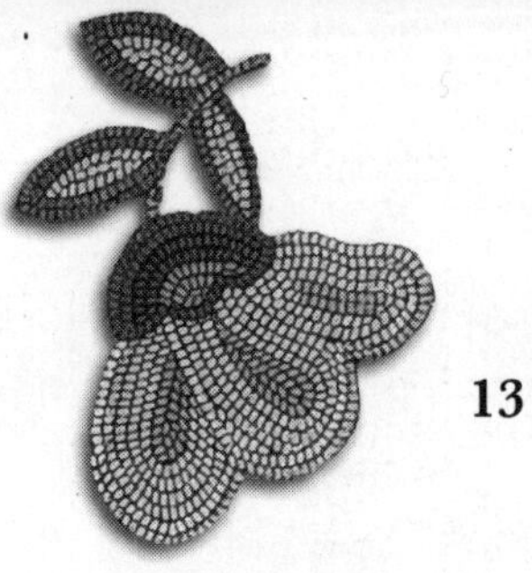

13

Connecting to Our Ancestors through Archaeology: Stories of Three Métis Women Academics

Kisha Supernant, Dawn Wambold, and Emily Haines

Introduction

The history of the Métis is often told through documentary and archival records.[1] These records tend to emphasize the role of prominent Métis men, such as Gabriel Dumont and Louis Riel, and contain fewer stories of women, children, and families. Recent historical scholarship has begun to tell the stories of our Métis grandmothers, but there remain gaps in our knowledge of their day-to-day lives.[2] In this paper, we tell our stories of connecting to our ancestors through our work as archaeologists and anthropologists, where digging into our pasts can bring us to the places where our ancestors lived, had families, built homes, and left behind belongings. These belongings and the lands that hold them are powerful teachers that help us learn about the vibrant and resilient lives of our ancestors, as well as help us understand the role that our grandmothers played in their families and communities.

This is the story of three Métis women and how our academic work as archaeologists has helped us connect with our ancestors, as well as strengthened our relations with our living kin. Archaeology is the study of the past through the material remains left behind by ancient peoples. For a long time, most of the study of the archaeology of Indigenous ancestors was done almost exclusively by non-Indigenous archaeologists, further distancing living Indigenous peoples from their pasts.[3] Archaeologists have also paid little attention to Métis cultural heritage, although the material remains of our ancestors' lives can be found throughout the homeland, and what work has been done has been from an outsider's perspective.[4] We are three Métis women academics who are working to reclaim our heritage and tell the stories of our ancestors from the belongings they left behind. In this chapter, we tell our stories of research, reconnection, and reclamation through archaeology.

Coming Home: Kisha Supernant's Story of Reconnecting

Archaeology is part imagination, part science, part storytelling. We are time travellers, using the material minutiae of lived experience to understand the past, weaving back together tapestries of existence with a fraction of the threads. We try to breathe life into those who came before us, to tell stories that are otherwise unspoken. For me, archaeology is also deeply personal, an act of reclaiming and resistance, of resonance with myself and my ancestors. It is not breathing new life so much as listening to their breath, recognizing that their lives and stories were never fully lost, although many have forgotten how to hear. If not for my own journey home, I may have been among them.

It was during my teenage years that archaeology caught my imagination. The ideas of adventure, exploration, and learning about things unknown were deeply compelling; at the time, I didn't have the self-awareness to understand why I might want to know more about ancient human identity and belonging. A child of a Sixties Scoop survivor, I grew up away from my homeland, disconnected from my community, although I lived with the trauma of my father's history in the foster care system. For a long time, I did not know where and to whom I belonged.

Universities, at their best, reshape and transform minds. On the first day of my university journey, I was unshakable in my belief that my path would allow me to walk in the footsteps of the earliest civilizations, discovering their secrets, exploring the unknown and exotic pasts. However, many signposts, wrong turns, and course corrections later, I finally found my path within archaeology. It took a return to my homeland to show me the way forward. In 2010, I was offered a tenure-track job at the University of Alberta in Edmonton, my father's birthplace. Soon after, I decided to explore Métis archaeology as a way to learn about who I was and to whom I belonged. This journey has taken me to the sites of Métis ancestors in Alberta and Saskatchewan, where I get to explore our history through the archaeological materials left behind by our ancestors. It has also taken me home to my living relatives, as through engaging in the archive, I have discovered my many generations of Métis ancestors who built their lives and families in the lands we now call Alberta. The work I do is designed to connect living Métis people to the vibrant, resilient lives of our relatives and to provide material evidence of our way of life throughout the homeland.[5] I also want to show how exploring our history on our own terms transforms the practice of archaeology[6] and how our places can teach us to be good relations.

I would like to tell you a story about one of these places.

A light breeze floats in from the west, bringing with it the promise of afternoon heat. On this late June morning, I crouch over a perfectly square hole, trowel in hand, breathing in ancient soil. The first thing that hits you about the soil is the smell. A sharp richness, steeped in the depths of time, rises from the newly disturbed earth under my trowel. I catch a glint of something buried in the dirt, a flash of blue that is almost absurdly out of place in the myriad of brown and grey tones of the soil. My breath catches with a thrill of excitement as I painstakingly scrape at the surrounding matrix. A tiny blue glass bead emerges, exposed to the light for the first time in the 150 years since it was first lost.

I close my eyes and a scene emerges in the speckled darkness behind my eyelids.

I am standing on a low hilltop, overlooking the crowded settlement just below. Cabins, three or four to a cluster, are spread out in dozens of groups between me and the not-too-distant lakeshore. A light snow lies on the ground, trampled into paths by multiple moccasined feet, large and small, with the overlying tracks of dogs, horses, and oxen. The cabins are mostly simple, single-room log constructions designed only to last the season, but from afar they appear snug and cozy, enwrapped in a dense layer of muddy clay that keeps out the worst of the winter chill. Each is adorned with a chimney

cheerily emitting smoke from the fireplace below, creating localized columns of grey reaching toward the bright blue sky. I breathe in the brisk winter air, my lungs contracting with the cold, and can almost taste the village, so laden it is with a cacophony of smell. Mud, smoke, and a light undercurrent of human are most prominent, with a dash of wet animal fur, meat, and waste as an aftertaste.

The sounds are as chaotic and comforting: the wail of a tired child, a woman's boisterous laugh, the bark of a dog fighting for food, a distant tuning of a fiddle turning into a full-fledged reel. The thud of an axe chopping wood for the ever-present fire reverberates through the clearing. A man calls to his brother, the language distinct but vaguely French, vaguely Cree. The response is playful, teasing, as they gather supplies for the coming hunt. Out of a cabin, a woman emerges, dressed soberly in a dark dress and fur robe, with a mere flash of blue and white on her feet as she walks down the packed snow path. She speaks to the man, handing him a new pair of beaded moccasins. Unbeknownst to her, one of the beads caught in the folds of her dress as she painstakingly beaded the moccasins in the darkness of the small cabin tumbles down into the snow, lost, forgotten.

The tiny blue bead has been measured, photographed, and removed to a new home where it can live a different sort of life. I have taken the beads lost by my relatives and am seeking to reweave them into some semblance of order, of understanding that which cannot easily be known. I think of the cousin I met a few years ago while talking to the community about my archaeology. I think of my Grandmother, whom I would never meet. I think of my aunts and uncles, disconnected from a sense of belonging but forever seeking. I think of my many generations of Métis ancestors who called these places home, interwoven into webs of relations through time and space. I think of my thousands of living relatives and the ones to come after us. For me, this is the power of archaeology, of standing in the places of our ancestors. I feel deeply privileged to engage with our ancestors' belongings and the work of reconnecting them into our webs of relations. There is power in the past, as the vibrant and resilient lives of our families through time can inspire us in the present and can support our future as Métis people.

I lay my hand down on the soil. I can feel them breathing, my ancient relatives, the lands and the waters. I can feel them breathing, my ancestors. Their breath fills me, heals me. I breathe with them, our heartbeats in sync.

I am Métis. I am home.

Grandma's Gauntlets: Dawn Wambold's Search for the Stories of Métis Women

Looking back, I realize that the awareness of my Métis heritage and my interest in archaeology were both recognized at approximately the same time in my life. When I was about ten years old, I remember asking my Dad if we were related to anyone famous. He proudly told me the story of our Great-Great-Great Uncle Gabriel Dumont. At the same time, I remember receiving a big heavy book about archaeology. This copy of *The Adventure of Archaeology* by Brian Fagan still sits on my bookshelf; nestled between the archaeology and Canadian history textbooks.[7] As a result of these two influences, my interest in my own personal family history developed alongside my much broader interest in the history of the world.

Around the same time, my Dad took me to the local museum to show me the beaded gauntlets that had been made by my Grandmother. I remember that they were labelled as being made by an "Indian woman" and that we were forbidden from opening the glass display case to touch them. Despite this, they were, and continue to be, a cherished connection to a woman whom I knew so little about. She had passed away when my Dad was only five; a loss in his life that continued to be felt as my siblings and I mourned for a Grandmother we had never known. Although my Dad could share stories told to him by my Grandfather, there was little that he could tell me about my Grandmother. Thus, I keenly felt the absence of the women's stories that had been passed down for generations before they were abruptly lost. This loss could not be replaced by the books on our shelves that told the stories of the Métis bison hunters and resistance fighters but rarely mentioned Métis women.

As I grew older, my interest in history and archaeology also continued to grow. However, it was pushed aside when I was told by a teacher that archaeology was done only in far-off places, a misconception that seemed to be validated by the photos of exotic excavation sites in *The Adventure of Archaeology*. Not wanting to leave the lands of my ancestors, I prepared for a technical career in the oil and gas industry but continued to take ancient history classes along with my courses in metallurgy and physics. It was not until my oil and gas career was firmly established that I discovered the importance of archaeology to development projects and that my homeland contained a rich archaeological past that rivalled that of any other foreign lands. With this in mind, and my career established, I continued to read everything I could about the past and finally returned to school part-time to complete an undergraduate degree in anthropology.

Recalling the absence of my Métis Grandmother's influence in my life, I joined Kisha Supernant's Exploring Métis Identity Through Archaeology (EMITA) project as a graduate student. The call for applications asked for students who were interested in the archaeology of gender, and it was this that made me realize that archaeology could help fill the gap left by the missing stories from my Grandmother. Working with the belongings left behind by the ancestors at three Métis hivernant (overwintering) sites, I have incorporated historical and feminist archaeology theory to help tell the story of the women and their families who lived at these sites.

Working with Kisha and the rest of her graduate students, including co-author Emily Haines, I have also found myself in the wonderful position of being able to incorporate theories and epistemologies related to Indigenous archaeology into my work. At its simplest, Indigenous archaeology can be defined as "archaeology with, for, and by Indigenous peoples."[8] Other theoretical aspects of Indigenous archaeology include the development of research practices based on partnerships with Indigenous stakeholders.[9] For me, this means that I am able to draw upon *wâhkôhtowin* and *keeoukaywin* as vital inputs into my work.

Wâhkôhtowin, the "state of being related,"[10] reminds me that the people who lived at these sites are our Métis ancestors. *Wâhkôhtowin* also implies a set of responsibilities and reciprocal obligations that we have for one another and includes our non-human kin: the animals, spirits, and landscapes that surround us.[11] As such, I have a responsibility to tell the story of these sites to the best of my ability. Furthermore, as I work with the ancestors' belongings from these sites, I find myself developing a relationship that can be described as "visiting" with the belongings. By visiting with the belongings and listening to their stories,

I engage in *keeoukaywin*; a Cree term that can be described as "the visiting way."[12] Through practising *wâhkôhtowin* and *keeoukaywin* in my work, I gain strength from the spirits of our ancestors, the wisdom of our elders, and the encouragement of my contemporaries.

The gauntlets made by my Grandmother are still in the local museum, but now they prominently display her name and identify her as Métis. I can also say that thanks to my position as a researcher, and the willingness of more museums to work with descendent communities, I was finally able to open the glass display case and hold my Grandmother's work in my own hands. When this opportunity finally came, I fought back tears as I gently removed the gauntlets from their display. I finally felt the physical connection to my Grandmother and the women who came before her. Although I started this academic journey for my own benefit, I have come to realize that my work is really for my Grandmother and all those who came before. My research is an opportunity for their stories to be told so that future generations can hear their voices. It is because of the spirits of the Métis women of my past that I can consider myself to be a strong Métis academic.

Family Teachings: Emily Haines's Journey to Anti-Colonial Archaeology

Being a Métis archaeologist in the Métis homeland, what is today known as western Canada, means incorporating family into my practice as a source of inspiration and knowledge. My father is a Métis man whose family networks have stretched widely throughout the Métis homeland over centuries. He has spent his life regularly practising what Janice Cindy Gaudet calls *keeoukaywin*, the visiting way, whereby he regularly visits his extended family and friends in and around Winnipeg, Manitoba. Gaudet holds that *keeoukaywin* is how we "anchor a sense of belonging, a sense of self, a sense of responsibility to family, community, and land."[13] As a child with little understanding of my father's Métis upbringing, this was simply a part of life. I now am able to recognize his actions as teachings. His visiting patterns implicitly taught me that maintaining connections is necessary work, which in turn relayed the concept of relational responsibility, *wâhkôhtowin*.

My father does not only visit people but places, too. The same relational responsibilities that lead my father to visit his loved ones have led us to visit myriad places with ritual regularity, including old houses where he or loved ones once lived, the site where the Red and Assiniboine rivers meet (known as The Forks), and the restaurant Salisbury House, which, not being available in Alberta, he cherishes as part of his Winnipeg experience. It is clear to me that what, who, and where he visits are deeply significant as anchoring points in his world. This is what pointed my attention to his recent visits to two sites associated with Métis nationalism: the gravesites of the Métis leader Louis Riel, Riel's wife and our cousin Marguerite Monet dit Bellehumeur, and their children; and the site of the Northwest Resistance of 1885 at Batoche, Saskatchewan. What motivated his visits to these places? What sense of belonging and responsibility could he be enacting?

Belonging to the Métis Nation involves sharing a history, culture, and familial ties. One of the many ways people belong to and connect with a history and a group is through material history. These are the places, belongings, and structures left behind by ancestors. Their importance is recognized and protected by Article 11 of the United Nations Declaration on the Rights of Indigenous Peoples,[14] which states that Indigenous peoples have the right to "maintain, protect, and develop the past, present and future manifestations of their cultures," whether that be through archaeological sites and materials or through traditions and ceremonies.[15] Article 11 supports the interpretation that material history is important to rooting ourselves in our history and nationhood today. We cannot visit what has not been preserved, and unfortunately, many of our historic sites have been destroyed, buried, or are simply unfound. Much of the cultural heritage made and owned by us is now held by national or provincial museums. Dawn's emotional reconnection with her Grandmother's gauntlets simultaneously illustrates the relational power of our material history and the formidable colonial barriers to achieving access.

As a practice concerned with uncovering what has been left behind by past populations, archaeology is one of the main methods we can use to find and preserve the places and belongings of our ancestors. However, I have often thought there is a danger that archaeology, as a colonial tool, could not possibly do the anti-colonial work required to forge grassroots connections between our ancestors and ourselves. Archaeology was introduced to the Americas through colonialism and has a horrific history of stealing and destroying human remains, cultural materials, and sacred places.[16] The work of many Indigenous archaeologists over the last several decades has truly changed a segment of the discipline by interrogating the colonial methods, goals, assumptions, and biases inherent to archaeological practice and shaping them to suit the needs of Indigenous communities. This work, and the necessity of knowing our history through our ancestors' belongings and places, has convinced me that archaeology can be valuable if used to meet decolonial or anti-colonial goals. To do this, I place the concept of resurgence at the centre of my research. Resurgence is a process of strengthening our connections to our ancestors, traditions, history, practices, and families as an Indigenous people.[17] As a pathway to knowing and connecting with our ancestors, what we uncover through and by archaeology can unsettle narratives told about us, provide a foundation for rejecting the colonial narratives about us, and strengthen our footing in our history and nationhood.

Colonial incursions have done much to separate Métis peoples from their history such that many of us know only a fraction of our nation's rich past. In this number are myself and my father. Still, he enforces connections to our nation through practising *keeoukaywin*. I imagine a time when he will be able to feel connection, and belonging, and enact relational responsibilities to places beyond the Riel gravesites and Batoche, as important as those are. I imagine connections to the multitudes of places and belongings dotted across the prairies as plentiful as stars in the sky. If we as Métis people practise archaeology with the vitality of our ancestors, families, communities, and nations at the core of our research agenda, I believe we can forge these connections to our history, connections that are vital to our modern existence.

Being Good Relations

Our experiences are varied but deeply connected. Through our individual stories and collective work, we are reconnecting to our ancestors, both human and other-than-human. We are also learning how to be good relations with each other and our academic colleagues, a practice that deepens and expands as we spend more time together with our relatives. Archaeology has long been an extractive and colonial discipline that co-opts Indigenous histories through a western analytical lens. As Métis women archaeologists, we engage the methods of archaeology through our own understanding of the world, informed by concepts and practices of *wâhkôhtowin* and *keeoukaywin*. Instead of merely measuring and analyzing the belongings of our ancestors, we also visit with them. We strive to be good relations to each other, the places of our ancestors, and the materials they left behind. We conduct our work in ways that benefit our living relatives by demonstrating where we were throughout the homeland. Through our practices and the practices of other Indigenous archaeologists, we are working to reimagine what archaeology can be.

Notes

1 Peterson and Brown, *The New Peoples*; Macdougall, Podruchny, and St-Onge, *Contours*.
2 MacKinnon, *Metis Pioneers*; Macdougall, *One of the Family*.
3 Atalay, "Indigenous Archaeology"; Watkins, "Through Wary Eyes."
4 Burley, Horsfall, and Brandon, *Structural Considerations*.
5 Supernant, "Archaeology"; Supernant, "From Haunted"; Wadsworth, Supernant, and Kravchinsky, "An Integrated."
6 Supernant, "Reconciling the Past."
7 Fagan, *The Adventure of Archaeology*.
8 Nicholas and Andrews, "Indigenous Archaeology," 3.
9 McNiven, "Theoretical Challenges," 28.
10 O'Reilly-Scanlon, Crowe, and Weenie, "Pathways," 30.
11 Campbell, "We Need to Return"; Wildcat, "Wahkohtowin in Action," 14.
12 Gaudet, "Keeoukaywin."
13 Ibid., 51.
14 UN General Assembly, *Declaration*.
15 Ibid., §11.
16 Mihesuah, "American Indians"; Deloria, *Custer Died*.
17 Corntassel, "Re-Envisioning."

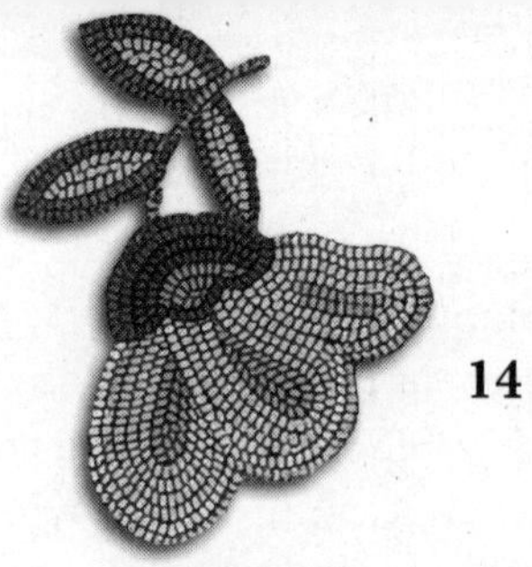

14

Métis Women Educating in the Academy

Yvonne Poitras Pratt and Jennifer Markides

The topic of how Métis people have experienced education, and how Métis women are currently involved as post-secondary educators, is an area that has received little attention over the years. With the politics of identity playing a large role in how others position us, we have primarily been subject to the whims of powerholders and others who may have very little to no understanding of how the Métis themselves determine collective belongingness and how we have made strides towards self-determination in recent years.[1] As teacher educators who work in a large research-intensive university in western Canada, we take up the opportunity to relay this missing narrative to others in hopes of asserting the ongoing and active participation of Métis people, with a particular focus on the agency of women, in the realm of higher education. We distill lessons learned through Métis involvement in educational initiatives to establish community-identified needs and values within education and, finally, we reflect on how our Métis identity impacts our roles within a faculty of education.

So, what impact does our Métis identity have on our roles as teacher educators working within a mainstream post-secondary institution? As Métis women, each working as faculty, we are in the position of negotiating complex political and educational landscapes that simultaneously exclude and involve us. Recruited as Indigenous educators, we were brought into the university based on our connections to our ancestral communities and, as a result, we are continually asked to bring our identities forward in our work. We teach from our lived realities that reflect colonial impacts and repercussions, and we share unique worldviews that may resonate with, or rile up, students and colleagues. Most students have learned Canadian history from a colonial perspective that has misrepresented our peoples in textbooks and curricula for as long as the Métis people have existed.[2] Knowing this, we are also cognizant that what we are sharing can be harmful to our personal well-being.[3] Teaching who the Métis are is a perilous privilege.

In contemporary times, there is a certain penchant for learning about Indigenous peoples propelled in large part by the work of the Truth and Reconciliation Commission of Canada (TRC)[4] but also driven by the fact that many Canadians find the topic of Indigenous peoples mysterious and even exotic and hearing previously unheard stories sparks great interest and intrigue.[5] Yet amongst this interest, there is also an underlying perception of First Nations and Inuit peoples as more "authentic" than the Métis. Many people assume they know who the Métis are—associating our identity with the term *half-breeds* or thinking we are simply mixed-blood, the first-generation offspring of colonial settlers and their First Nations partners.[6] By this logic, any union of a First Nations person and non-Indigenous person would yield Métis children to this day. This simply is not true. Thus, teaching about the Métis begins with the task of addressing the many misconceptions of who we are.[7] The rightful claim of being Métis means we are entangled in a complex web of diverse heritages, political assertions, and kinship relations that assert inherent and collective responsibilities.

As compared with our First Nations and European kin, the recognition by others of the distinctiveness of the Métis marked the ethnogenesis of our nationhood.[8] In "Deconstructing Métis Historiography: Giving Voice to the Métis People," scholars Leah Dorion and Darren Préfontaine once noted that "nobody knows for sure when the first Métis person lived or when contact first occurred . . . it is therefore not surprising that the process of 'being and becoming' Métis is one of the most interesting areas of Métis studies."[9] Over time, Métis scholars have added their voices to the scholarly conversation, asserting that being Métis is not a matter of simply being mixed-race; rather, being Métis means your ancestral lineage is connected to a distinct political and cultural landscape unique to Canada.[10] Certainly, questions of identity and political involvement tend to dominate any discussion surrounding the Métis and, given our complex and rich history in these lands now called Canada, this should not be surprising. As teacher educators, we dedicate our efforts in this chapter to sharing educational experiences specific to the Métis and purposefully hone in on the contributions of Métis women.

Historical Forms of Métis Education: A Holistic Approach

The topic of Métis education is one that reflects experiences as diverse as our peoples. As a post-contact people, we have had the privilege of learning traditional ways from our maternal ancestors as well as having experience and varied exposure to Western formalized learning spaces. These informal and formal learning spaces represent a holistic approach to Métis education, one that has always valued the contributions of women as leaders. Métis scholar Leah Dorion and co-author Darren Préfontaine maintain that "in the past, most Métis societies were matrilineal and matriarchal. Métis women's roles in the family and community were valued and fundamental to the preservation of Métis culture."[11]

In a recent chapter focused on adult education from a Métis perspective, it was shared that "historical accounts reveal that the Métis were educated in both First Nations and European ways, across informal and formal settings, and that economic alliances, gender roles, and religious forces were dominant factors in how formal education was delivered and, in many cases, imposed on learners."[12] In the early years, and in the informal spaces of home-based schooling, Métis women were primary care providers as well as educators of their young children. Historical accounts demonstrate the ways in which traditional practices from First Nations kin were being passed onto subsequent generations of Métis through oral traditions and experiential learning activities, at the same time print literacy was being promoted as a necessary skill for economic and social advancement. These multiple literacies reflect the valuing of diverse traditions emanating from both maternal and paternal lineages, representing a fundamentally holistic approach to education.[13] The influence of the Catholic church, and other religious denominations, was also considerable in Métis families in early times, as were the trading companies Métis were aligned with during the fur trade. In some cases, company policies groomed young Métis males to become front-line workers at fur trading posts while other companies sent Métis children overseas to Europe to gain access to formal education.[14] No matter what type of education Métis children were subject to, it is obvious that they were learning multiple and often contrasting perspectives that helped them navigate complex relationships as they grew older.

Seen as cultural mediators, Métis women were often sought out by newcomers/settlers for their expert knowledge and skills, including their command of multiple languages.[15] Since the historical record has proven strongly biased in reporting predominantly male-only activities, there are only fragments of how Métis women played a substantial role in Canada's history.[16] However, recent research is revealing how Métis women served as valuable sources of knowledge for many of the more recognized leaders of historic times.[17] Aligning with ancestral traditions, some of these activities have been captured for posterity in songs or poems that relayed intergenerational transmission of knowledge traditions from multiple ancestral lines.

> If someone had a headache, or a fever or the flu
>
> A daughter of the country knew exactly what to do
>
> She'd make a special medicine from a flower or a tree
>
> That she learned from her grandmother who was a Chippewa or Cree
>
> And who did they pass their knowledge to?
>
> May I tell you bluntly?
>
> [Refrain] It was those shawl-wearing, rabbit-snaring, moccasin-making, bannock-baking, floor-mopping, wood-chopping, snowshoe-mending, garden-tending, berry-finding, pemmican-grinding, hide-cleaning, hair-preening, child-rearing, persevering . . . Daughters of The Country![18]

Political Organizing and Governance as Educative Forms

Recognized as fur trade experts with continent-wide trading networks under their control, the Métis would also have been schooled through experiential learning where younger family members would be carefully groomed to take over the family business as the next of kin. In many ways, this type of learning could be seen as an early apprenticeship model. In focusing on economic participation as the primary driver behind learning, there has been a tendency to focus on how young Métis men were being trained to enter the fur trade economy, yet it is good to remember that young Métis women would also be learning tricks of the (fur and other) trade.[19] Since Métis families were traditionally matriarchal and matrilineal, young Métis women would be expected to know detailed familial records, where each of these families resided, and the particular trading commodities associated with each family or alliance.[20]

As the Métis started to politically organize and coalesce around a shared governance model, life lessons would naturally extend into political and military tactics. The Rules of the Buffalo Hunt, for instance, set out strict behavioural rules for proper conduct and also detailed rather severe repercussions for any violation of these rules.[21] The intellectual forays of the Métis into political and military strategizing would formalize over time and strengthen with the encroachment of the newly formed Dominion of Canada into their ancestral homelands.[22] More recently described as an impressive stand-off considering the relative numbers of Métis compared with armed and military-trained Canadian soldiers, this particular chapter in Canadian history would culminate in the eventual military defeat of the Métis in 1885. The execution of Métis leader Louis Riel was a painful final lesson meted out by the colonial power holders.

Post-1885 Diaspora and Learning Survival Tactics

As one might imagine, the golden days of the Métis would darken considerably after their defeat at Batoche in 1885. The political disruption following the Resistance and the takeover of Métis homelands through an unscrupulous scrip system, deemed North America's "greatest land swindle" by Métis rights lawyer Jason Madden,[23] would naturally pre-empt educational concerns for a time. In what might be termed a *post-1885 diaspora*, the economic prowess of the Métis would shift to everyday means of survival, and for many Métis who could "pass" as white, survival would mean turning their back on their cultural upbringing and ancestral communities by attempting to blend into settler communities. For others who could not, or would not, easily assimilate into the newcomer/settler society, times would prove extremely hard.

Howard Adams provides a glimpse into life at St. Louis, Saskatchewan, where the racial divide ran dangerously deep:

> These two European White supremacy groups created an ethnic, racially-divided society that subordinated and excluded Métis from their communities and elevated themselves as superior people. As Métis, we felt this discrimination deeply. . . . We were secluded mostly from the White Europeans who came into our community only when they needed our labour and resources. . . . White people set themselves apart from us, never inviting us to their cultural or even political functions. They were welcome to our social activities, but never came. . . . Because of the different levels of status, Métis do not have the same benefits and privileges. For example, Europeans have warm houses, adequate food, nice clothes, and medicine when sick.[24]

In recalling these childhood memories, Adams offers a first-hand account of how the Métis were seen as convenient sources of labour one moment but then socially rejected in the next moment. Tellingly, this passage also depicts the extreme levels of poverty Métis experienced, where even the basic necessities of life were wanting.

Unlike First Nations, who were subject to the residential schooling requirements within the Indian Act, the Métis experience of formal schooling was haphazard and often contingent on how outsiders viewed either their physical expression or life circumstances.[25] For many Métis children who were darker-skinned or who were barely surviving, their presence in Indian residential schools would help to fill student quotas and justify federal funding for this lesser form of schooling.[26] For those Métis who could "pass" or were considered "assimilated" by others, their children entered the provincial schooling system alongside newly arrived immigrant children. Children who were more visibly Métis or surviving extreme poverty were either routed to residential, industrial, or day schools, or they were simply ignored by the incoming colonial governments.

Reflecting the confusion around Métis identity at the turn of the last century, which sadly continues into the present day, one school superintendent reveals a flagrant white saviour attitude in the following remarks: "Not only are our schools every day removing intelligent Indian children from evil surroundings, but they are very often ministering to a class which would be outcasts without such aid: I refer to the illegitimate offspring of white men and Indian women who are thrown upon their mother's support, and who have no legal status as Indians. This great charitable work, which parallels the efforts put forth by white communities aided by Provincial, Municipal, or private endowment, must be carried on by the Dominion Government, aided by Christian missionaries and missionary societies."[27] The confusion around Métis and mixed-blood children seen here continues today alongside the "unresolved issue of jurisdiction and control [that] is at the heart of the breakdown in Métis education."[28] Nonetheless, this lack of knowingness by others of who the Métis are has not kept our communities across the Métis homeland from moving forward.

Leadership and Community-Led Métis Educational Initiatives

Shortly after the 1885 Resistance, the Métis began to organize politically once again, and these efforts increased after WW II in concert with other marginalized groups (including groups such as the American Indian Movement and the Congress of Aboriginal Peoples) who together represented the emergence of social justice movements in support of minority interests. Starting in the 1970s, Métis academics and leaders such as Howard Adams, Maria Campbell, and Emma LaRocque[29] stepped forward to argue for the importance of education and the need for Métis self-determination. Their selfless efforts helped to keep the educational interests of the Métis on the community radar, even if they were not always on the forefront of provincial and federal agendas.

In *An Institute of Our Own: A History of the Gabriel Dumont Institute,* Lisa Bird-Wilson notes the influence of the American Indian Movement (AIM) in the 1970s "on Saskatchewan Aboriginal people . . . as the Métis political body took up the AIM example and held a number of sit-ins and other forms of public protest."[30] From all accounts, these militant strategies proved effective as the governing Saskatchewan party conceded to several requests from the Métis, namely issues surrounding housing, adoption, and foster home placements, along with education provision. Speaking to community members who took part in these rallies, Bird-Wilson notes the Métis were disciplined for grassroots organizing in the 1970s and the resulting strong sense of solidarity eventually paved the way for political reform. No doubt greater momentum was gained through the release of the 1972 *Indian Control of Indian Education* publication that pointed out how education was being used as a tool of assimilation in First Nations communities. The Métis too raised concerns about inadequate curriculum, poor teaching resources, inadequately trained teachers, and lack of representation on school boards with high Métis student populations.[31] At a 1976 cultural conference, Métis attendees identified education as a top priority and the "imperative goal [was] to develop an Aboriginal education and cultural institute for Métis and Non-Status Indians"; this call for self-determination became the impetus for the "first Métis owned and controlled post-secondary institution in Canada"[32]—what is now the Gabriel Dumont Institute (GDI). The Métis initially proposed that "Aboriginal teachers would not be trained in the imposed and arbitrary standards of the dominant Euro-Canadian population, but would rather come into the classrooms and teach in Aboriginal languages, and in culturally appropriate ways";[33] however, this vision soon collided with provincial teacher accreditation requirements. In blending the two distinct approaches to teacher education, the highly respected Saskatchewan Urban Native Teacher Education Program (SUNTEP) was born. These impressive educational initiatives are credited to the incessant lobbying of the government by a unified and determined group of Métis who were able to make the case for Métis-specific education. Credit is also extended to a group of sympathetic and social justice-driven provincial bureaucrats who knew funding the Institute was the right thing to do. Notably, while GDI was viewed as holding a culturally based mandate for Métis knowledge and traditions, it was also seen as an appropriate avenue to teach mainstream Canadians about the Métis.[34] Some forty years later, GDI successfully operates through provincial government support and the upholding of its initial vision: "the early GDI founders and leaders saw the education of the Métis and Non-Status people as closely connected to the aspirations of self-determination and self-government,"[35] where "culture is intrinsically bound to our educational endeavours and sense of self-determination."[36]

Other Métis learning institutes exist across the Métis homeland and include the Winnipeg-based Louis Riel Institute and its "Adult Learning Centre [that] is a non-traditional high school for adults. Our centre is learner focused and we strive to create an academic environment that is safe, comfortable and supportive."[37] The provinces of Ontario and British Columbia have designated ministries of education within their elected provincial organizations but have yet to formalize learning institutes. In the *Métis Education Report: A Special Report on Métis Education* prepared by the Métis National Council for the Summit on Aboriginal Education, the authors point out the lack of Métis-specific data as a major challenge in justifying funding requests. One of the greatest impediments to realizing further educational growth across the Métis homeland is the "jurisdictional barriers and funding and capacity constraints on Métis educational authorities."[38]

In Alberta, the first ever Métis Education Conference was held in 1990, hosted by the Métis Nation of Alberta, where over 200 attendees from diverse sectors relayed a series of recommendations relative to educational concerns. One of the most significant concerns raised at this 1990 conference was the issue of racism and the lack of mainstream understanding of the unique positioning of the Métis. In 2012, the Alberta-based Rupertsland Institute (RLI), an affiliate of the Métis Nation of Alberta, took up the formal mandate of education and has since grown from a staff of one to a small staff of four Métis educators who oversee Métis-specific curricular resources, host professional development workshops on the Métis, and liaise with the provincial government on education initiatives. Writing from an Alberta perspective in 2013, Jennifer Paulson, Yvonne Poitras Pratt, and Guido Contreras assert that jurisdictional issues continue to plague RLI in terms of meeting their education mandate. Noting that provincial funding can be arbitrarily removed means "leaving Rupertsland Institute without an established education policy, no personnel, and effectively no capacity to contribute to the K-12 education of Métis students in Alberta . . . [yet] a responsibility to move forward on the Métis Education agenda without any dedicated resources"[39] remains. Through this observation of a clear injustice, we are reminded that we are "always already political"—this is a Métis reality.

The Political Landscape of Métis Education Today

The political landscape is shifting to reflect a nation in transition, one that is committed to responding to the TRC's 94 Calls to Action through genuine and meaningful actions, yet the Métis remain largely absent from conversations specific to reconciliation. Noting a predominant focus on First Nations' involvement in residential schools, the Métis are seeking to broaden national dialogue to consider how the Métis have also suffered greatly from a colonial past of grave injustices.[40] With Indigenous education receiving greater attention and prioritization in recent years,[41] academic institutions and educational systems have increasingly prioritized the need for Indigenous representation and voices in a variety of teaching and leadership roles. In many cases, Métis, and in particular Métis women with the requisite academic credentials, are stepping into academic positions in higher learning to assert these truths (see Forsythe, Chapter 11). While the prevalence of Métis scholars in academic positions reflects the growing numbers of Métis citizens across the country and our drive for self-determination, our growing presence in the academy is not without controversy.

As our historical and contemporary record reveals, Métis people have continually been cast as rebellious traitors, assimilated "half-breeds," or inauthentic "Indians."[42] Not fully First Nations. Not fully settler-Canadian. Yet both. In some cases, we are hired for our ability to bridge diverse worlds, just as we have done for generations. Other times, we are discounted for not being First Nations. Being a Métis scholar means proving our worth and right to be in academic positions to those who may have little to no understanding of who the Métis truly are, and it also means being called upon time and again to serve the wider interests of both Indigenous and non-Indigenous communities. Fortunately, Métis have been recognized for hundreds of years as hard-working and tenacious peoples with the inherent ability to bridge disparate worlds. Just as Métis women have held the place-specific knowledge and stories that have been essential for our survival over the years, we now share lessons learned as Métis women within our academic positions.

Conceptualizing Métis Education as Thought Leadership, Community Advocacy, and Cultural Renewal

More and more frequently, Indigenous scholars are advocating to have Indigenous knowledge systems recognized and shared within formal academic institutions through the involvement of respected Elders with whom they hold relationships. Métis and First Nations Elders are being invited into courses, such as in the Indigenous Education: A Call to Action master's program at the University of Calgary, as traditional knowledge keepers who can help university-trained academics bridge community knowledge traditions into the academy in respectful and inclusive ways.[43] By establishing respectful relationships with Elders and recognizing non-Western forms of educational attainment, universities are making space for Indigenous education practices and creating opportunities for intergenerational teaching and intercultural learning. Métis educators are uniquely positioned, as a self-determining group,[44] to work within the "in-between" spaces of Métis communities and academe to advocate for equity-driven practices such as the valuing of Métis knowledge traditions alongside other Indigenous peoples'. Other mentorship is tacit—exemplified in the ways that the academics prioritize service to the Métis Nation and mentor new scholars into the work. Being invited to serve our Métis community is an honour and a daunting responsibility. Working with the Nation exemplifies the interconnectedness of self and community, where actions must reflect the interests of the collective good. The Métis academics who have come before us and the strong Métis scholars of today model thought leadership, community advocacy, and cultural renewal towards the collective self-determination of Métis people.

In terms of the importance of cultural inclusion, Métis-specific courses are beginning to appear in institutions that serve larger Métis populations, yet many of these programs are still in their infancy. The University of Alberta boasts a Faculty of Native Studies, currently operating under the leadership of Métis scholar and Dean Chris Andersen. In this setting, Métis scholars find not only a safe but also an empowering space to articulate their Métisness. Speaking to how Métis pedagogies might be realized in post-secondary settings, Métis scholars Adam Gaudry and Robert Hancock maintain that "land- and community-based approaches to Métis scholarship and pedagogy"[45] are what is required. In thinking about Métis education, we see a more holistic paradigm that includes both formal and informal learning spaces, and one that is driven by community needs and interests.

Our Roles as Métis Women in the Academy

Our roles and responsibilities span many spheres. Beyond the responsibilities we carry as part of our institutional roles, we also shoulder significant responsibilities in our Métis communities. As we are hired to bring our indigeneity forward in our research and teaching, Indigenous scholars are recognizing a misfit between what is expected and what is counted for academic tenure and promotion with regard to Indigenous scholarship,[46] although promising movements are emerging with Declaration on Research Assessment (DORA) as an exemplar.[47] As Métis within the academy, we are mentoring, and making space for, the next generations of Métis. Our advocacy also has bearing on the trajectories of other minoritized scholars. For some, entering into the academy was a harsh and lonely space that can feel disconnected from Métis community and cultural values and where our community work was not as valued as other forms of research. Fortunately, the landscape is changing. And while we cannot write about Métis education without discussing Métis identity politics, we similarly cannot write about individual challenges without recognizing the political advocacy of the Métis Nation in terms of our inherent rights. Being held in these kinship relations creates an impetus for us, as Métis women in the academy, to lead others by example, be the voice that brings Métis voice and vision into the institutions, and, as educators, work to support programming that reflects Métis values and knowledge.

Notes

1 *Daniels v. Canada*; Gaudry and Andersen, "*Daniels v. Canada*"; Martel, "*Daniels v. Canada*."

2 Adams, *Prison of Grass* (1975 ed.); Adams, *A Tortured People*; Dorion and Préfontaine, "Deconstructing"; LaRocque, *Defeathering the Indian*; LaRocque, *When the Other*; Sealey and Lussier, *The Metis*.

3 Markides, "Being Indigenous"; Markides, "Examining"; Poitras Pratt, *Digital Storytelling*.

4 Truth and Reconciliation Commission, *Final Report*.

5 King, *The Truth*.

6 Andersen, *"Métis."*

7 Isaac, *A Matter*; LaRocque, *Defeathering the Indian*; LaRocque, *When the Other*.

8 Devine, *The People*; Macdougall, Podruchny, and St-Onge, *Contours*.

9 Dorion and Préfontaine, "Deconstructing Métis Historiography," 17.

10 Andersen, *"Métis"*; Andersen and Adese, "Introduction"; Macdougall, "The Myth"; Shore, *Threads in the Sash*; Voth, "The Race Question."

11 Dorion and Préfontaine, "Deconstructing Métis Historiography," 13.

12 Poitras Pratt, "A Family," 17.

13 Canadian Council on Learning, *Redefining*.

14 Blumlo, "The Creoles."

15 Murphy, "Public Mothers."

16 Dorion and Préfontaine, "Deconstructing Métis Historiography."

17 Kermoal, "Métis Women's"; Macdougall, *One of the Family*.

18 Freed, "Daughters of the Country."

19 Leclair, Nicholson, and Hartley, "From the Stories."

20 Hourie and Carrière-Acco, "Métis Families," 56.

21 Louis Riel Institute, "Buffalo Hunt."

22 Teillet, *The North-West*.

23 Muzyka, "What's Métis Scrip?"

24 Lutz, Hamilton, and Hembecker, *Howard Adams*, 19.

25 Truth and Reconciliation Commission, *Final Report*.

26 Ibid.

27 D.C. Scott, *Annual Report*.

28 Métis National Council, *Métis Education Report*, 1.

29 Adams, *Prison of Grass* (1975 ed.); Adams, *A Tortured People*; Campbell, *Halfbreed* (1973 ed.); LaRocque, *Defeathering the Indian*; LaRocque, *When the Other*.

30 Bird-Wilson, *An Institute*, 1.

31 Ibid., 13–14.

32 Ibid., 10.

33 Ibid., 12.

34 Ibid., 27.

35 Ibid., 30.

36 Métis National Council, *Métis Education Report*, 1.

37 Louis Riel Institute, "Why Choose Us?"

38 Métis National Council, *Métis Education Report*, 5.

39 Paulson, Poitras Pratt, and Contreras, *Métis Education in Alberta*, 1.

40 See, e.g., the *Métis Memories of Residential School Survivors* (2021), https://www.muralmosaic.com/metis-memories/; and *Métis Voices* (2020), digital stories and community-led teaching resources, www.metisvoices.ca.

41 Association of Canadian Deans of Education, "Accord"; Truth and Reconciliation Commission, *Final Report*.

42 Campbell, *Halfbreed* (1973 ed.); LaRocque, *Defeathering the Indian*; LaRocque, *When the Other*.

42 Campbell, *Halfbreed* (1973 ed.); LaRocque, *Defeathering the Indian*; LaRocque, *When the Other*.

43 Poitras Pratt and Bodnaresko, *Truth and Reconciliation*.

44 See Poitras Pratt and Lalonde, "The Alberta."

45 Gaudry and Hancock, "Decolonizing Métis Pedagogies," 7.

46 Louie, "Aligning Universities' Recruitment."

47 The University of Calgary has revised their *Academic Processes and Criteria Handbook* that sets out requirements for academic tenure and promotion to include the all-important aspect of community engagement—an area of vital importance in an Indigenous faculty role.

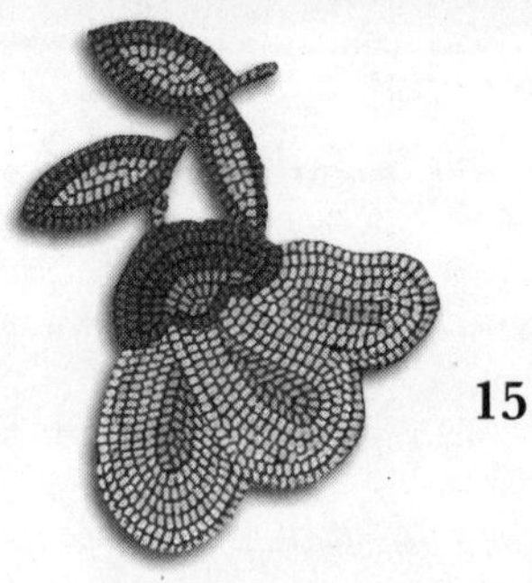

15

Structural and Lateral Violence toward Metis Women in the Academy

Lynn Lavallee

Indigenous peoples of Turtle Island have occupied positions in academia for decades, and they are increasingly holding administrative positions with the goal of making the institutions more accountable, welcoming, and open to the diversity of Indigenous knowledges. For Metis, and women in particular, the journey in academia can sometimes be met with anti-Indigenous racism, misogyny, and *misog-roozh* (intersection of misogyny and anti-Metis discrimination against women, two-spirit, transgender, and non-binary people), but also lateral violence from those within the Indigenous community. While scholars are increasingly speaking about colonial violence and misogyny in the academy, less attention is being paid to the issues among Indigenous people, specifically the political challenges between First Nations, Metis, and Inuit on Turtle Island, north of the colonial border (Canada). Further, with increasing numbers of incidents involving individuals falsely claiming to be Indigenous—also known as *pretendians*—the gaze on Metis people as not being quite enough has amplified.[1] This chapter will explore lateral violence affecting Metis women in the academy and offer some strategies to encourage a collegial environment.

The intersectional characteristics and marginalization of identities within Indigenous communities further complicate experiences of lateral violence. Lateral violence and internalized oppression play out regularly in Indigenous identities, specifically with regard to Metis women as being not enough, not "Indigenous enough."[2] It is important to note that lateral violence couched with misogyny lands differently on two-spirit, transgender, and non-binary people. The experiences of trans, non-binary, and two-spirit Indigenous scholars who experience lateral violence are beyond the scope of this chapter, but they also warrant further discussion and attention. The intersection of lateral violence, misogyny, and anti-Indigenous racism was discussed in detail at a recent forum related to misogyny within the Indigenous community, and Dr. Percy Lezard coined a term for the intersectionality of misogyny and the experiences of non-binary, transgender, and two-spirit identities within the Indigenous community: *misogyny kʷil.*[3] Misogyny kʷil means *red* in Sqilxw; it and related terms such as *misogyny miskwaa* (*red* in Anishinaabemowin) and *misog-roozh* (*red* in Michif) are derived from the work of Moya Bailey and misogynoir that speaks to the experiences of Black women and anti-Black misogyny.[4]

The terms *lateral violence*, *internalized oppression*, *crabs-in-a-bucket*, and *crab mentality* have all been used somewhat interchangeably and are now commonplace in discussions regarding Indigenous peoples. Some early work on lateral violence in the field of nursing focuses on Indigenous peoples. For example, Jody Underwood describes lateral violence as involving "mistrust or misuse of people of the same race, profession, or gender" taking place "among populations that are depressed and powerless."[5] She recounts a story told to her by a Native American angler about "catching crabs and throwing them into a bucket" and goes on to share that these were "Indian crabs" who were trying to escape but were pulled down by the rest of the crabs in the bucket.[6]

On the Navajo Reservation, middle school teacher Beth McCauley,[7] in true anthropological fashion, reported on conditions among children, noting that lateral violence and internalized oppression are an everyday reality for Hopi people, who experienced abandonment and rejection from their own community. Regardless of whether the idea of lateral violence first emerged from the discipline of nursing, through anthropological observations of lateral violence in Indigenous communities, or an Indigenous angler sharing the story about crab mentality, lateral violence and internalized oppression are commonly understood by Indigenous people.

Martina Whelshula grew up on the Colville Reservation in Washington State, and her doctoral dissertation[8] reflects her own experiences of lateral violence among Indigenous peoples. She positions lateral violence among Indigenous peoples as internalized violence and trauma from the deep and profound scars left from over 500 years of colonial wars. Whelshula cites Eduardo Duran and Bonnie Duran,[9] who note that individuals can relate to being both the recipient of lateral violence and the aggressor. Others have identified this internalized violence as being part of the colonial hangover, for example in original work on the post-colonial and colonial hangover.[10]

Whelshula furthers the concept of lateral violence, describing linked behaviours, such as passive aggressiveness, with an individual's search for power and control related to emotional dishonesty, sense of inadequacy, dependency, and fear of intimacy.[11] As a behaviour of lateral violence, passive aggressiveness requires more than one person, and it stands to reason that in the context of lateral violence, individuals can fluctuate between aggressor and recipient of aggression, particularly in prolonged relationships. Academia is a workplace where many people have tenured careers working for decades with one another, and for Indigenous peoples in particular, the playing out of lateral violence and passive aggressiveness can become deeply rooted. Scott Wetzler and Whelshula discuss passive aggressiveness as being a result of one's inability to express hostility and behaviour rooted in concealed anger projecting onto the other person.[12] On the surface, passive-aggressive behaviour appears as innocence and generosity. The passive-aggressive person attempts to rouse anger by "constantly giving you little tastes of . . . hostility in doses just large enough to irritate you."[13] Whelshula details a story of being asked a seemingly innocent question by someone who underneath was angry about a particular circumstance. The continued simple questioning resulted in Whelshula expressing anger while the instigator remained calm and almost smug.[14] The trap of lateral violence and passive-aggressive behaviour can lead to lack of clarity about the interchangeable role of aggressor and victim. Becoming aware of this is a critical step in moving forward in a positive way.

Particularly in long-term relationships, like those in the academy among colleagues, lateral violence and passive-aggressive behaviour serve as forms of psychological abuse that can align with gaslighting, specifically when the objective of the passive-aggressive behaviour is to seek control and power. Gaslighting is typically deployed over a long period of time;[15] similar to lateral violence, it is rooted in social inequality and plays out in interpersonal relationships.[16] While the definition of gaslighting involves psychological manipulation to the point where the *victim* questions their own sanity, scholars such as Angelique Davis and Rose Ernst have furthered the notion of gaslighting to collective groups or the macro-level, particularly related to racial gaslighting for African Americans. These authors argue that racial gaslighting is upheld and reinforced by white supremacy as follows: "The process of racial gaslighting invites intersectional and multiplicative understandings of domination and resistance precisely because the process is a binary of normalization versus pathologization that can take place with or without individual agency. For those who are aware of racial gaslighting, it can be almost impossible to combat their pathologization by the dominant narrative, due to the ubiquitous nature of white supremacy."[17] This kind of pathologizing is often exploited onto the original victim with the creation of a false narrative. It is frequently deployed against individuals who challenge anti-Indigenous racism, anti-Black racism, and colonialism, and who attempt to speak truth. Subsequently, these false narratives are upheld by the supremacy of whiteness and thrive in the colonial academy.

Complicating whiteness further is the notion of the pretendian who, because of their "whiteness," can further weaponize colonial structures against Indigenous people. It is not technically lateral violence when a pretendian is involved, but one of the first lines of defence when someone is challenged for making false claims to indigeneity is that this challenge is an act of lateral violence. In this way, the pretendian effectively becomes the master (pun intended) not only of declaring lateral violence, but executing it, particularly when they are still in the *role* of the Indigenous person upheld by colonial structures and institutions. Therefore, the term *lateral violence* can apply in the case of the pretendian because they are using their false Indigenous identity to garner support to be weaponized against Indigenous people, especially Metis.

Metis can become easy targets of the pretendian feigning First Nations identity given the well-established lateral violence and erasure of Metis by other Indigenous groups. Laura Forsythe positions this erasure and lateral violence within pan-indigeneity and the umbrella term *Indigenous* that tells Metis people they are not enough.[18] Pretendians capitalize on this in their divisive tactics. Pretendians who use false narratives in lateral violence are strategically cunning in convincing non-Indigenous people to buy into the deceitful narrative. The person who can more easily *raceshift* is better able to utilize the structures that uphold whiteness; because these false narratives are often created against individuals who are not the "palatable Indian,"[19] they are easily believed and upheld. The unpalatable Indian in academia is one who attempts to make change and consistently challenges systemic colonialization. They are academic warriors, but their passion and conviction are framed as uncivil, yelling, uncollegial, and aggressive. This is analogous to labels applied to Black women, who are often categorized as aggressive when they are simply being assertive.[20]

For Metis people, racial gaslighting can contribute to feelings of not being "Native enough" and acquiescing to their First Nations and Inuit relations. Even among those who have made false claims to First Nations communities, Metis are often seen as being less than—even less than the pretendian. I have had personal experience with this: as a Metis woman and scholar, my knowledges, experiences, and my very being is erased and eclipsed by legitimate First Nations persons, as well as those who falsely claim to be First Nations. My being as a Metis woman has been dismissed by some, but I am grateful to be seen and recognized by the other First Nations and Metis relations who matter. I battle racial gaslighting daily by remembering the teachings I have gathered as a *Oshkebawis* (helper) over the years for Vern Asin Harper and others, going to ceremony, and remaining confident and humble in knowing my Metis and First Nations relations. I fight the pathologization for my ancestors and for the next generations.

Once the narrative of the pathologized and aggressive Indian is secured, you will sometimes hear embedded in these false narratives the notion of *Who's Next*. Pay attention to the narratives created by "alt-right" activists, white supremacists, and people who are accused of being a pretendian, anti-Black, and/or anti-Indigenous. For example, in response to the removal of statues that symbolized white supremacy, Donald Trump tweeted the following on 17 August 2017: "Robert E. Lee, Stonewall Jackson—who's next, Washington, Jefferson?"[21] Canada is no different in upholding the white supremacist narrative of "Who's Next." After the 6 January 2021 Capitol Hill riot led by white supremacists in the United States,[22] the Trudeau government learned of involvement by the Canadian-born alt-right white supremacist Proud Boys organization and designated it a terrorist organization.[23] Soon after, the Who's Next narrative began (see, for example, "Proud Boys Face Canada's Anti-Terror Law But Who's Next?").[24]

At worst, the Who's Next narrative gains sympathizers who are then used by the original aggressor to fuel the pathologizing narrative against the original victim. When lateral violence aggressors (pretendians included) recruit sympathizers, this solidifies their position and further marginalizes the victim. Even people making false claims to indigeneity use this narrative to garner support when challenged about their false claims. The emboldened pretendian can exclaim, "If *my* identity can be questioned, who's next?"

The Who's Next narrative in lateral violence often involves silent bystanders[25] who are afraid of speaking for fear of the gaze being placed on them—being *next* or perhaps worse, being labelled as anti-Indigenous or racist. Lateral violence playing out among non-Indigenous audiences or colleagues creates opportunities for the bystander to offer verbal support in a hallway or via email but never in a group setting at the time of the behaviour. Parallel to the notion of collective racial gaslighting,[26] the bystander thus contributes to the ongoing colonial mindset of divide and conquer.

The indicators and characteristics that one might see in circumstances of lateral violence include passive-aggressive behaviour, gaslighting, and pathologizing narratives, all of which are supported by the Who's Next discourse. Pretendians have become the masters of declaring and inciting lateral violence. Some might view this claim as a catastrophizing perspective, but many Indigenous scholars can attest to this pervasive pattern in the academy.

What can be done to create a more welcoming environment for Metis women scholars specifically? The remainder of this chapter focuses on policies and procedures that are commonly employed in dealing with the prevalent issues of lateral violence within institutions.

Issues involving lateral violence typically align with harassment, discrimination, and/or incivility policies that are complaint-driven.[27] The colonial academy and the complaint-driven process are not conducive to dealing with racial inequity, let alone experiences of lateral violence. Given the complexity of lateral violence, including the features of passive-aggressive behaviours, gaslighting, pathologizing narratives, pretendianism, and the Who's Next narrative, academic institutions are ill-equipped to provide an environment that does not perpetuate the harms of colonialism. Post-secondary harassment and discrimination policies are tragically inadequate in dealing with lateral violence and often contribute further to the erasure and division of Indigenous peoples and the marginalization of Metis women, two-spirit, transgender, and non-binary people.

In a complaint-driven process, it becomes the responsibility of the victim to fight the harassment, bullying, or lateral violence.[28] However, as in the criminal justice system, the complaint-driven process is often weaponized against Indigenous people where Indigenous people can be more easily complained against, accused, investigated, and sanctioned. Much like in the criminal justice system, complaints are more likely to be lodged against Indigenous people and taken up by the institution as meeting a threshold of investigation. Within the colonial narrative, it is more plausible that Indigenous people are not civil and are instead angry or hostile. Therefore, the true victim can sometimes be the person being complained against.

Adding to the complexity of this issue, most academic institutions are unionized environments. Unions are part of the colonial structure, and consequently, they may support whiteness and/or misogyny. Unions also typically shy away from member-to-member disagreement, so issues between Indigenous peoples are often not supported. Unions focus on challenging the employer and non-unionized administrators, and as a result, issues between Indigenous people are not well addressed. In the case of student-driven complaints, most institutions avoid bad publicity, dealing with complaints by keeping them quiet.

Once a complaint-driven process is enacted, all parties are sworn to confidentiality, essentially further isolating the victim—whether the victim is the actual complainant or the respondent. This requirement of secrecy and confidentially is one of the reasons we hear little, if anything, about complaints of racism and discrimination, although academics are increasingly beginning to write about these processes.[29] The complaint process is often used against those who are marginalized in the academy, as the policies themselves support the status quo (i.e., whiteness and/or misogyny). Sara Ahmed noted that it is often more difficult for people of colour to be considered justified complainants, and that complaints are more easily lodged and investigated against racialized and Indigenous people. For example, in the high-profile case of Dr. Carrie

Bourassa, past scientific director of the Institute of Indigenous Peoples Health at the Canadian Institutes of Health Research (CIHR) and a professor at the University of Saskatchewan, Indigenous faculty raised concerns about Dr. Bourassa's questionable Metis identity claims and brought a formal complaint through an integrity policy at the university. The university responded privately to the Indigenous complainant that there was no justification for the complaint; however, after a revealing exposé of Dr. Bourassa's fraudulent claims by the CBC,[30] the university eventually responded and terminated Dr. Bourassa. The university and CIHR responded only after being subjected to public exposure: the Indigenous faculty who initially brought the complaint forward internally at the University of Saskatchewan were ignored, and the university initially supported a white woman posing as Indigenous. To reiterate: the institution acted only after public disclosure of the fraudulent identity claims.[31]

University administrators are aware of the procedural issues related to complaints. A complaint can be formally lodged, with immediate sanctions and a decision to go to third-party investigation employed, without a full synopsis of allegations being provided to the respondent. These third-party investigations can take years, and often the respondent to a complaint is not made aware of the full complaint for months. Franz Kafka's dystopic classic *The Trial* detailed an individual being arrested and prosecuted, with the nature of the crime never being revealed. Somewhat analogously, the university typically does not provide details about a complaint until after an investigator meets with the complainant. Administrators of academic institutions understand that during an investigation, a complainant can add to the initial complaint, while surveillance of the respondent results in restrictions against academic freedom. Sanctions can be imposed, such as not attending meetings where the complainant is present or speaking about issues related to the content of the complaint, often restricting academic freedom depending on the nature of the complaint.

For an Indigenous person who is wrongfully accused or an Indigenous person who attempts to lodge a complaint, the complaint process is far from restorative. Indigenous academics have also noted that proposals for Indigenous mediation and/or restoration processes are often denied. This might be related to the fact that Indigenous approaches close the circle by bringing together all parties, including witnesses, with the goal of bringing individual and collective truth to the circle—rather than secretive processes that fuel falsehood. The complaint-driven processes in most academic institutions are not concerned with restoration to relationship. The main concern is preserving the reputation of the institution and upholding the status quo: whiteness and misogyny.

Overall, it is vital to reflect upon the challenges related to the complaint-driven process to create an alternative approach to dispute resolution. This will require more discussion to expose problematic procedures and policies. As noted earlier, one of the most significant issues with this process relates to confidentiality. Once a complaint is formalized, the complainant, respondent, and witnesses are often strictly instructed not to discuss the matter with anyone, even after the complaint process ends. Confidentiality is imposed, citing the need to uphold the integrity of the investigation; however, even after the fact, parties are often sworn to secrecy. Confidentiality transforms into secrecy with the goal of protecting the colonial institution: this secrecy does not allow for any conversation about bettering the process or any restorative function with relationships. For example, if witnesses are called, they are not permitted to discuss the matter, even with the complainant or respondent. They often do not learn the results of the investigation, so false or validated complaints are never discussed, meaning that a false narrative may be perpetuated. There is no hope for restoration under the veil of secrecy. Further, secrecy in the complaint process isolates individuals: for Indigenous people who are faced with defending complaints or being the respondent, this adds to the marginalization one experiences in the academy.

Further, individuals can leverage the confidentiality clause as a tactic to further isolate and gaslight, supporting the mechanisms of lateral violence discussed earlier in the chapter. The confidentiality clause in the hands of the master pretendian is the ultimate weapon; it can surrender Indigenous people, especially Metis people, into the hands of the colonizer and erase Metis identity. The confidentiality clause precludes conversations about the marginalization of Metis identity, particularly with regard to Metis women, two-spirit, non-binary, and transgendered people and their experiences with misog-roozh.

What might be an alternative approach to dispute resolution in the context of ingrained lateral violence within the colonial academy?

Can an Indigenous approach be adapted within an environment that upholds the structures of white supremacy, misogyny, and misog-roozh? Can an Indigenous and Metis approach be used in a unionized and litigious environment? How can an Indigenous approach be inclusive of Metis women? The answers to these questions are still unclear because many individuals within the institution are resistant to restoration from an Indigenous perspective and are resistant to any change in policy or change in status quo. However, policies clearly need to be decolonized for Metis women, two-spirit, transgender, and non-binary people to thrive in the academy. It may be possible for Indigenous and Metis ways of healing to be taken up in the colonial academy by turning to traditional teachings and ceremony.

If institutions and their administrators truly seek to be accountable to reconciliation, Indigenization, and decolonization, they must first dismantle the processes that support lateral violence, including further erasure of Metis and Indigenous people by pretendians. It is vital to be aware that these policies are harming Metis and Indigenous people, and to move beyond simple land acknowledgements and blanket statements related to reconciliation and decolonization. Current complaint-driven policies and procedures do not allow truth to come forward and must be dismantled. These processes protect whiteness, misogyny, and misog-roozh and do nothing to contribute to restoring relationships in academia. They do not consider the complexities of Metis citizenship.

A restorative process should not be an alternative approach—it should be written into institutional policies and procedures. Additionally, a restorative process should not be named an Indigenous approach. People will not opt for an Indigenous process. In fact, labelling a process as Indigenous is likely to act as a deterrent for those who are fearful of Metis or Indigenous people—pretendians included—and those who know that this kind of approach will bring people together, close the circle, and allow truth to be told. Restorative processes are not necessarily Indigenous or Metis but will allow for the veil of secrecy to be lifted. Secrecy is the most harmful aspect of the current complaint-driven processes. A restorative process is needed to bring everyone together and dismantle the structures that allow false narratives to be perpetuated.

An effective restorative approach would not allow bystanders who witness lateral violence or the harms of pretendianism to stay silent.

Staying silent contributes to harm: as with bullying behaviour among children, violence feeds off an audience. Lateral violence aggressors and pretendians bank on fear. Those who observe ongoing lateral violence without acting are accomplices of lateral violence and pretendians. Sitting silently while gaslighting occurs furthers the role of accomplice to that of abuser: it is difficult to gaslight without co-conspirators.

It is critical to recognize one's own role in the intersection of lateral violence and pretendians when engaging in restoration—and perhaps more importantly, self-preservation. One way to move forward is to reflect on scared teachings. Another vital element is speaking one's truth. This may be difficult, but setting intentionality to speak one's truth bravely, couched with kindness, can help individuals acknowledge their own worth—while holding themselves and others accountable.

I conclude with one final recommendation: know when self-care is needed and retreat to ceremony, community, and family.

Notes

1 Tait et al., "Pretendians."
2 Forsythe, "Métis Women."
3 Lezard, DiNova, and Lavallee, "Misogyny kʷil Misogyny."
4 Bailey, *Misogynoir Transformed.*
5 Underwood, "Nurse Experiences."
6 Ibid., 71.
7 McCauley, "Students."
8 Whelshula, "Healing through Decolonization."
9 Duran and Duran, *Native American Postcolonial Psychology.*
10 Johnson, "The Post-Colonial Hangover"; McGill, "An Institutional Suicide Machine."
11 Whelshula, "Healing through Decolonization."
12 Wetzler, "Living with"; Whelshula, "Healing through Decolonization."
13 Wetzler, "Living with," 239.
14 Whelshula, "Healing through Decolonization."
15 Spear, "Gaslighting."
16 Sweet, "The Sociology of Gaslighting."
17 Davis and Ernst, "Racial Gaslighting," 764.
18 Forsythe, "Métis Women."
19 L. Lavallee, "Is Decolonization Possible," 124.

20 Daniel, "Teaching While Black."
21 Stieb, "Drawing the Line."
22 Murphy et al., "At Least 150 People."
23 BBC News, "Proud Boys."
24 Clarke, "Proud Boys."
25 Bannerji, *The Dark Side.*
26 Davis and Ernst, "Racial Gaslighting."
27 Mackenzie, "Racial Harassment."
28 Ibid.
29 Ahmed, *Complaint!*
30 Leo, "Indigenous or Pretender?"
31 Pratyush, "Carrie Bourassa's Suspension."

Part Three:

Research Methodology

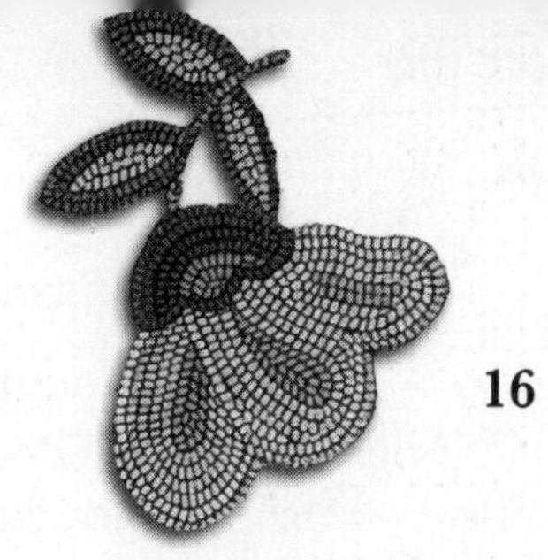

16

Métis Research and Relationality: Auntie Governance, the Visiting Way, and Kitchen Table Reflections

Kirsten Lindquist, Shalene Jobin, and Avery Letendre

> *In 1932, my grandmother's uncle, Joseph F. Dion, alongside James Brady, Felix Calliou, Malcolm Norris, and Peter Tompkins, known as the "Métis Five," formed the Metis Association of Alberta (MAA), four years after the 1928 formation of L'Association des Métis Alberta et les Territoires du Nord-Ouest. Dion was elected president and served until his passing in 1960. As part of his commitments, he travelled extensively across Alberta, frequently visiting with Métis people across settlements, communities, and landscapes. Almost ninety years later, in 2016, I had a similar opportunity to travel across Alberta to visit with Métis people from the various regions of the Métis Nation of Alberta (MNA) with Dr. Shalene Jobin, and (at the time) research assistant Avery Letendre, as part of a research project initiated by the Métis Nation of Alberta.*
>
> —Kirsten Lindquist

This project was called into action by a citizen's ordinary resolution at the Métis Nation of Alberta's (MNA's) eighty-seventh Annual General Assembly. The resolution, which was passed by the Assembly, called for research to develop a Governance Framework Model.[1] This research project, the MNA Governance Framework Review, was one of many processes to engage with Métis citizens to legally transition the nation's governance framework as an Association (Societies Act of Alberta) into a nation with a self-governing constitution, in relationship to the provincial and federal government.[2] As of this writing, the Métis Nation of Alberta has formed the Otipemisiwak Métis Government.

The following reflective commentary on the research process, methods, and methodologies is shaped by our relational positionalities to this project as co-authors, and is also grounded through our relationship to each other, our Métis kin network, and Métis women's scholarship, public leadership, and activism. These relationships are highlighted throughout our work on the MNA Governance Framework Review. We hope to contribute to the lineages, genealogies, and networks of Métis women's historical and contemporary knowledge and scholarship, which this co-edited collection represents.

We each have a unique relationship with the MNA and Métis communities. Dr. Shalene Jobin is Métis through her paternal line.[3] As the director of the Indigenous Governance and Partnership (IGP) program, Shalene was responsible for implementing the MNA Governance Review research project. As part of this research, she mentored Kirsten and Avery in a leadership role in practice. Kirsten is Cree-Métis through her father and her grandmother, and is a citizen of the MNA. Her grandmother's family comes from the Moose Mountain homestead and Kehewin Cree First Nation. Avery Letendre is the administrator of the Indigenous Governance and Partnership Program. Avery is a Euro-Canadian settler, and her husband is an MNA citizen.

We begin with a background on the research project, which leads into a description of our research methodologies and a section on Métis women's leadership. In the methodologies section, we review the guiding literature from Métis academic grandmothers, aunties, and kin, including a reflection on our academic Aunties and research positionalities. In the section on Métis women's leadership, we profile Métis women and collectives who have contributed in significant ways toward what Daniel Voth calls indignant governance and indignant disobedience. Taken together, this chapter highlights Métis women's leadership, provides examples of Métis research methods and methodologies, and provides reflections on Métis governance and leadership—academic, government, and grassroots.

The MNA Governance Framework Review

The MNA is the government for Métis people in Alberta and is governed at both a provincial and regional level. A provincial president and vice-president, as well as six regional presidents and vice-presidents are accountable to Métis citizens living within their respective regions.[4] However, Métis citizens also have the opportunity to directly participate in the nation's governance each year at the Annual General Assembly. In comparison with the Alberta provincial and federal representative legislative bodies, Métis governance and government processes are a hybrid between representative and direct democracy.[5] As we briefly introduced in the preface, the MNA approached the Faculty of Native Studies following the eighty-seventh Annual General Assembly to conduct research on governance frameworks. As a result, the MNA and the Indigenous Governance and Partnership program developed a formal research partnership that was guided by the MNA governance advisory committee.[6]

The research partnership and process was citizen- and community-led, which is also reflected by the resolution put forth in 2015. Working directly with the MNA governance advisory committee, we developed a research plan to provide several opportunities for Métis citizens' input and direction as part of the review, at both the regional and provincial levels. Focus groups and individual interviews were conducted with administrative staff, affiliate staff, political representative leaders, and citizens connected to their respective regions. Citizens were invited to participate in focus group consultations at each of the six regions: Peace River, Lac La Biche, Slave Lake, Bonnyville, Edmonton, and Calgary. The research team facilitated these focus groups with citizens, focusing on Métis governance topics such as consultation processes, program and service delivery, community engagement, and approaches to decision making. At each focus group gathering, there was an Elder or knowledge keeper in attendance who started with a prayer and intention for good conversation and relating. We also shared food together as part of the conversation. All participants were gifted with a Faculty of Native Studies coffee/tea mug.

In addition to interviews and focus groups, other opportunities for community feedback included paper-based workbooks at the eighty-eighth Annual General Assembly (2016), as well as access to an online fillable version of the workbook. Main themes emerging from community feedback were integrated with the summaries from the historical governance, policy, and academic literature reviews. An interim report-back presentation was also made at the eighty-eighth Annual General Assembly at Métis Crossing/Victoria Settlement.

In January 2017, we finalized a sixty-page final report, which was provided to the MNA and disseminated at the eighty-ninth Annual General Assembly (2017). The report was based around a twofold governance framework: (1) a structure to understand, administer, and implement the foundational values, vision, rights, and responsibilities of the MNA, and (2) a mechanism to organize and address the recommendations that, in turn, inform and shape the governance framework. This included twelve key governance recommendations and four potential options for governing structures to support the MNA to work towards self-government.[7]

The MNA governance processes, Annual General Assembly, and bylaws are shaped by provincial legislation, the Societies Act, which provides the MNA access to provincial and federal funding. On 27 June 2019, two years following the final report on the MNA Governance Framework Review, the MNA signed the Métis Government Recognition and Self-Government Agreement with the federal government. This agreement signified eighty-nine years of Métis organizing through the Societies Act in Alberta and was the result of intergenerational political organizing and nation building. Following this historic agreement, the MNA ratified a constitution to replace the Societies Act.

MNA Self-Government and Gendered Métis Nation–Building/Organizing Narratives

Through nation building and obtaining recognition for self-government, the Métis nation has been sustained by the perseverance and contributions of men and women within the nation.

> ***Jobin:*** My parents always taught me to be proud of being Indigenous, specifically Métis (paternal) and Cree (maternal). My late father was Métis, born in a small homestead in Big Prairie, outside of Grouard, Alberta (north of High Prairie). When my dad was almost two, his dad, Joe Jobin (m.

> Helen Chalifioux), drowned in a slough on their land after a day of haying. Joe Jobin was born to Louis Jobin and Olive Dumas in Big Prairie sixteen years after Joe's parents fought in the 1885 resistance. Louis Jobin was a lieutenant secretary for Louis Riel and a freighter during the fur trade. Louis' brother, Ambroise Jr., died fighting during the 1885 resistance. In 1985, our extended family camped in Batoche for the 100-year commemoration of the Northwest Resistance. At seven years old, I remember music and dancing and my sneaker tips melting after being a little too close to the fire while drying off. A special memory I have is one evening sitting around the campfire with people singing and visiting all around me and looking up to the sky to see the northern lights in all their splendour, appearing to dance to the music.

As part of connecting to a cohesive national and homeland identity, Métis people and communities invest in collective memories that link nationhood to a shared nationalism. The Métis National Council and its provincial governing members accomplish this task by providing a shared public history that begins with historical sovereign narratives, most often evoking the memory of Louis Riel and Gabriel Dumont in relation to the 1885 Northwest Resistance. However, there are historical accounts by Métis women involved in the Northwest Resistance, and missionary records, that demonstrate how "women were active agents or played an important supply role outside the trenches, challenged Dumont and Riel's battle strategy, and were subjected to the humiliation and plunder of the victorious and vengeful North-West Field Force."[8]

When nationalist narratives are built around male figures like Riel and Dumont, by way of omission, Métis women and two-spirit, queer, and/or non-binary Métis persons are relegated to the private sphere, a space where their political memories are subordinated to those of Riel, Dumont, or other male "warriors," resulting in imbalanced contributions to Métis nationhood narratives.[9] Jennifer Brown points this out by writing, "it is all too easy to learn more about the men than the women; but new kinds of systematic study can redress the balance, contributing richer perspectives not only on individuals and families. [*sic*] but on metis social history in its broadest sense."[10] Additionally, as Voth poignantly remarks, "if we reflect on the great narratives that still dominate Métis politics and Métis nationalism, we can see many of the so-called great men of Native history. Cuthbert Grant, William Hallett, William Dease, Louis Riel Jr. and Sr., James McKay, Charles Nolin, Gabriel Dumont all come to mind. One is hard-pressed to name or even point to Indigenous women in this conception of the nation."[11]

Existing Alberta Métis public history narratives and scholarship focus on the history of the political organizing work of men, like Joseph Dion and the Métis Five, yet there are many stories of Métis women working and organizing alongside these men that have yet to be published into the canon of Métis Studies, and more broadly shared as public history. Heteropatriarchal, settler colonial influences on Indigenous governance have contributed to the male-centric shape this public history has taken. Even as we write the vignettes of our own family histories and connections to Métis nationhood in this chapter, we reflect on how this male-centred Métis public discourse can become embedded in family histories that are passed down through the generations.[12] Métis women have been and are integral to labouring and organizing in the struggle for nationhood and self-government. In the next section, we explore examples of how this nation-building work has been approached in academia, politics, and activism through gendered, kin-centric practices.

Métis Women's Research Methodologies

As part of our reflection on this project's research processes and methods (i.e. focus groups, questionnaires, dissemination), we recognized that some of the processes, such as travelling to the different regions in Alberta, sharing meals over conversation, gifting, and upholding and enacting kinship responsibilities, embodied Métis women's governance principles and practices.

Kinship-centred governance principles-in-practice such as wahkohtowin/wahkootowin, kîhokewin/keeoukaywin (the visiting way), kitchen table governance/theory, and (academic) Auntie mentorship are core to Métis women's research methodologies.[13] For many Métis-led research projects, these governance teachings originate from Maria Campbell, a Métis knowledge keeper, granny, and matriarch. Campbell was one of the first Native women to publish an autobiographical narrative, providing a public, yet intimate insight into gender-based violence, demonstrating the compounded impacts of both racism and sexism experienced by Indigenous women.[14] Through telling her story, she dismantled the perceived divide between the personal and the political in Indian Country.[15] Through intergenerational mentorship, Campbell has shaped many of the Métis women that we now know as our academic Aunties. The growing collection of published Indigenous women (and gender queer) narratives, as well as the expanding scholarship focusing on Métis concepts of nationhood through the lens of gender-centric kinship,[16] can diversify the male-centred national narratives that are often at the heart of Métis nationalist public history.[17]

These kin-centric governance principles as/and methodologies continue to be woven into the scholarly work of the next generation. wahkootowin (wahkohtowin), a concept Métis scholar Brenda Macdougall learned not from historical records but from being in relation with Maria Campbell, "is invoked in ceremonies, prayer, and daily conversation."[18] Guided by wahkootowin, Macdougall's research focuses on the role of Métis women and their maternal relatives in nation building across the prairies, as what she terms "kinscapes."

Also mentored by Campbell, Janice Gaudet practises keeoukaywin, a word gifted by Campbell, meaning the *visiting way*. Keeoukaywin is "a living expression of wahkotowin that resists colonial dominance."[19] In practicing this resistance, Gaudet connects keeoukaywin to Sherry Farrell Racette's "kitchen table theory" where everyone is welcome. In describing kitchen table logic, Farrell Racette demonstrates the multi-modality of the kitchen table and its creative spatial potential "where men, women and children worked, dreamt and created."[20]

> ***Lindquist:*** wahkohtowin and keeoukaywin remind me that visiting our kinship relations also includes our more-than-human relations, ancestors, and the spirits of the landscapes. During our travels to the different regions, I felt compelled to carry extra tobacco in my pack. Shalene and I visited the shores of Lesser Slave Lake following our conversations with citizens from Region 5. We also visited Lac La Biche and Peace River following our conversations in Region 1 and Region 6, respectively. The practice of offering tobacco to introduce and orient myself to these powerful water relatives reminded me how these beings shape places and people.

> After conversations in Region 2 (my home region), Shalene and I spent the evening at my parents' home. I often feel that to really know me, you need to visit the land I grew up with. And I was grateful to share this kinscape with my mentor. A year later, I shared a similar experience with Avery when we attended the Assembly in Peace River to share the final report with citizens. The visiting way not only extends to Métis citizens and our kinscapes, but also between each other as research colleagues. During the hours we spent together during the drive, we held space for conversations, learning more about each other, and in this way, strengthening the kinship bond between us.
>
> ***Letendre:*** Years later, I can see both the collective and individual strengths of the nation. Reflecting on this [research] project, the underlying value of relationality and inclusivity —of wahkohtowin—is apparent, embodied by the project team. This Cree and Métis concept and law of wahkohtowin is truly profound . . . to search out in others and uphold their inherent relationship to yourself, in order to have connectivity and right relations . . . in order to have peace. This is a mode of leadership and a form of sheer wisdom that is not lauded enough. wahkohtowin, put into action, is a marker of strength. Of personal significance, wahkohtowin has had positive repercussions for my family, by connecting us closer to the Métis nation and local community . . . making inroads where colonialism has brought separation. Drawing people in as relatives, however near or distant, has been and continues to be a strength found in Métis women that is manifested as a matter of course—in families, communities, friendships, vocations, and formal leadership roles. The reverberations from this ethic are immeasurable.

Anderson, in her reflection on moving into the autumn season of her work, also connects Farrell Racette's kitchen table methodologies to her responsibilities as an academic Auntie in mentoring the next generation. The spatial location of the research lab and the kitchen table blend together in a project that Anderson is working on with her university, the "Grannie's cabin/Nokum's house."[21] Here, Anderson intends to not only academically train but also nurture "students across disciplines, host workshops on food and family, and land-based practices, and foster and model Indigenous women's leadership."[22] Research, ceremony, social and environmental justice organizing, and of course, food, are shared in this intergenerational gathering space.

Academic Aunties

This research project demonstrated how Auntie mentorship and leadership can create space and nurture the next generation.

> ***Letendre:*** Indigenous academics often play a key role in making space for students to grow. They are known to excel at providing mentorship and opportunities for people within and outside of the academy. In short, what Indigenous academics regularly demonstrate is an ethic of giving. When I was invited into the governance research project for the MNA, it was very humbling and such an honour. As a settler student of Indigenous Studies, I hoped to be able to contribute in a meaningful way and was keenly aware of my shortcomings on the topic! Grateful to be overseen by knowledgeable Indigenous academics, Dr. Shalene Jobin, Dr. Chris Andersen, and Kirsten Lindquist, I entered into this project with eagerness to hear what the people of the MNA would express. In reviewing the words of Métis people on the topic, it was clear that they were passionate about Métis culture, citizen and community well-being, and the future of the nation—to be continually strengthened, defined through a new governmental structure, and properly recognized. This, in and of itself, was heartening.
>
> ***Lindquist:*** One of the main teachings I've learned, from both studying and observing the Métis women mentioned above in scholarship and practice, is the ability to facilitate and weave many stories and viewpoints into a cohesive narrative. Shalene facilitated and weaved many perspectives during our focus group conversations. Through observing her in practice, she taught me how to manage different viewpoints

> and address conflict. The citizens respected Shalene because she approached the conversation humbly and respectfully; however, she was firm around the intentions of knowledge sharing to ensure that all voices were heard. Through Shalene, I started learning about practising wahkohtowin as a research methodology. While we are researchers, we are also relatives with roles and responsibilities. Following in the footsteps of the Métis women academics before us, wahkohtowin is central to our research and relating practices. Not only do I feel guided by a network of strong academic Aunties, I also reflect on the influence of political Aunties, and the grassroots network of Métis women and youth, queer, 2S, and trans/non-binary people that have taught me about diverse ways of leading and showing up for their kin and communities in various governance spaces.

As described above, Anderson, as an academic Auntie, blends the research space with kitchen table methodologies. During the focus group sessions, we similarly found that office boardroom tables and hotel conference tables blended into a familial and generative conversation space, as exemplified in kitchen table methodologies/theory. The next section profiles two Métis women politicians who have integrated their experiences of kitchen table and boardroom politics to address gender discrimination.

Multi-Spatial Métis Women's Governance

Kitchen table governance centres Indigenous women's roles in governance and blurs the discussion between the public and private. In our experience of working with the MNA, Métis women have brought the specificity of women's kitchen table relationality into the political realm. In our research, we witnessed Métis women, as leaders, inherently challenging and changing a historically male-dominated space. While we observed strong Métis women doing the work of making and remaking the nation in the 21st century, public narratives of the Métis Nation still remain fertile ground for rearticulation. As mentioned earlier, Métis scholar Daniel Voth puts forward two Métis women-centred frameworks: indignant governance and indignant disobedience.[23] In the former, he argues that Métis women require actual political power and empowerment in the nation. Why indignant? Voth explains how indignation is a concept directly tied to the Métis "indignation meetings" where principal ideals of land, gender, and the impacts of colonization were held.[24] Indignant is a useful concept to describe being angry at unjust treatment, such as violence towards Indigenous women and disempowerment of Indigenous women in governance. In our research specific to MNA governance, it appears that Métis women do hold political power—indignant governance. During our 2016–2017 research process, five of the six regionally elected president positions in the Métis Nation were held by Métis women.[25] Currently (2021), in the six Métis Nation regions in Alberta, where each has an elected regional president and vice-president position, five are women.

> ***Lindquist:*** There are Aunties in the political realm, like Métis women Audrey Poitras and Muriel Stanley Venne. I first met Audrey Poitras through her nieces, Maureen Moneta and Kristy Isert. I have known Maureen Moneta and Kristy Isert since I was three years old, and their mother, Isabel Myshaniuk, was my town mom. We are still connected over thirty years later, and I am humbled by their accomplishments in their respective workplaces, as well as their contributions to their families and communities. I am also proud to be an Auntie to their children. The first MNA governance event that I attended was a MNA special vote. There can be up to 500 citizens at the Assembly, and everyone has an opportunity to take to the floor and speak at the meeting. Observing Audrey address questions demonstrated her strength as a leader who listens.

> ***Jobin:*** During our research project, I had family members who were actively involved in the political and administrative arms of the nation. My aunt (my father's sister), Beatrice (née Jobin) Demetrius, was the senior genealogist for the MNA. My father's cousin, Marlene Lanz (1943–2018), served twelve years as president of MNA Region 3 and was on the advisory committee for our research project as the MNA co-minister of governance and registries. These and other family relations bring another layer of accountability to scholarship, being accountable to our aunties.

We offer two profiles of Métis women who have political power in the Métis Nation. We do so in order to add to the public narratives of Métis women who are doing the work of the nation and to demonstrate indignant governance and indignant disobedience.

Audrey Poitras

For twenty-five years, the MNA has been led by a Métis woman president. President Audrey Poitras is an excellent example of a strong Métis woman and leader. Born in 1950 and from Elk Point, Alberta, Ms. Poitras became a certified accountant in 1990. She was involved in founding Métis Locals 1885 and 999 and was a key initiator of the Alberta Métis Women's Organization. Ms. Poitras was the first woman elected as president of the MNA in 1996 and held that position until 2023. When first elected, there was only one other woman elected on the fourteen-member governing council, but during her tenure there have been as many as nine women on the council at one time.[26] President Poitras states: "There is more acceptance of women leaders. We see it not only in the Métis Nation. We see it in the First Nations. We see it in corporate industries, banks. . . . When I was first elected, generally, I would walk into a room and there would be me and a whole bunch of men. Today you see a lot of women in leadership roles."[27]

What becomes apparent is how Métis women are actively involved in kitchen table governance and how this takes shape in various leadership spaces in all aspects of Métis society, including public office. We see that Métis women are taking the philosophies of kitchen table governance (creativity, action, etc.) and bringing their own leadership style into the political realm. Voth articulates an indignant governance that orients "the way Métis govern themselves with reference to connections between Indigenous women and the land," and that is "operationalized in the nation's practices of governance."[28] Within Ms. Poitras's twenty-five years as MNA president, she has placed great importance on land through land negotiations,[29] the creation of Métis Crossing,[30] and self-government.[31] We contend that Ms. Poitras's long-standing leadership, prominence, and contributions to the Métis Nation have been a demonstration of indignant governance.

In addition, Voth articulates that, "Indignant disobedience seeks to guard against the demand for women to take up obedient and subservient positions in the service of unity within a nationalist movement."[32] Indignant governance must be joined with an indignant disobedience to operationalize the types of Métis nationalism needed to address gender discrimination and violence in our communities.[33]

Muriel Stanley Venne

We see indignant disobedience exemplified in Métis women like Muriel Stanley Venne. From 2008–2012, Ms. Stanley Venne served as provincial vice-president of the MNA. In 1994, Ms. Stanley Venne created the Institute for the Advancement of Aboriginal Women (IAAW) in Alberta to recognize Indigenous women's "role, value, and achievement"[34] in society, raise awareness, and respond to challenges faced. To achieve the former, she led the creation of the Esquao Awards—a ceremony dedicated to honouring the strength, resilience, and beauty of First Nation, Métis, and Inuit women in Alberta. To achieve the latter, the IAAW, composed of First Nation and Métis women, has advanced Indigenous women's rights through advocacy, education, grassroots support, and program development. For example, in 2016, the IAAW partnered with LEAF to intervene in the appeal of the *R v. Barton* court case for the killing of Métis mother, sister, and grandmother Ms. Cindy Gladue.[35] After tireless work from many, Bradley Barton was eventually convicted of manslaughter. Métis women like Venne exemplify the indignant disobedience needed for the future of the Métis Nation.

Grassroots Governance

wahkohtowin and keeoukaywin/kîyokêwin have been described and implemented as Métis research methodologies above. However, more broadly, they are teachings and values for being in good relation in all areas of governance. Being indignantly disobedient and being in good relation are not mutually exclusive. Enacting kinship responsibilities also means challenging colonial and capitalist structures and practices in our communities. Building the Métis Nation can happen through elected avenues, but it also happens through the everyday actions[36] of Métis people and grassroots organizing. An example of a grassroots project that enacts and embodies these values and practices is the Mamawi Project Collective.

The Mamawi Project Collective

While Métis youth in Alberta have many opportunities to engage with intergenerational knowledge exchange and learn about MNA governance and government through Elder and youth conferences and specific youth activities during the Annual Assembly, there are other grassroots projects that connect Métis youth across provincial boundaries to share stories and learn from each other's experiences. One of these projects that centres the kin-centric governance principles discussed above is the Mamawi Project Collective. The Mamawi Project Collective, a grassroots collective, utilizes social media, storytelling, and in-person gatherings to connect young Métis people across the Métis homeland. The collective gathered together with Elder Maria Campbell in July 2019 in Saskatchewan.[37] She shared the teaching of kîyokêwin (visiting) as a core governance principle in rebuilding relations. The collective recently published an online zine that showcased multi-media storytelling about visiting. As a grassroots project that is separate from the provincial councils, the collective also acts to encourage critical thinking and challenging colonial practices, including those within our communities and nation. Indignant disobedience is a practice that young people can enact to hold each other, our communities, and our nation accountable with care, as part of kinship responsibilities.[38]

Concluding Reflections for Better Relations

In this chapter, we have introduced a research project completed with the MNA that was women-led and engaged with Métis women research methodologies and, more broadly, governance principles. These methodologies include wahkohtowin, keeoukaywin (the visiting way), kitchen table governance, and academic Auntie mentorship. Reviewing this research project together has provided space to focus on not only the methods of research (i.e., focus groups, questionnaires, dissemination), but the methodologies as well—how we related to each other during the research and in the moments in-between. By utilizing these Métis women research methodologies, we have learned more about each other's family/relations and engaged with these kinscapes during road trips in a relational, visiting way.

We reflect back and share learnings in order to encourage further academic discussion about the role of gender within Métis politics and governance. We have recognized gender as an area for greater embedded focus in the Indigenous Governance and Partnership Program and its governance framework.[39] While the Indigenous Governance and Partnership framework makes space for leadership in a wide range of roles, it is important to be reflexive in community-led research and teaching on this subject. We realize how a gendered analysis should be included in all aspects of the research process. To include gender in a focused manner means that the voices and narratives of Métis women and self-identifying two-spirit and/or queer Métis persons are centred and heard in governance spaces.[40]

Examples of indignant governance and indignant disobedience include profiles of significant Métis women leaders Audrey Poitras and Muriel Stanley Venne. Additionally, there are research and grassroots projects that are rooted, directed, and informed by Métis youth in various leadership and scholarship roles, such as the Mamawi Project, as described in this article, as well as 2Land2Furious, Métis Kinscapes, and Walking with Our Sisters. We are encouraged by the futurities that Métis women are building into and the visionary aspects inherent in each of them. In our reflections together, it is evident that Métis women are leading in a variety of spaces, including grassroots community organizing, politics, academia, and beyond.

While published and public material on leadership in the Métis Nation has a history of centralizing men, and while even our own personal kinship ties and stories can subconsciously be male-centred, there is a wealth of historical and contemporary examples of strong Métis women whom we want to see recognized, whom we have learned from, and continue to lift up. Our narratives of the nation should be expanded to not only include women, two-spirit, and non-binary people, but also include those doing the work that is not typically seen as within the realm of formal politics. This chapter has contributed to some of the written work that highlights specific accomplishments of Métis women in politics and governance, with the hope that it will positively influence scholarship, teaching, and research for many across Turtle Island. Gender-based discrimination can be implicit, and we see great utility in directly asking gendered questions in Métis governance, scholarship, teaching, and research in order to counteract this and build a different future.

Notes

1 Métis Nation of Alberta, "2015–16 Annual Report," accessed 18 March 2021, https://albertametis.com/app/uploads/2021/07/AnnualReport_2014-2015.pdf.

2 Métis Nation of Alberta, "Timeline," accessed 15 March 2021, https://albertametis.com/metis-in-alberta/timeline/.

3 Jobin upholds her Métis ancestry and identity but does not qualify for citizenship as she is Cree First Nations through her maternal line and has citizenship with Red Pheasant First Nation.

4 Métis Nation of Alberta, "About," accessed 18 March 2021, https://albertametis.com/who-we-are/.

5 Citizens are able to bring forward ordinary and special resolutions to the citizenry at the Annual General Assemblies and they each have direct decision-making powers through a direct vote. In this way, they exercise direct democracy because these votes determine whether the resolutions will pass or be defeated. During this forum, citizens are able to comment upon and debate the merits and drawbacks of the resolution. The MNA features representative democracy because there is an elected president, vice-president, and elected regional presidents and vice-presidents who are accountable to citizens for the political service in the nation.

6 Jobin, Lindquist, and Letendre, *Métis Nation of Alberta*.

7 Ibid., 5–6.

8 Payment, "'La Vie,'" 26.

9 Voth, "'Descendants'"; Welsh, "Voices of the Grandmothers."

10 Brown, "Woman as Centre," 45.

11 Voth, "'Descendants,'" 98.

12 Indigenous Studies is inherently a continually self-reflective space.

13 K. Anderson, "On Seasons"; Farrell Racette, "Kitchen Table Theory"; Gaudet, "Keeoukaywin"; Macdougall, *One of the Family*.

14 Campbell, *Halfbreed* (1973 ed.).

15 Million, *Therapeutic Nations*, 62.

16 Hodgson-Smith and Kermoal, "Community-Based Research"; Macdougall, *One of the Family*.

17 Adese, "Restoring the Balance"; Payment, "'La Vie'"; Voth, "'Descendants.'"

18 Macdougall, *One of the Family*, xii.

19 Adese, "Restoring the Balance"; Payment, "'La Vie'"; Voth, "'Descendants.'"

19 Gaudet, "Keeoukaywin," 55.

20 Farrell Racette, "Kitchen Table Theory."

21 K. Anderson, "On Seasons," 211.

22 Ibid., 210–11.

23 Voth, "'Descendants.'"

24 Ibid., 88.

25 Métis Nation of Alberta, "2016–17 Annual Report," accessed 24 August 2023. https://albertametis.com/app/uploads/2021/07/AGA-Report-2017-for-Website.pdf.

26 CFWE Radio, "Audrey Poitras, President of the Metis Nation of Alberta," https://www.cfweradio.ca/news/indigenous-woman-in-the-21st-century/audrey-poitras-president-of-the-metis-nation-of-alberta/ (accessed 21 March 2021).

27 Ibid.
28 Voth, "'Descendants,'" 87–88.
29 Métis Nation of Alberta, "Recent Agreements with Canada and Alberta," accessed 26 March 2021, http://albertametis.com/metis-rights.
30 Métis Crossing, "About."
31 Métis Nation of Alberta, "Governance."
32 Voth, "'Descendants,'" 87.
33 Ibid., 105–6.
34 Institute for the Advancement of Aboriginal Women, "About Us."
35 Women's Legal Education and Action Fund, "IAAW."
36 Corntassel, "Re-Envisioning Resurgence."
37 The Mamawi Project Collective, *Kîyokêwin*.
38 Atter, "'It's About Feeling Seen.'"
39 Jobin, Lindquist, and Letendre, "Indigenous Governance Programming."
40 Métis in Space, "Back 2 the Land."

Doris McDougall and Marlene Vandale, River Road Métis Festival, 2018.

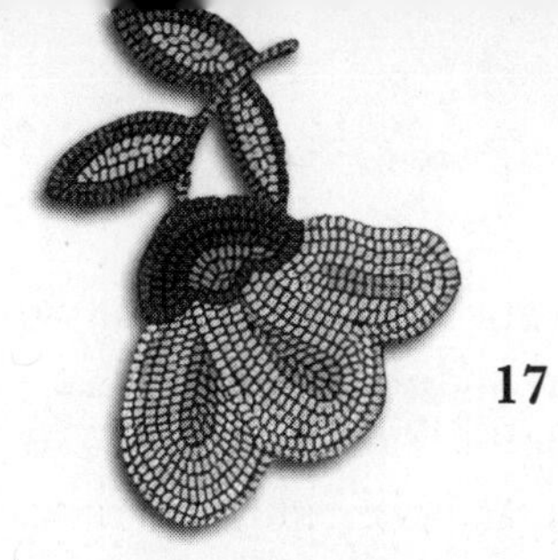

17

Lii Taab di Faam Michif / Métis Women's Kitchen Table:

Practising Our Sovereignty

Janice Cindy Gaudet and Angela Rancourt

Dedication

We dedicate this work to the late Michif Matriarch Marlene Vandale. Even though she left this world before we could share this chapter with her, we know that she is still with us. She has advised us throughout this project and continues to do so. She is alive in our hearts, and she is a perfect example of why Lii Taab di Faam needs to prosper.

Marlene Vandale was born in 1949 and was the eldest of nine children. Her mother, Eva Lafontaine, was originally from the Batoche area and her father, Albert Richard, resided in the Métis community of St. Louis. Marlene speaks about her mother's relations in Montana, and her memories of her father sawing ice from the South Saskatchewan River in order to provide financially for their family. As the first-born child, she had various responsibilities in keeping the household happy and healthy.

In 1967, Marlene married her life partner, Sonny Vandale. Marlene and Sonny had four children of their own and also graciously welcomed a number of children into their family through the fostering system over their lifetime. Many of them still come back to visit from time to time. It is obvious that, with Marlene's gentle soul and kind heart, at her kitchen table and in their home, these children realized that they were family.

Marlene took pride in the Michif language. She and Sonny spoke Michif with each other frequently and she explained that while their children understand it, they are hesitant to speak it. She worried that the Michif language is being lost, and wanted to see more and more people speak it!

Acknowledgement

We recognize that this work is possible because our ancestors defended our rights, our land, our peoples, our language, and our ways of life. Our Michif grandmothers, mothers, sisters, and aunties compel us to stand up firmly and lovingly to ongoing harm, and they continue to help us return to the power of Métis women's kitchen table.

We are grateful for the encouragement and wisdom shared by Métis Matriarchs Sophie McDougall and Maria Campbell.[1] We also acknowledge Graham Andrews, our Michif relative, for sitting with us at Lii Taab and for sharing, listening, and entrusting us with the wisdom of his Matriarchs (also respected as his noohkooms), Leona (née McDougall) and Nancy Boyer (née Anderson).

Responsible Research: Situating Ourselves in Relation to Lii Taab di Faam Michif

In the ways of our grandparents who engage in conversation by asking "Who do you belong to?," "Who are you related to?," we situate ourselves by ensuring that our Métis kinship connections are respected, and in doing so we unsettle the power structures of the academy, which insists that we situate ourselves as experts within a certain field of study. In doing so, we share why this work matters to us as we come together as Michif, drawing strength from oral histories and our aunties' and grandmothers' ways to help strengthen family and community. In this way, we connect with our specific roles and responsibilities in relation to Lii Taab di Faam Michif.[2] This is the beginning point of community-engaged research, but more importantly, it is our responsibility to the place and the people that guide our story of belonging at Lii Taab.

Janice Cindy Gaudet

I am the youngest daughter of Norma (Morrison) and Sylvio (Gaudet). I grew up in the farming community near Bellevue, Saskatchewan, with my five older siblings. My mom is the daughter of Auxile Lépine (born in Duck Lake, Saskatchewan) and Norman Morrison (born in Hoey, Saskatchewan, son of Harriet Bremner and Jack Morrison), who raised their ten children on their first home quarter purchased in 1928 in the Hoey area. Auxile is the daughter of Margaret Boucher and Maxime Lépine, Jr. Some of the first families who made their homes in St. Louis were Maxime Lépine, Sr., and Josephete Lavallee, and Jean-Baptiste Boucher and Caroline Lesperance. I am so proud to be learning from the generation of Métis women belonging to the rich stories of this region. Learning with and from Métis women keeps me connected and grounded to this place. I learned about our values of generosity, visiting, and sharing guided by and at my mom's, maymairs', and aunties' kitchen tables. For me, they were as important as, if not more important than, the church altar. In many ways, Lii Taab was and is our home altar kept up by our Matriarchs. The sharing at Lii Taab in creating Lii Kaart made me reflect on what our Métis Matriarchs have fought for so many to have, a good life—miyo pimaatisiwin.[3]

Angela Rancourt

I am the first of three children born to Leslie Rancourt and Betty Morrison. I currently reside in, grew up in, and teach in the community of St. Louis. My maternal grandfather, Duncan Morrison, is the son of Auxile Lépine and Norman Morrison. The Lépine family is well-known in the area for their great contributions to the 1885 Resistance in Batoche as well as their commitment to the Métis way of life for generations that followed.

Our community has always immersed our children in the Michif way of life, even when it was labelled as less valuable. As a child, one's way of life is simply that, no questions asked. As we grow older, we begin to question where these traditions came from, how they were able to survive colonization, how we will continue to pass these valuable ways of living on to future generations, and most importantly, why it is necessary to hold on to these ways of being. In looking to answer these questions, many researchers find themselves lost in a pile of literature, attending numerous conferences and interviewing endless numbers of people. I, however, found myself down the street from my own home, at a kitchen table covered with fried chicken, bannock, and snacks, in the company of our local female Elders. That kitchen table is where I learned to reclaim and practise our sovereignty through our Michif language.

My role as an educator in our community has provided the opportunity to participate in passing these traditional values and practices on to our youth. Many of our youth no longer have that kitchen table to learn from, but I am hopeful that my classroom can play the role of a similar setting—a place where we visit, learn, and grow with each other.

Situating Place and People

The St. Louis community, located on the banks of the South Saskatchewan River, is a vibrant community first settled by Métis families in the late nineteenth century. It is located approximately sixty kilometres south of the city of Prince Albert, and twenty-five kilometres east of the historic site of the 1885 Métis Resistance in Batoche, Saskatchewan. The St. Louis region was historically a hub for vibrant trading and gathering activities along the central North and South Saskatchewan river systems. The kinship region includes the Métis communities of Batoche, St. Laurent, Duck Lake, Halcro, Red Deer Hill, and MacDowall, among other former Métis settlements such as Boucherville, Petite Ville, Fish Creek, and Lepine Flats. Trading, freighting, and visiting occurred on the rivers and the overland-connected trails within this region.[4] There is little contemporary research on the vibrancy of this part of our homeland and on Michif women's governing ways.

With this in mind, we introduce our mataant, Doris McDougall, a Michif woman who held and guided—in multiple ways—our Michif language project at her kitchen table. Doris was born in the St. Louis area in 1935. She is the second of seven children to Mederic McDougall (whose great-great-grandfather was Peter Fiddler, married to Mary Muskegeon) and Marie Anne Lépine, granddaughter of Maxime Lépine (Sr.) and Josephette Lavallee. Doris spent the first five years of her life living in a region called Lépine Flats, which is approximately seven miles west of St. Louis. The families that lived in this region were all Métis, and the language spoken by everyone was what is now known as Michif. In 1941 her family moved to St. Louis, where Doris started school. The children were encouraged to speak what was considered to be "proper" English and French. Nevertheless, the Métis way of life was very important to the McDougall family. They faithfully attended the local Métis monthly political meetings, provincial meetings, and rallies. Doris was also close to her first cousin Howard Adams, a Métis activist. They often met and discussed the plight of the Métis people at the kitchen table.

The Significance of Lii Taab di Faam

In this chapter, we share our story of Lii Taab as inseparable from our community-engaged language project, co-created with Michif Matriarchs from St. Louis, Saskatchewan. The Lii Kaart aen Michif project was, as Métis Maria Campbell pointed out, a way in which we practised our sovereignty. This practice involved a) learning from our female Michif Matriarchs; b) reclaiming women's kitchen table spaces (Lii Taab di Faam) as systems of authority; c) the ways of visiting with one another; and d) appropriately sharing the gifts of what we know. We hope this chapter inspires a return to the ways of Lii Taab di Faam for many generations to come.

Graham Andrews explained during one of our many visits working on this chapter that the late Michif Matriarch Leona Boyer née McDougall decried European-led and -influenced scholarly attempts to isolate, categorize, and define the language of the Michif people. She specifically bristled at labelling our language as "Michif." In addressing, particularly, the efforts of non-Indigenous scholars, she explained that "they are only talking about the words we speak. We are Michif; we are our language."

Our understanding of the nuanced ways of being Michif originated in our mothers' wombs, where we first heard our language, one that emphasized our connections to the world around us. Following our graduation from this "first classroom," as infants, toddlers, and young children—regardless of gender—we spent the majority of our time in the company of our mothers, grandmothers, and aunties at or near Lii Taab di Faam Michif. As a result of multiple colonial interventions, including separation from our land and our people, the proliferation of Christianity at the expense of our "savage" traditional ways, residential schools, and our common experiences as targets of Indigenous cultural genocide, the critical role of our matriarchy as knowledge stewards was devalued and silenced, and systematically, Lii Taab started to become an isolated structure rather than a focus that provides the most dynamic way to meet ourselves and our responsibilities. Lii Taab is the simplest and most profound way to support the energy of keeoukaywin (the way of visiting), a way of being in relation that operationalizes our kinship way of governing ourselves. Patriarchal culture has attempted to domesticate our sovereignty, isolating the ontology of Lii Taab to a "physical structure" in the kitchen, and in doing so, colonizing and depoliticizing Michif women's bodies and ways of good governance. Yet, Lii Taab is about practising sovereignty. This is evidenced in our Lii Kaart aen Michif project, which honoured the source of our creativity, learning, friendship, and exchanges, taking us beyond the physical structure of Lii Taab. It is a point of balance carrying its own consciousness, whereby pimaatisiwin (life) itself is supported to be in constant movement, reinforcing our Michif interconnectedness to people and place.

Reasserting and returning to Métis women's governing authority as expressed through Lii Taab is a decolonial act, as it unsettles the historical degradation of Indigenous women's spiritual and political authority upheld at Lii Taab.[5] Although Métis women's knowledge as recorded in writing remains minimal, we are part of each other's stories, often returning to our grandmothers' and aunties' kitchen tables to understand their living experiences and therefore ours. We have also experienced how incomplete views and narratives of a homogeneous Métis identity make us vulnerable to predatory behaviours, founded upon our story of being outcasts, never fitting into the white or "Indian" worlds, and often being referred to as a mixed-race or forgotten people.

Regenerating the epistemological significance of Lii Taab di Faam Michif is an effort to delink from white possessiveness, to feel sovereign once again. While there is much research on the harmful consequences of colonial oppression, violence experienced by Indigenous women, and the shattering of our kinship relationships, our aim is to share the strength, intelligence, gifts, and resilience of Métis women who are the heart of this project and the heart of our lives. Our approach lived as Lii Taab di Faam Michif reasserts our inherent right and responsibility to practise our sovereignty as expressed in the Lii Kaart project. Other scholars have referred to kitchen table methodology in their relational and dialogical research approaches.[6] We add to their contribution by recognizing that the kitchen table goes far beyond a physical structure. As Dr. Cheryl Troupe reminded us in her presentation at the Gabriel Dumont Institute Culture Conference on 6 February 2020 that "women's agency is in their kitchen as they own their property."[7] She was referring to the historical context of Métis women's governing roles and cultural and economic contributions to family, community, and land connectivity. A social and economic understanding of the kitchen table situates Lii Taab as a simple yet complex form of governance, an expression of practising our sovereignty in respectful relationship to pimaatisiwin.

Theoretically and practically, Lii Taab regulated the life force inside and outside the home, including the spiritual and physical worlds upheld by women's agency. As Diane Payment explains, "These [Métis] women had agency. Their moral, emotional, rhetorical, and political resources were manifold. They were the bosses in their homes and were responsible for the education and survival of future generations. They got together to work at activities such as sewing, herb-gathering, and berry picking. They also helped each other in core community and family functions such as health care and childbirth. There were at least two practising midwives in each community along the South Saskatchewan River."[8]

Dr. Kim Anderson's extensive research on life stage roles and responsibilities discusses extensively the authority that the grandmothers held within the family and extended family.[9] As respected decision makers, they considered first of all the well-being of children. This included decisions about, but not limited to, when to harvest and gather, equitable food sharing and economic distribution, arranging marriages, administering justice, and watching over the safety of the children. Dr. Sherry Farrell Racette also explores and applies "Metis Kitchen Table Talk" as a legitimate, Métis-specific methodology of knowledge making, learning, and being in relation.[10]

When discussing the role of Lii Taab with our local Michif Matriarch Sophie McDougall (born 1928 in St. Louis, Saskatchewan), she explained the significance of the kitchen table: "It was so important in our home. I would even put my babies on the table when I was busy mixing my bread. I had two apple boxes for the twins and two mattresses inside. They were content. It was nothing fancy, but it worked." She went on to say, "We did not have much material things but there was values. You ate around the table, you prayed around the table, you received visitors around the table, you made gallettes, bread, jam, preserves, canning at the table. You even butchered at the table. My children did their homework around the table. The table was used for many things."[11] Graham, who was raised by Sophie's mother and his maataants, knows that those women, his aunties, watched and knew everything from Lii Taab.

The Lii Kaart aen Michif Project

Inspiration

The inspiration for a Michif-specific Lii Kaart project came from a visit with Ainu women in their community (Indigenous people in Japan).[12] They proudly shared with me (Cindy) their language revitalization project, a deck of cards with fifty-four Ainu words translated into English and Japanese. Given that playing cards at Lii Taab was, and remains, a common practice in our Métis families, the deck was shared with Doris McDougall at one of the many visits and conversations at her kitchen table. With the growing concern over Indigenous language loss, including our Matriarch stories, we discussed the possibility of a similar, Michif-specific language project produced as a deck of playing cards. Related to this expressed concern was the need for place-based language resources that honour the gifts and stories of place and people, interrupting the notion of the "right" Michif and who has authority to determine this rightness.

Doris initially dismissed the idea because of the seeming lack of interest among the younger generations in learning Michif. She also respected her generation's concerted effort to perfect their English and French. After all, she said, "they had tried to brush the Michif out of them, so why on earth would we put our energy towards reviving or preserving the language?"[13] I (Cindy) shared that many of the younger generations were longing for nuggets of Michif knowledge, especially women's stories. Although initially unsettled by Doris's lack of interest, I became aware of the deficit view that I had adopted in terms of language loss. While the narratives of cultural loss are prevalent, I had lost sight of our Matriarchs' concerted efforts to "adapt" and "succeed" in a settler-colonial context despite the "brushing out" efforts. "Brushing out" is a reference to colonial efforts to put down the Métis for being Métis, and to assert assimilatory practices, such as valuing French and English over Michif in schools and in family and community life.

Notwithstanding the government's concerted efforts to undermine Métis people's lives, Doris was demonstrating what it meant to practise sovereignty. She embodied sovereignty, meaning owning herself, her position, and her right to refuse my (Cindy's) invitation. Without ever saying so, she pointed to her generation's labour to perfect settler languages for their families' well-being and survival. It is not often that we read or hear about the choice to "assimilate" and the valiant effort to do so. Later that week, I stopped in for an unplanned visit. To my surprise, Doris had a two-inch stack of 300 handwritten Michif words. She had selected the words from the Gabriel Dumont Michif Dictionary, which she felt reflected the Michif that was still being spoken in St. Louis.[14] When I inquired as to why she had changed her mind, Doris shared that after some time thinking about it, she realized the project would be valuable as a resource for schools, so that people would know the Michif still spoken in the St. Louis area. She felt that some good would come out of promoting the interest of Michif, given that the Métis are too often not thought of.

Doris's Kitchen Table

In spring 2018, at Doris McDougall's kitchen table, the Lii Kaart project took its creative shape, becoming a fifty-four-card playing deck including fifty-four Michif words translated into French and English, six historical images, four place-based themes as the suits—Our Foods, Our Land, Our Relatives, and Numbers—and an accompanying 111-page classroom resource. A local female Métis artist, Jennifer Brown, was invited to brighten the card deck with her vibrant and unique art. It was because of our kitchen table conversations and way of visiting that we (Doris, Marlene, Angela, and Cindy) committed to this research creation initiative. Together, we shared the vision of the project and set up regular meetings to discuss and dream up possibilities for this co-creation, including the themes, words, stories, knowledge, art, and the six historical images embedded in the cards. Ideas, stories, laughter, and food were part of every visit. University of Alberta funding and ethics protocols advanced this responsible community-engaged research. We were supported with honorariums, printing, materials, research assistance, local artwork, travel costs, cultural protocols, and gifts. As part of our responsible research, to ensure that knowledge creation was made accessible and could be celebrated in and with the community, we launched the first print of Lii Kaart aen Michif and its accompanying curricular resource as part of the St. Louis River Road Métis Festival in September 2018.

Lii Kaart included English and French translations in order to make distinct the language differences, so as to reassert the value of Michif as its own sovereign language. Lii Kaart included images on each Ace that reflect our Métis heroes, both male and female: Gabriel Dumont, Madeleine Dumont (Wilkie), Louis Riel, and Marguerite Riel (Monet di Bellehumeur); and for the jokers, two historical Canadian figures: Sir John A. Macdonald and Major-General Middleton. Our conversation on the choice of John A. Macdonald on a joker card was sobering, as it involved the word zhamayn (never). Resilient statements such as "You will never do this again" and "You never succeeded to eliminate us" were spoken by our Matriarchs. We sat in a sobering silence of truth, hardship, and resilience. Without further discussion, we took the necessary steps to validate the accuracy of historical images with our local, provincial, and federal archives.

The photos on Lii Kaart furthered our awareness of the historical role of Métis women and their all-too-often-forgotten stories. Our choices generated dialogue around Lii Taab, and different perspectives, given the diverse generations involved in the project. We were alarmed at the fact that we had been socialized to prioritize the victory of Métis male heroes, with little knowledge of their wives. This awareness inspired me (Angela) to integrate these images into the accompanying curricular language resource for schools, universities, and family and community kitchen tables, which served as an additional learning tool. The images provided an opportunity for my students to see the faces of the women who stood by our Métis heroes, and provided names and stories to accompany the great influence of Lii Faam in sustaining their families' lives. I also reconfigured my elementary classroom setting in the way of Lii Taab—a classroom full of fifth- and sixth-grade students, situated in the heart of Michif, in the village of St. Louis, where the school is made up of over 96 percent Indigenous students. The physical reconstruction of the classroom into a Lii Taab setting allowed us to transform the relationships we had with one another, our language, and ourselves. The themes and words chosen had meaning for who we are as Michif people living in a specific place, with a specific history.

Our Matriarchs Giving Voice and Meaning to People, Places, and Stories

The storytelling method brought insight to all of us involved in the project. Learning through stories is a well-respected Indigenous approach to knowledge sharing. Stories are a crucial point of reference for understanding experiences, life, and the world.[15] Stories elucidate the wisdom of place and people. There is strength in these stories. They breathe life back into the oral way of creating knowledge. Many of the Lii Kaart words chosen reflect the work in which Métis women took part. Marlene and Doris identified Michif themes that were meaningful to them. This project quickly became about more than learning Michif words; we were learning about the people, places, and stories that live within each word. In the Métis way of visiting (keeoukaywin),[16] two Matriarchs were sharing their experience of culture, history, and ways of life. For example, when we asked Marlene to translate the first theme, she said, "It is our people's world, the world around us"; in the language, "la vii di moond, la vii toot alaantoor." This took on a new meaning; for her it was about relationships with all that she is part of. She lived Michif.

We learned about our traditional foods—"nutr maanzhii ordinayr." This included the strategic process of gathering, harvesting, and preparing foods from the land or grown in gardens. We were reminded how our families relied on the diversity of skills and foods, such as berries. The traditional economy of berries served at our Matriarchs' kitchen table in pies, jams, and syrup sustained the sweetness in life. We learned about the ways in which the river sustained life for Métis people—the types of fish, and the skills needed to survive during times of scarcity and beyond. Travel for gathering food was at times extensive, and it took incredible effort as a family system. As an example, Doris shared a vivid memory of the hazelnut bushes located across the river, and the big trip across the river on horseback with gunny sacks full of hazelnuts. We learned about nutr paraanti (our relatives) and the ways in which Métis kinship systems help us care for one another through the relational obligations that accompany our distinct roles and responsibilities.

Beyond Words: Practising Our Sovereignty

Indigenous language revitalization initiatives cannot and must not be awakened outside of the context of our spaces and stories, and the lives of our Matriarchs. Michif does not have to be linguistically understood in order to be spoken or lived. We understand and live Michif-ology in the way we are traditionally in relation to Lii Taab di Faam Michif; by this, we mean how we traditionally express ourselves through our culture, genealogy, environment, experience, history, and connection to people and land. This became evident in the place-based stories that our Matriarchs shared to accompany the selected Michif words in the Lii Kaart project.

Together, we came to experience Lii Taab di Faam as living and breathing space that extends to the land, people, and places. Epistemologically, Lii Taab di Faam must remain a central placeholder for us as Michif to practise our sovereignty—to know and to regulate ourselves; to own ourselves, our bodies, our minds, our responsibilities, our history, our land, our stories, and our ethics. Lii Taab is, for us, an equalizing force that begins at an early age, teaching us as children to be knowers of our specific roles and responsibilities through each life stage. Our respective gender roles, too, define how we live well. Lii Taab requests something of us, individually and collectively, that is not necessarily scripted or clearly defined until we sit, talk, and listen. As such, the Lii Kaart aen Michif project became an extension of and an inseparable connection to Lii Taab. This is no surprise, given that Lii Taab di Faam Michif has provided for and sustained our families, physical systems, and values for generations. Lii Taab invests in helping us to know our place in the world around us. Sophie McDougall, who is committed to sustaining the Michif language, helped us to imagine life without Lii Taab di Faam. She spoke of the isolation that would occur; the feelings of insecurity, anxiety, fear of failure; and feeling and living out of balance. Lii Taab has certainly been, and continues to be, overwhelmed by our colonial history of interference, harm, domination, punitive measures, and efforts to co-opt. Yet we attest that its spirited strength, produced and lived by generations of Michif Matriarchs, ensures an unshakeable and safe approach to pass through adversity and live and be well.

Sovereignty needs to be reimagined by centring Michif women's approaches, knowledge, and stories upheld at Lii Taab di Faam. Otherwise, we risk reproducing a fragmented sovereign nation, malnourished generations longing for our noohkooms, mataants, maamaas, suers.[17] Returning to Lii Taab di Faam helped us to reimagine our sovereignty from within the Matriarchs' practical and complex responsibility as household pimaatisiwin regulators. This is, as Marlene reminds us, to keep our household healthy and happy.

Notes

1 We use the words grandmother/maymair/noohkoom or auntie/maataant to show respect to our Matriarchs and the caring ways of Métis peoples' kinship systems. It is indicative of our value system that these ways are a collective responsibility and demand relational accountability. This is the way we do our best to live today. Out of habit—and even within this chapter—we use the term Métis and Michif interchangeably. In our shared experiences as Michif people, our language, culture, history, relationships, and cosmology are inseparable from one another. It is our mission to reclaim and reinstate our traditional teachings for the rightful stewardship of Michif Matriarchs.

2 Lii Taab di Faam Michif translated in English refers to Métis Women's Kitchen Table.

3 Pimaatisiwin is a Michif concept described by Graham Andrews as a recognition that "I am a part of life. Life is good because of how I am in relationship with life itself. This is a prayer in a single word."

4 Payment, *The Free People*.

5 K. Anderson, *Life Stages*.

6 Farrell Racette, "Kitchen Table Theory"; Flaminio, "Kinship-Visiting"; Flaminio, Gaudet, and Dorion, "Métis Women Gathering"; Gaudet, "Keeoukaywin"; Kovach, "Conversational Method"; Kovach, "Emerging from the Margins."

7 Troupe, "Women's Agency."

8 Payment, *The Free People*, 255.

9 K. Anderson, *Life Stages*.

10 Farell Racette and Mattes, "Métis Kitchen Table Talk."

11 Sophie McDougall, personal communication, 30 October 2019.

12 The meeting took place at the International Conference on Policy towards Indigenous Peoples, 2–4 December 2017, at Hokkaido University, Japan.

13 Doris McDougall, personal communication, 2018.

14 The Gabriel Dumont Institute delivers Métis-specific educational programs and services.

15 Archibald, *Indigenous Storywork.*
16 Gaudet, "Keeoukaywin."
17 Michif kinship concepts meaning grandmothers, aunties, mothers, and sisters.

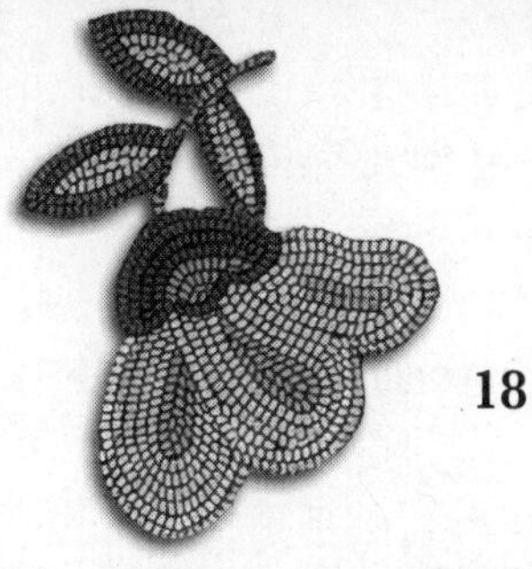

18

Wahkotowin:
An Approach to Indigenous (Land-Based) Education

Nicki Ferland

Just before I started my graduate studies, I wrote an article for *Red Rising Magazine*'s Language issue. In "Michif: Another Gift for Our Children," I wrote, "I'm committing to learn Michif, and I'm inviting other Métis to join this journey."[1] At the time, my wife cautioned me that this constituted a kind of contractual obligation, at a spiritual level at the very least. I was so nervous to put those words out into the world because it meant that I was establishing relationships and, therefore, relational accountability with others driven to a Michif language resurgence. In my second year of coursework in the University of Saskatchewan's Master of Education (MEd) program with a concentration in Indigenous land-based education, I was learning more about the relationship between the land and language, so I enrolled in language courses at the University of Manitoba under the tutelage of Michif language specialist Heather Souter.[2] It was an opportunity to honour my commitment, and to forge relationships with other language learners. Later, our daughter, Mireille, was born, and my wife and I committed to raising her in ceremony, on the land and with the language, which are all intrinsically connected within a relational worldview. Now, as I embark on my PhD studies, I am still committed to learning the language and especially looking forward to learning the language through the land. To me, this defines wahkotowin—the kinship structures, relationships, and relational accountability that exist between all things. With its pedagogical focus on relationships—with people, place, land, language, and even concepts and ideas[3]—the MEd program offers wahkotowin as an approach to Indigenous education.

Introduction

When I tell people about my program of study, some wonder if obtaining a traditional Indigenous education in the Western academy is an oxymoron. Universities, unintentionally or otherwise, continue to extract knowledge, cause harm, and be unwelcoming sites of racism and discrimination for Indigenous learners. Historically, education was used as an assimilation tactic, a tool to eradicate Indigenous languages, cultures, and traditions. These tendencies are still common within most educational institutions, where Western credentials are privileged above Indigenous knowledge, Indigenous identity is stifled, tokenized or stolen, and dusty volumes are prioritized over the living libraries that are Indigenous knowledge holders. In Waianae on the island of Oahu, Christopher Oliveira said, "Every time we lose a kūpuna,[4] we lose a library."[5] The University of Saskatchewan's Master of Education (MEd) program with a concentration in Indigenous land-based education, however, helps students access the relational pedagogies and "deep knowledges" embedded in the land[6] and stored within knowledge holders while completing a rigorous course of study that satisfies university graduate degree requirements. We just had to leave the classroom behind for a more traditional site of learning: the land.

In this chapter, I share my experiences as a Métis learner in the MEd program. I explore the core values and approach to this unique Indigenous education, including wahkotowin, consent and protocol, oral knowledges, Indigenous pedagogies, and queering education. I begin by describing the MEd program and cohort model, emphasizing the importance of relationality, and conclude with a discussion of the influence that the MEd courses have had on my own work and scholarship in urban land-based education.

The Indigenous Land-Based Education Master of Education

The University of Saskatchewan's Master of Education program offers courses with a land-based focus. The website explains, "This focus includes intensive land-based field institutes where students take graduate level courses framed within an Indigenous paradigm and taught primarily by Indigenous faculty. The land-based courses support and accommodate students who are unable to commit to long periods of study away from home. Students are required to live on-site for the duration of field institutes (approximately two weeks each) so that contact hours with faculty, Indigenous communities and the land are maximized. Land-based field institutes are supplemented with on-campus or online courses."[7]

Our cohort completed courses in Opaskwayak Cree Nation (Manitoba), on the islands of Oahu and Hawaii (Kingdom of Hawaii), and in Chief Dry Geese territory of the Yellowknives Dene (Northwest Territories), as well as online. The final field institute, a canoe trip along the Saskatchewan River Delta planned for the summer of 2020, was cancelled due to COVID-19.

The Guardians of the Galaxy

The MEd Indigenous land-based concentration is coordinated by the brilliant queer scholar, educator, and Jedi Master Dr. Alex Wilson. Alex is a two-spirit[8] Cree woman from Opaskwayak Cree Nation. Our cohort was called the "Guardians of the Galaxy,"[9] in part to distinguish our group from previous Padawan learners.[10] The 2018 cohort[11] included twenty graduate students. Four non-Indigenous students joined a predominantly Indigenous-identified cohort, which included Métis, Cree, Anishinaabe, Mi'kmaq, Pueblo (from Jemez Pueblo and Isleta Pueblo in New Mexico), and Kānaka Maoli (from the Kingdom of Hawaii) learners. The students represented a range of life stages, urban/reserve experiences, land-based practices and experiences, and professional backgrounds (though the majority were classroom teachers). I am a two-spirit Michif[12] mother, learner, and (land-based) educator working with university-aged learners.[13]

Principles of an Indigenous Education: The MEd Approach

Below, I present an approach to Indigenous education drawn from experiences collected during our land-based graduate program of study. I explore the often interdependent and sometimes overlapping values, practices, and pedagogies that informed our learning, including relationality and relational accountability, consent and protocol, oral learning, Indigenous pedagogies, and queering pedagogy and praxis.

I also highlight the ways that the MEd approach aligns with a Métis paradigm and pedagogy.

Wahkotowin

Wahkotowin means kinship structures. Wahkotowin informs how we are related to, and relate to, the natural world, other spiritual beings, our past and future ancestors, as well as ancestral knowledges. Brenda Macdougall (Métis) maintains that wahkotowin—our relationships with land and each other,[14] and the ensuing obligations and responsibilities we have for these relationships—is foundational to Métis identity.[15] There are many stories from our courses and learning that embody relationality and relational accountability. Indigenous ontologies are relational, and relationality is therefore a core value and main objective of an Indigenous education. Below, I illustrate the role of wahkotowin in an Indigenous education.

Dr. Alex Wilson, the MEd land-based concentration coordinator, relied heavily on wahkotowin to plan the field institutes. The Elders and guest scholars we learned with and from during land-based courses were her relatives, friends, and acquaintances. We visited territories where Alex was connected, including her home in Opaskwayak Cree Nation territory (Treaty 5), and worked with Elders and knowledge holders with whom she has personal relationships. This exemplifies wahkotowin; it is relationality in practice. Through these experiences and introductions, we learned about and reflected on the importance of acquainting learners with radical thinkers and radical energy that leads to "radical collaborations."[16] Pua Case, a Kānaka Maoli land guardian and protector of Mauna Kea, recognized that the "speakers, leaders, and activists that you invite into your classrooms can change young people's lives, paths, and direction."[17] She suggested that our cohort and each of us within our own small and large communities "form a hu'i,"[18] a community that comes together to practise language and culture.

During the first online course (sandwiched between our field institutes in Opaskwayak Cree Nation and the Kingdom of Hawaii), our cohort created a Messenger group to chat privately amongst ourselves. That Messenger group is still in use today. It is an ongoing resource for us as learners and educators, as well as a place to maintain connection as friends and relatives. In practice, our relational accountability for each other manifested as community building, teamwork, personal and professional support, idea sharing, meaningful group work, and celebrating each other's milestones (children, marriages, and more) and accomplishments (academic, professional, and other).[19] The kinship relationships that we have developed with each other over the last few years, and our relational accountability to those relationships, endures.

Honouring reciprocity is one of our responsibilities as learners and educators.[20] Alex invited us to bring meaningful gifts to the field institutes to give to knowledge holders and guides. Gifts included dried sweet corn from the Pueblo communities, contemporary Métis sashes, Indigenous art from various territories, handmade art, and more. In Chief Dry Geese territory (Northwest Territories), Elder and guest instructor Paul Mackenzie (Dene) gave students individualized pocket knives carved from caribou antlers. He taught us to make birchbark canoes and antler jewellery. He guided us on many hikes (having laid many of those trails himself) and generously shared his knowledge about plant medicines. He gifted me with two large birchbark canoes for my wiidigewin ceremony.[21] I spent a lot of time with him, heeding his wisdom and admiring his skills, and during this time, he mentioned that he would like to work with deer antlers. When I returned home, my father and I prepared a set of deer antlers, which I shipped to Paul in Dettah (Yellowknives Dene settlement), along with photos of our cohort and of Paul and me. It is an important relationship to which I feel accountable and duty-bound (but also honoured) to reciprocate.

There was another relationship that was the focus of our graduate education: the primary and enduring relationship between learners and the land. The field institutes were designed to maximize our time with land, and the journaling assignments (discussed below), repeated in every course, were designed to help us explore and connect to our own cosmologies[22] and Indigenous worldviews. Our observations and learning remind us that land is our first teacher;[23] that land is teacher, content, and process;[24] and that land is not just the site of learning but the pedagogy.[25]

Consent and Protocol

Consent and protocol are another important aspect of Indigenous education. Consent and protocol are also pedagogically and spiritually required in Métis education and research.[26] Robert Hancock (Métis) reminds us about our obligations when living in or visiting another people's territory, and remarks, "as Métis we know about . . . being good guests."[27] Our cohort was invited to each community that hosted a land-based field institute. Consent is an important part of our relationship with the land. Erin Konsmo (Métis) and Karyn Recollet (urban Métis) remind us that "there is a need to practice consensual relationship building with the waters, the stars and each other."[28] Being invited and welcomed onto different places is a way to acknowledge and respect the relationship that the land has with its original people. In each of the communities we visited, we were received by local Indigenous people in their own traditional territories.

In Hawaii, when we arrived on the Big Island, we headed to the Hawaiian Force, a radical T-shirt shop, to meet Luana Neff (Kānaka Maoli). Luana welcomed us to the island with an oli (chant) and spoke of Pele and her 2018 flow (the eruption of Mount Kiluaua) as both intentional and intelligent. Luana also shared an important protocol: we should make an offering to Pele as soon as possible upon our arrival to the Big Island. So, we changed our plans and headed to a steam vent on the rim of Kilauea caldera that evening. It was late, after a long day of travel, and many of us were tired and sore. We were energized, however, when the blistering steam vents balanced the cold wind while we made our offerings. This experience was a pedagogical reminder of the flexibility and protocol that the land expects from us.

Oral Learning

Privileging Indigenous voices and oral knowledges is an important pedagogical principle of Indigenous education. Our courses centred Indigenous teachers and sources. In our field institutes, the readings were almost exclusively written by Indigenous scholars and knowledge holders. We also learned from "guest speakers" like Crystal and Omar Constant (Cree), knowledge holders from Opaskwayak Cree Nation who took us gillnetting and taught us about food sovereignty, and from many other inspiring educators and land protectors. We interviewed Elders about their own land-based learning practices and traditional ecological knowledge. Over the course of three field institutes, we met with dozens of Indigenous scholars (including Drs. Stan Wilson and Peggy Wilson, Manulani Meyer, Peter Hanohano, Rebecca Sockbeson, and Praba Pilar), teachers, Elders, and knowledge holders. By sharing their worldviews, land ethics, and pedagogies, they helped us explore and develop our own.

Oral sources are essential to an Indigenous education. Cree Métis scholar "[Emma] LaRocque views 'the oral' as intrinsically 'Native.'"[29] Whether we grew up hearing our stories or not, we are culturally inclined to transmit and receive oral knowledges. The Gabriel Dumont Institute reports that "the oral tradition has always been a key component of Métis culture."[30] The opportunity to explore Indigenous scholarship directly from Indigenous knowledge holders (Elders, academics, and radical youth) is invaluable to students. During our program of studies, our cohort met and engaged with many of the Indigenous knowledge holders whose work we were studying. On the final day of our Hawaii study tour, I found myself riding shotgun along the coast with Dr. Manu Meyer. As we drove past a cousin's surf shop, Manu spoke of the special relationship that Kānaka Maoli (native Hawaiians) have with the sea. "Surfing saved the Hawaiians,"[31] she said. More than just a fun pastime, surfing embodies the relationship between the Kānaka Maoli and the sea—respect, beauty, intimate knowledge, and innovative design garnered over millennia of learning from the land. While I might forget some of Dr. Meyer's written wisdom, I will never forget riding in that small truck with Aunty Manu, surrounded by the deep greens of native foliage and the wise words of a land-based scholar.

Indigenous Pedagogies

Indigenous pedagogies grounded in a specific paradigm are essential to an Indigenous education. Adam Gaudry (Métis) and Hancock (Métis) explain that as a "land-based Indigenous people . . . a considerable amount of Métis pedagogical knowledge can be learned from Métis knowledge holders and Métis who grew up on the land."[32] The authors acknowledge that "a critical part of developing Métis pedagogies that are well-rounded and consistent with Métis ways of life is the re-establishment of relationships with the land and with Métis communities."[33] In addition to storytelling and experiential pedagogies, prayer and ceremony[34] were common pedagogical themes in our land-based field institutes. Instructors were also very intentional about developing an Indigenous paradigmatic land ethic and centring community service/helping as both pedagogy and purpose of an Indigenous education. In Stoney Point Camp (Opaskwayak Cree Nation), we bathed in Clearwater Lake with biodegradable soaps. In Hawaii, we cleaned kalo (taro) patches at Ke'ala Farm, weeded at Ma'o Organic Farms, and helped the Pāhonu restoration and limu planting in Waimanalo. These activities helped us learn about the symbiotic relationships between land, humans and more-than-humans, and our knowledges. Like these experiences in the Kingdom of Hawaii, Métis land-based education is "an immersion in Métis worldviews that sustain [cultural] practices."[35]

The MEd program of studies and land-based activities were honed over time by many land-based educators and Elders.[36] Assignments were designed to meet graduate degree requirements, including journal-length academic papers, as well as develop Indigenous literacy. Sandra Styres (Kanien'kehá:ka) explains, "Indigenous literacy is based on reading the cosmos—it is about reading all the things around us that are not necessarily the written word but nevertheless contain valuable information."[37] In "Queering Land-Based Education during Covid19," Alex Wilson describes the student practice and exercise of observing, reflecting, and journaling about certain astronomical features over the course of our master's work. The objectives of the assignments were to link features like the moon, sun, and stars to our cosmologies. These journaling activities were embedded in all field institutes. Over time, we began to explore and articulate our own Indigenous paradigms and uncover the pedagogical practices that honour those paradigms.[38] Exploring Métis cosmology through MEd assignments has been a wayfinding journey of discovery and connection to my own Métis worldview.

Relationality was a focus of our education. Wahkotowin is a Métis concept;[39] pedagogically, Métis ways of teaching and learning align with the Indigenous education described above (the MEd approach) and its pedagogical focus on relationships. Our cohort used familial terms to refer to some of the knowledge holders whom we met. They were not Drs. Meyer and Hanohano to us, but Aunty Manu and Uncle Peter. These personal relationships distinguish Indigenous education from Western education. In Western education, educators have sole authority and expertise, as well as professional boundaries that inhibit personal relationships. An Indigenous approach recognizes that relationships are the objective of education, and that learners also have valuable knowledge and experiences. On our first day as graduate students, on campus for a two-day graduate student orientation (the first and only time most of us ever set foot on campus), we left our classroom behind, sat in a circle in the grass, and told each other about ourselves and our communities. It was a moment of early but eager connection—a sudden recognition that we would be brought together several times over the course of the next two years and beyond to learn and grow with each other. We continued to meet in a circle, sometimes around a fire, at least once a day during the field institutes. These circles were our opportunity to reflect and debrief together. In this way, we contributed to the learning of our peers, and expanded our own understandings of the land, the course content, and our experiences.

In conversation with a colleague and myself, Rocky Cree Elder Keith Anderson acknowledged that "relationship—being together—is the ceremony."[40] An Indigenous education centres relationship, and it is thus a ceremony in and of itself. The MEd program provided a powerful reminder that we are all sacred beings,[41] and that our classrooms, land-based or otherwise, are sacred spaces.

Queering (Land-Based) Pedagogy and Praxis

Queering was another important pedagogy and practice of our Indigenous education. In "Queering Land-Based Education during Covid19," Alex Wilson writes, "Hawaiian scholar Kalaniopua Young . . . describes 'queering' as an act of 'transforming poison into medicine' (personal communication, 18 January 2019). From that, we understand queering as a 'reconstructive practice,' one centred on the radical reclamation and reassertion of our 'self-as-relationship.'"[42]

For me as an educator, queering has meant questioning my assumptions about content and pedagogy (what and how I learn and teach), confronting heteronormativity and Eurocentrism in education (what I have been conditioned to think is normal and good to learn and teach), and calling attention to gender and sexuality (challenging the cis/hetero narratives and norms of education). Konsmo and Recollet explain that "binaries . . . also force heteronormativity onto land, water, plants and animals. After all, gender normativity wasn't only forced onto our bodies, but also onto our lands simultaneously."[43] Queering education challenges the heteropatriarchy and settler colonialism that impact land, gender, and pedagogy, while also challenging the gender and other binaries and hierarchies that we as educators project onto the land and our students.

In July 2020, MEd students participated in Dr. Wilson's Queering Land-Based Education course (EFDT 898).[44] The course was one part of an entire program of studies whose bedrock was queering pedagogy and praxis. All MEd professors and the majority of guest scholars and knowledge holders were women or 2S/LGBTQ+ people. Queering was an intentional pedagogical practice. "Queer and non-cis gendered [people] tell different stories [about the land]. This is why we tried to have only queer or trans people as our guides."[45] Consider which land-based practices and roles we value, who we think typically fills those roles,[46] who generally facilitates and participates in land-based education, and who is typically excluded or othered. Female- and two-spirit/LGBTQ+–bodied people are often excluded, ignored, and unstoried.[47] Queering land-based education ensures that "when you're on the land, all the socially constructed hierarchies around gender, around sexual orientation, around race, or around class disappear."[48] Queering education and other aspects of the MEd approach have contributed significantly to my own pedagogy and praxis.

Urban Land-Based Education: A Métis Approach

The MEd program has significantly informed my own work and scholarship in urban land-based education.[49] Early in my studies, I switched to the thesis stream[50] and focused my research on urban Métis land-based education to counter entrenched settler narratives and establish Métis place in (historical and contemporary) urban society. As an urban Métis person living in Winnipeg (Métis inhabitation in this area predated the Red River Settlement), I know that our stories are rooted in the land. My research is a (re)membering and (re)claiming of urban land and Métis community. Winnipeg is a Métis place with shared prairie First Nations jurisdiction.[51] Our historical and contemporary presence is visible in multiple neighbourhoods and historic landmarks. In Winnipeg, we are immersed in "storied landscapes,"[52] which chronicle Métis experiences. My research focuses on women and two-spirit/LGBTQ+ Métis people's stories about and relationships with the land. Uncovering these hidden narratives is central to my research.[53] In these ways, my research is contributing to oral knowledges, the development of urban Métis pedagogies, and queering Métis land-based education.

Urban land-based education helps learners establish relationships with the natural and built environments in which we exist, (re)story urban land as Indigenous land,[54] and unearth the ancestral knowledges rooted in the land. My research seeks to (re)connect Métis people to the land to (re)member who we are and where we come from. Métis academic Victoria Bouvier remarks, "being Michif is not linear, it is cyclical."[55] We reconstruct the past in the present. The Métis are a land-based people[56] with deep roots in the prairies.[57] The ways of knowing, being, and doing that informed Métis relationships with land—the Laws of the Buffalo Hunt, our spirituality, and more—continue to influence us in their present-day manifestations.

Our experiences in the Master of Education program with a concentration in Indigenous land-based education reveal that students can access and enrich Indigenous knowledges through a land-based education while completing a course of study that meets graduate degree requirements. The MEd approach demonstrates the importance of particular values and practices to an Indigenous education, including relationality and relational accountability, consent and protocol, oral knowledges, Indigenous pedagogies grounded in a specific paradigm, and queering education. This approach has greatly influenced my own Métis studies. In a Métis education, the land is our classroom and teacher, and the curriculum is wahkotowin.

Notes

1 Ferland, "Michif," 101.

2 Heather Souter is now a faculty member in the Department of Anthropology at the University of Winnipeg.

3 S. Wilson, *Research Is Ceremony*.

4 Kūpuna means "grandfather" or, colloquially, "Elder."

5 Christopher Oliveira, personal communication, 5 January 2019. This chapter intentionally relies heavily on personal communication, with scholarly references cited as needed, to draw attention to the importance of oral sources and oral knowledge. In a similar vein, I occasionally use the first name of scholars rather than the more formal last name, not to diminish their expertise, but to emphasize our relationship.

6 Alex Wilson, personal communication, 14 May 2020.

7 University of Saskatchewan, "Educational Foundations."

8 *Two-spirit* is a contemporary term used by North American Indigenous people whose gender and sexual expressions do not fit within normative gender and/or sexuality binaries. The term is inclusive of Indigenous people who identify on the LGBTQ+ spectrum as well as those who do not use these labels; see Ferland, "This is Indigenous Land."

9 So named by Geraldine Delorme, a member of our cohort, on 6 November 2018.

10 Earlier cohorts of the MEd land-based concentration were called Padawan learners, which is a reference to Jedi apprentices from the *Star Wars* franchise.

11 I am intentionally listing the first year of our program of studies instead of the last to acknowledge that several learners in our cohort were still completing their coursework (or thesis, in my case), while nearly three-quarters were awarded their degrees in Fall 2020.

12 I use Métis and Michif interchangeably to refer to the Red River Métis, distinct from people with (sometimes tenuous and long ago) Indigenous ancestors (incorrectly called the eastern métis or new métis), or people born of First Nation and European(-descended) parents or ancestors (people of mixed parentage or ancestry).

13 My parents are both descended from scrip-bearing Métis people. My forefathers arrived from France in the 1600s, while my foremothers have been here since time immemorial.

14 This includes land in its entirety (earth and rocks, water and sky), humans and more-than-humans, ancestors, and future generations.

15 Macdougall, *One of the Family*.

16 Manu Meyer, personal communication, 4 January 2019.

17 Pua Case, personal communication, 8 January 2019.

18 Ibid.

19 In Fall 2020, many students from our cohort graduated. An in-person convocation was cancelled due to COVID-19. While disappointing, the online celebration allowed Elders, knowledge holders, teaching assistants, guest scholars, and MEd professors to participate in the virtual gathering. Our cohort met online to celebrate the graduates, and Alex shared a video that included dozens of personal congratulatory messages for the graduates. It was a special evening that celebrated our relationships with knowledge and with one another.

20 S. Wilson, *Research Is Ceremony*.

21 A Midewiwin "union of souls" marriage ceremony.

22 Our peoples' origin stories and paradigms, including our ontology (what we know), epistemology (how we come to know), and axiology (why it is important to know).

23 Meyer, "Acultural Assumptions"; Bang et al., "Muskrat Theories"; Meyer, "Hoea Ea"; Styres, Haig-Brown, and Blimkie, "Toward a Pedagogy."

24 A. Wilson and Murray, "Queering Indigenous Land-Based Education."

25 Simpson, *As We Have*.

26 My distinctly Métis research methodology offers gifts and plant medicines to research participants. In addition to the University of Saskatchewan's research ethics process, I participated in the Manitoba Métis Federation's Manitoba Métis Community Research and Ethics Protocol to receive formal consent and approval to work with Métis citizens on Métis-centred research in Winnipeg. Despite the persistent stereotype that Métis people do not pass or accept tobacco, all of my Métis research participants accepted tobacco (an agreement to participate in the research, and a way to honour knowledge-sharing protocols), sage (for smudging ceremonies, as all interviews would be held virtually due to COVID-19), and other gifts (tea, jam, and Métis art). I also offered tobacco and participated in sweat lodge ceremonies and the Sundance prior to selecting my research topic for guidance and consent from

the land, which is an important participant in the research process. These activities describe a legitimately Métis research methodology (Fiola, *Returning to Ceremony*) and demonstrate the importance of consent and protocol in the methodological process.

27 Hancock, "The Power," 41.

28 Konsmo and Recollet, "Afterword," 241.

29 Eigenbrod, "The Oral," 92.

30 Gabriel Dumont Institute, "Oral History."

31 Manu Meyer, personal communication, 11 January 2019.

32 Gaudry and Hancock, "Decolonizing Métis Pedagogies," 19.

33 Ibid., 20.

34 Prayer and ceremony include giving thanks before every meal, working with medicines, feasting, smudging ceremonies, sharing circles, and more.

35 Gaudry and Hancock, "Decolonizing Métis Pedagogies," 20.

36 Alex Wilson, personal communication, 9 February 2020.

37 Styres, "Literacies of Land," 25.

38 A. Wilson, "Queering Land-Based Education."

39 Hancock, "The Power."

40 Keith Anderson, personal communication, n.d.

41 Peter Hanohano, personal communication, 7 January 2019.

42 A. Wilson, "Queering Land-Based Education," 91.

43 Konsmo and Recollet, "Afterword," 250.

44 I did not take this course, as my daughter was born the week before it started. For more information, see A. Wilson, "Queering Land-Based Education."

45 Alex Wilson, personal communication, 14 March 2019.

46 Hunting and other harvesting activities, for instance, have been heavily impacted by patriarchy. In the *Briarpatch* "The Land Back" issue, Tanya McCallum, a Woodland Cree member of our MEd cohort, is interviewed about hunting and patriarchy. She reminisced about her great-grandmother, recalling, "She talked about how hunting used to be a partnership between the male and the female: they both went out, they both hunted" (A. Wilson, "Becoming Intimate").

47 A. Wilson, "Skirting the Issues"; Spillet, "Gender, Land, and Place."

48 A. Wilson and Laing, "Queering Indigenous Education," 134.

49 Ferland, "Kishkeetamawin."

50 The MEd with a concentration in Indigenous land-based education is a course-based master's degree.

51 Riddle, "Mâmawiwikowin."

52 Styres, "Literacies of Land," 28.

53 For instance, Métis culture is transmitted by Métis mothers (Laliberte, "Being Métis"), but although they raised generations of Métis communities while fathers travelled, few of their stories have been told.

54 Bang et al., "Muskrat Theories."

55 Victoria Bouvier, personal communication, 20 November 2019.

56 LaRocque, *When the Other*.

57 Riddle, "Mâmawiwikowin"; Andersen, *"Métis."*

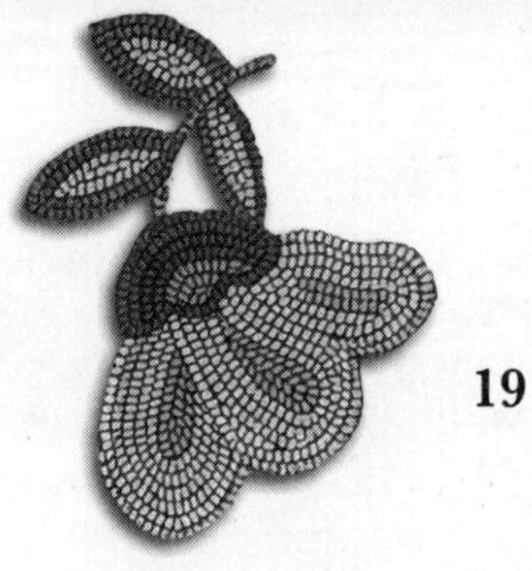

19

Kaa-natoonamaan taanshi chi-ishi-natoonikeeyaan:

My Search for How to Research Things (in a Queer Métis Paradigm)

Lucy Fowler

As an early-career Two-Spirit Métis scholar, I have not typically felt connected to the research methodologies I have employed. The methodologies I have used in my earlier research, while thoughtful, do not always hold space for the complexities of my positionality and the research that I dream of doing. This short chapter delineates kaa-natoonamaan taanshi chi-ishi-natoonikeeyaan—my searching (or groping) for how to research things.

In keeping with the recognition that place and relations are integral to knowledge in Indigenous research and in affirming ties with Indigenous communities and kin, I want to begin by telling you who I am and what has shaped me. Taanshi Kiyawaaw, Lucy Fowler pi wambdi to wiyan d-ishinikaashon, Winnipeg d-oschin. Aeñ Michif niya. My Métis ancestors are Sinclairs, Cummings, McKays, and Prudens, and some of them took scrip in St. Andrews, Manitoba. I also have family from Sioux Valley Dakota Nation and settler family from the Orkney Islands and Carlow, Ireland. I have been guided and surrounded by strong Indigenous women throughout my life, and have sought guidance in my burgeoning career as a Métis academic from others who have forged this path ahead. I approach the topic of a queer Métis research paradigm with humility, as I know only a small fraction of the knowledges of our homelands, and understand even less.

To do research in an ethical way with Indigenous peoples demands the use of such a paradigm, rooted in Indigenous knowledges and an Indigenous worldview. In the early years of my research career, I had little experience working exclusively within an Indigenous paradigm. My master's work employed an Indigenous métissage framework, utilizing interviews and standard hand-coding practices to find recurring patterns and frequently discussed topics, which I then wove back together into shared stories that I retold through a sash metaphor. I was (and am) proud of that work, but as I progress in my career, I look to problematize my previous work and prioritize those things that are important to me, including nation building, amplifying queer voices, and addressing anti-Blackness.

Métis scholar Nicki Ferland has noted a problem with Métis research focusing on such blended paradigms as I utilized in my own master's research, paradigms that reflect both western and Indigenous worldviews. Ferland asserts methodologies can be combined, but that the use of the term métissage reinforces the misconception that to be Métis is simply to be a mix of Indigenous and non-Indigenous ancestry.[1] This distinction, which had not occurred to me while working on my thesis, has since stuck with me, and I knew that I would have to find another path for my work to come. I dream of a methodology that is shaped by my aunties' voices, holds space for community, and allows for subversion or queering[2] of expectations around what constitutes robust and significant data collection within the field of education. I am in search of a methodology that better represents my community.

Much has been written about Indigenous research paradigms and methodologies, and there is a growing body of literature on Métis-specific methodology. As evidenced by other chapters in this collection, the kitchen table research paradigm fits within a Métis epistemology quite firmly. In an Indigenous Methodologies class with Dr. Margaret Kovach, Dr. Kovach tasked each of us with imagining a metaphor for research. After some thought, a kitchen table during a holiday dinner emerged for me as the metaphor that best fits my idea of an Indigenous methodology. A holiday dinner at my auntie's house has a usual cast of characters, but they do change—people move away and move home, have other obligations, move to the spirit world—and even so, the dinner continues. The continuity is due to the nurturing, loving, and work done with the older family and the young. Without this dedication to passing on knowledge to further generations, the family dinner would fizzle out. The younger generations aren't learning from just one person, because with only one perspective, the meal would be unbalanced. It takes the combination of many gifts and personalities to make the experience so enjoyable.

Like with research, there is no true end to family gatherings—there is no final meal, and it is not possible to hear every story, or learn every teaching, or understand every conversation. The holiday plate, too, reflects research as there is no one set outcome—each plate is subjective and self-created, and we may not all agree about what should be included. As I search for my own place within Métis research methodologies, I hold these ideas close to my heart.

At family dinners, as within our Métis communities, there are also difficult conversations to be had. The heteropatriarchal ideals that colonists brought to these lands have seeped their way into our family structures as much as our governments. The men in my family often arrive to enjoy the food prepared by the women and sit back to rest while the women clean up at the end. My own Métis government, for all the good and even incredible things they have achieved for our nation, has the lowest number of women in Cabinet positions of any Métis government,[3] and closed-door meetings determine the direction of our nation without centring the voices and perspectives of Two Spirit, women, youth, and queer folks. I envision and hope for change, but change in governments and in families is often slow.

It is important to note that it is not only the men who need to examine their perspectives. Queer experiences are also often ignored or undermined within the broader Métis community, especially in ceremonial spaces. Alex Wilson discusses the "cultural disruption" that happened to our communities through colonization, the effects of which we are still feeling today, including limiting ceremonial access to community members based on perceived gender.[4] As a straight-coded person and one whose perceived gender mostly matches my gender identity,[5] I am not policed in ceremony in the same way that others are—but I have still been told many times to stay away from ceremonial spaces without a skirt or to be sure to keep my legs closed (instead of crossed) if I sat on the ground, as though if my knees were not together, my vagina would somehow disrupt the ceremony. These heteropatriarchal ideas are perpetuated by women and men alike.

These difficult conversations must also include interrogating the ways in which Black Métis people are treated within our communities. Anti-Black racism exists within Indigenous communities, too, with Black Indigenous peoples often erased from conversations, not believed to be part of the community they claim, and excluded from discussions of sovereignty as Indigenous peoples.[6] Too many of our discussions across the Métis nation focus on the experiences of white-coded Métis people who struggle with feeling as though they belong in neither First Nations nor white communities. While this is certainly a shared experience for many, the discourse of Métis-as-white-passing erases Black Métis people, as well as Métis folks who are visibly Indigenous.

I see these issues—nation building, supporting queer Métis community members, and addressing anti-Black racism—as integral cogs in the next research paradigm I will employ. I also see these issues as dishes at the holiday table, which may previously have been relegated to side dishes or not prepared at all but I will now centre as new staples of the meal. I may not have yet uncovered or grasped the recipe I will use, but as I learn from and with my community, the process becomes less a grope in the dark and more a targeted search, with a vision to strengthen and support my nation. I invite you to join me at this holiday table, and strengthen our nation with me. Añ saañbl apitaak p miitshotaak (Let's sit and eat together).

Notes

1 Nicki Ferland, personal communication, 2020.

2 Alex Wilson describes queering for Indigenous educators as both deconstructing what is taught and how it is taught and reconstructing teaching practice through relationality (A. Wilson, "Queering Land-Based Education," 5).

3 Saunders and Dubois, *Métis Politics*, 108.

4 A. Wilson, "Our Coming-In Stories," 2.

5 When I refer to straight-coded, I use the term similarly to white-coded—upon meeting me, most do not recognize that I am queer and instead assume I am a heterosexual woman. I write that my perceived gender mostly matches my gender identity as I identify most often as a woman and use she/her pronouns, but I am comfortable being referred to as they/them and at times prefer it.

6 Beals and Wilson, "Mixed-Blood."

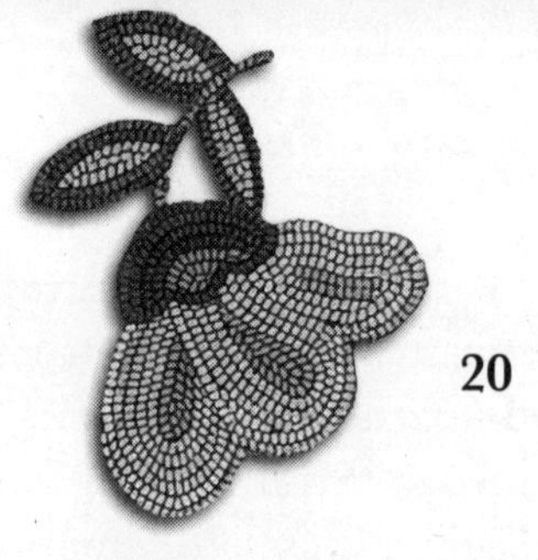

20

Differentiating Métis Feminism

Robline Davey

Indigenous Feminisms: Key Commitments and Grounding Principles

This chapter focuses on Canadian Métis feminist scholarship, but before I go into details about Métis feminism, key foundational scholarship originating from countries with similar colonial origins warrants a brief discussion. Countries such as New Zealand and Australia and certain states in the United States, such as Hawaii, have informed Canadian discourse. The need to build on this literature is evidence of the gap in literature on Indigenous feminisms in the Canadian context, and even less scholarship exists on the topic of Métis feminism.

Indigenous feminisms is placed within a relational framework, as a "multisphered concept with the family as the centre, surrounded by clan identification, then tribe and tribal relationships, which can mean relationships with state and federal governments."[1] Gina Starblanket argues that a critical gender lens preserves Indigenous plurality, providing an analysis of the connections between gender, sexuality, and oppression.[2] Structuring feminism in a binary way oversimplifies the spectrum of ideologies, undermining Indigenous women's approaches to decolonization.[3] Using the plural form also reminds us of the multiplicity of communities across Canada, including Métis people who are often rendered invisible under the umbrella term Indigenous. The notion of "Indigenous" or "Aboriginal" as one people is a convenient overarching term that has aided colonization, currently and in the past.

Recent scholarship has framed "Canada as a colonial settler state infused with racist conceptions of Indigenous peoples."[4] Métis scholar Emma LaRocque asserts that feminism can be described as a framework to view "how social systems work to privilege men and disadvantage women."[5] Mainstream and Indigenous feminisms diverge in the intersectionality of Indigenous women's identities. Differences centre on ways in which heteropatriarchy is reinforced by colonialism, including how racism and misogyny impact Indigenous women.[6] Indigenous feminisms combine political activism, critical race theory, and feminism, describing the approach as "libratory critical theoretical"[7] and several theories include the promise of transformation for a post-colonial world, offering alternative positive solutions for society in general.[8]

Joyce Green[9] points to a gap in the literature, calling for an increase in the application of Indigenous feminist frameworks, and I would add a necessary Métis feminist framework. Despite this gap, a recent growing body of Métis feminist scholarship has emerged in which Métis scholars explore matriarchal roles and responsibilities, academic contributions,[10] and women's roles in political and economic spheres;[11] and validate emerging and existing women's methodologies such as gathering and visiting (kiyokewin),[12] including keeoukaywin, the Visiting Way,[13] and the Kitchen Table Methodology,[14] which refers to ways in which women engaged in important conversations in the private sphere versus the public sphere largely inhabited by men.[15]

Central Concepts of Indigenous Feminisms

Key to Indigenous feminisms are the foundational feminist understandings of heteropatriarchy operating through settler colonialism and resulting in the current societal standards.[16] Intersectionality impacts how Indigenous women experience societal, institutional, and family structures, not considered by whitestream feminism,[17] which serves women who do not experience marginalization due to racism. Denise Lajimodiere, an American Indigenous scholar, refers to critical Indigenous feminist theory, which incorporates how gender can inform the understanding of colonial ideology.[18] The notion that gender is a colonial and heteropatriarchal construct[19] leads to a critique of whitestream feminism, which addresses oppression related to gender only.

Indigenous feminisms, including Métis feminism, seek more than just parity with men of the same class. Maile Arvin et al. list several concepts integral to Indigenous feminism—land, sovereignty, futurity, and decolonization, criticizing the inclusion of Indigenous feminisms under the umbrella of feminism. "Centering settler colonialism within gender and women's studies instead exposes the still-existing structure of settler colonialism and its powerful effects on Indigenous peoples and settlers."[20]

Indigenous feminisms use a lens through which to analyze, critique, and transform current standards, reimagining society using Indigenous worldviews. Looking at the contradictions between democracy and the colonial past is an integral aspect of this viewpoint. In bell hooks's foundational work on Black feminism, she defines feminism as a transformative paradigm—capable of transforming societal norms, including aspirations to rebuild society with considerations for all human rights, traditions, and cultures. Building on Paulo Freire's foundational concepts, it connects colonial oppression to the internalized oppression of marginalized peoples.[21]

Governmental tools of oppression have uniquely impacted Indigenous women. The Indian Act, residential schools, land dispossession, the Sixties Scoop, and Indian hospitals all eroded family structures and women's value and role in society. The Indian Act provided policies to build a Canadian citizenry by reorganizing existing complex and often matrilineal kinship and governance.[22] Indigenous feminisms is about integrating settler colonialism, heteropatriarchy, and heteropaternalism with an analysis of how colonial systems interrupted and replaced family structures and matrilineal lines of succession.[23] Ignoring power relations, gender roles, and sexuality affected the production of cultural memory, culminating in negative stereotypes as well as erasing Indigenous family kinship structures by imposing Western norms.[24]

Several scholars allege that establishing Western gender roles was instrumental in divesting Indigenous peoples of land,[25] which impacts the Métis directly through the scrip system. Arvin et al. remind us of blood quantum metrics and patrilineal systems that were enforced to curtail land claims, limiting women who married off-reserve from maintaining Indian status,[26] highlighting the importance of using gender and decolonization lenses to recover pre-contact knowledge, rather than relying on settler observations. It is critical that Indigenous women are not characterized by a mythical past or solely defined by their relationships with white men,[27] which is specifically relevant to Métis people due to our fur trade origins. Rayna Green explored stereotypical representations of Indigenous women, the Pocahontas perplex, which explores the origins and reasons behind binary identity constructions resulting from Christian biases and Eurocentric worldviews that led to often stereotyping Indigenous women as Princess/Squaw or Drudge, which are predicated on relational descriptions of identities originating from contact.[28]

Key Issues

Key issues are varied and wide-reaching, including missing and murdered Indigenous women (MMIWG), poverty, stereotypical depictions, the criminal justice system, colonialism, racism, sexism, sexuality, land and environmental health, community wellness, health and wellness, identity, violence against women and children, sovereignty, political liberation, and oppression.[29]

Controversy around the term feminist exists. Many activists, scholars, and theorists discuss the tension and do or did not identify with Indigenous feminisms,[30] preferring the label "activist" to the "F-word."[31] Among other things, this was a reaction to the way feminism originated to address gender equality within their class, by white women, without concerns for intersectionality, culture, or racial oppressions generated from colonialism or slavery. In contradiction, several scholars express the value of a feminist analytical framework with an anti-colonial lens for decolonizing policies and institutions.[32]

Sovereignty, Legal Rights, Responsibilities, and Land

From a legal perspective, Gina Starblanket argues that a combination of heteropatriarchy and colonial oppression have created society's current conditions, eroding women's power and autonomy. Indigenous feminist activism began early—their pleas for interventions into patriarchal governments and demands for self-governance are some of the first instances of activism. Constitutional negotiations did not account for gender, and Indigenous governments replicated patriarchal power structures, excluding and further marginalizing women's voices and different concerns.[33]

Indigeneity can be described as place-based; our geography defines us, and our worldviews are informed by our relationship to the land.[34] Manulani Meyer conveys the importance of this connection: "the dispossession of land and access to the ocean have been so materially and spiritually destructive to Indigenous peoples."[35] Self-governance, jurisdiction over land, and policy development through Indigenous protocols are critical to Indigenous feminisms, directly tied to cultural resurgence.[36] Sovereignty extends to include Indigenous peoples who reside on and off policy-driven Indian reservations, which includes Métis who were divested of a land base. Passing culture intergenerationally is difficult when a community is divested from an original land base,[37] which had a devastating impact on the cohesiveness of the Métis people. An Indigenous gender lens is critical, including a Métis perspective, given that resource extraction is argued to impact women disproportionately.[38]

Cultural Resurgence and Traditionalism: Gender Roles and Complementarity

History has largely been documented by settlers which marginalized Indigenous experiences.[39] Several scholars indicate that women had more agency pre-contact. Living off the land allowed for increased gender role flexibility,[40] which decreased after colonization.[41] Settlers misunderstood tribal "kinship systems, gender roles, social values, and tribal spirituality,"[42] characterizing their work as the "hardships of men or drudgery."[43] Biased Western observations resulted in inadequate and incorrect depictions of pre-contact gender relations,[44] contributing to false notions of gender roles and replication of Western norms,[45] reinforced by missionaries.[46] For example, during the fur trade, Euro-patriarchal notions of labour transformed women's autonomy,[47] resulting in an increased reliance upon men. Travel meant women were left at home, limiting their agency,[48] erasing their voices from political conversations, but Métis scholarship challenges this characterization of limited agency for Métis women.[49]

Eurocentric views of women's diminished capacities for physical labour due to their reproductive capabilities and dividing responsibilities became a determining factor in limiting Indigenous women to the domestic sphere.[50] Menstrual cycles are linked to the lunar cycle, giving women access to higher spiritual powers with the ability to interrupt ceremony. In the colonial context, this was reimagined and reinterpreted to mean that women were unclean, dirty, amoral—linked to sexuality, which shifted women's perceived value, reinforcing heteropatriarchy, and denying women the agency over how to conduct themselves ceremonially.[51] Several scholars have explored the concept of complementarity, that different roles—even if denoted by gender—were equally valued.[52] But Emma LaRocque questions this view. Do balance and complementarity extend to equality, equity, empowerment, or equal voices in political spheres? Relying on tradition ensures patriarchal dominance over women by asserting that women should only be defined by maternal, nurturing roles.[53]

Métis Feminism: Defining Our Unique Experiences

These colonially constructed identities were designed to divest people of their lands.[54] The legacy of land dispossession combined with colonization impacted Métis women adversely.[55] As previously mentioned, various mechanisms were employed to disenfranchise women from their communities, effectively preventing children from obtaining status. Métis people are not governed by the Indian Act, the expectation being that as half-breeds, we would assimilate easily.[56] Many of us did pass as white or French-Canadian, as my grandparents did, posing problems for Métis women who were not able to pass—unable to obtain services, employment, health care, or funding tagged exclusively for those with First Nations status.[57] The results of these policies and the invisibility of the Métis have had ramifications for access to education, equity, and health care. Additionally, government timelines for equitable access to health care have not been met,[58] reducing Métis Elders' life and health span today.

Using a specifically Métis feminist framework to analyze any societal challenge allows us to parse out concerns unique to specific populations. LaRocque notes that universal discussions "conflate and collapse concepts of culture and tradition," identifying a gap in research for discourse that honours the variety of Indigenous cultures.[59] For these reasons, it is integral to engage in Métis-specific research in order to contribute to the emerging scholarship that identifies Métis-specific priorities for health and education, preferably through a Métis feminist lens. Colonization is not often considered a modern determinant of health.[60] Yet, fewer opportunities impact income levels directly, resulting in lower rates of economic stability. Loss of culture and family traditions, combined with not being able to identify as Métis, caused intergenerational trauma uniquely different from that of First Nations. Road allowances and migration had negative impacts on well-being and health. For example, Diedre Desmarais takes up the issue of specifically Métis women Elders in poverty, connecting it directly to colonization.[61]

Unique determinants have reduced Métis women's opportunities, impacting our communities adversely. Being denied access to land through the fraudulent scrip system resulted in a higher than typical level of mobility to seek opportunities elsewhere away from our home communities, or live in impoverished road allowances on the edges of town. Separating the Métis from their land base affected the cultural cohesiveness due to cultural fragmentation and poverty,[62] resulting in a lack of cultural transmission intergenerationally, limiting the protective factors of culture. Additionally, the lack of identification as an Indigenous group under the Indian Act meant that the Métis did not fall under the responsibility of the government policies like First Nations communities, resulting in less compensation being available. Reacting to this exclusion has become an integral component of Métis political culture.[63]

Métis scholars document the ways in which female kinship relationships were central to the structure and boundaries of Métis communities, despite economic changes, community movement and migration, physical relocations, and political upheaval.[64] Despite male-dominated accounts of the Métis Nation, scholars remind us of the matrilineal and kinship-oriented structures of Métis families and communities and evidence of women's integral role in communities—they were often capable hunters, trappers, fishers, businesswomen, even building cabins and running dog teams.[65] Contrary to the notion that trade was the domain of men, several scholars document Métis women's highly desirable beadwork, which resulted in the autonomy to engage in commerce.[66] It is well documented that Métis families joined buffalo hunts, contrary to the notion that all Métis women remained at home.[67]

Additional scholarship shines a light on the political activism of women of the Métis Nation,[68] despite the fact that the national narrative is rooted in male stories. Jennifer Adese argues that women played a vital role and uses a Métis feminist approach to contemporary Métis politics.[69] Despite assertions to the contrary, several scholars validate the reality that Métis women were active in community issues, involved in various activities such as recruiting organization participants, supporting public male leadership through fundraising using the domestic domain.[70] For Métis women, this role evolved to be increasingly visible and public by the 1960s and 1970s. As a comment on the existence of women's public activism, Adese recounts the story of Annie Bannatyne, a prominent Métis woman in the Red River Settlement, reacting publicly to harsh words by an official.[71]

For those who grew up in the 1950s and 1960s, opportunities were not readily accessible or even available. Many lived in poverty, existing in survival mode, which resulted in lower economic stability and higher poverty rates. Education is another determinant of health, which can vastly improve the economic stability of a family and affect all other determinants.[72] With an increase in economic stability comes access to other factors that can improve well-being and quality of life. Desmarais uses the example of access to a pension.[73] With the current employment landscape changing, this may not impact future generations, but stable pensionable jobs were not available to everyone in the past. Without a pension, many Métis Elders rely solely on Old Age Security, Canada Pension Plan, and the Guaranteed Income Supplement, which is an insufficient fixed income to support oneself, especially as inflation rates are beginning to soar and Canadians are facing a recession.

Desmarais ties a lower financial security to government neglect.[74] Relying on the fact that Métis were considered Canadian citizens, the government denied them a collective land base, educational opportunities, and funded health care. This lack of identification has resulted from the absence of a national registry and governing body that is responsible for overseeing and delivering funding for healthcare. This often excludes the Métis for the purposes of data collection and reporting, as in the MMIWG report[75] and a dearth of health data.[76] The resulting impacts are particularly damaging for women. Indigenous women experience more violence than any other group in Canada.[77] In one study by Métis Nation British Columbia (MNBC), Thanks for Listening, a survey of eight to ten questions resulted in over 400 quantitative and qualitative responses, evidence of the desire for our stories to be heard and documented from our own perspective.[78]

Sarah Hunt calls for an ethic of care towards one another, supporting decolonization in every interaction, rather than reproducing gender violence and heteropatriarchy.[79] As a learning sciences scholar, my intention is to contribute to the emerging scholarship by defining and using Métis feminism and culturally specific methodologies to investigate connections between culture, technology, and equity. As previously stated, decolonizing and dismantling heteropatriarchy are beneficial not just for Indigenous women but for all women.[80] Starblanket articulates my argument for using a Métis feminist lens to explore any topic: "Indigenous feminist modes of analysis can help make space to engage in critical conversations around gender and patriarchy as we negotiate this new terrain, and to keep these discussions going in the everyday."[81] It should be central to understanding Métis women's experiences to think critically about the conditions of our lives, and how they may impact our daily interactions, including experiences of educational access, and digital interactions, and how this may inform educators to create "safe spaces which are conducive to and open to marginalized voices and contradict normative points of view informed by settler colonialism, [creating] opportunities to integrate into our collective unconscious,"[82] thus confronting patriarchy and colonialism from a specifically Métis lens.

A Métis-specific lens is valuable to evaluate the conditions that Métis women find themselves subjected to daily, including technology used in higher education, because the same colonial structures contextualize everyday life. Using a Métis feminist lens can illuminate and challenge heteropatriarchal norms that are accepted or assumed; and allow us to use an ideological, critical, and activist framework to transform learning spaces, educational technology development, and pedagogy; and inform ways that learning communities are facilitated or organically develop. Based on the concept that heteropatriarchy can be dismantled from many angles,[83] using a specific Métis feminist lens can support educators to challenge and deconstruct colonial and gendered representations in the curriculum. It can also be used to examine how gender and power relations impact interactions within technology-mediated discourse, which is critical to improving educational access and experiences, given that this is one of the determining factors for Métis women to improve their own life and health span.[84]

Notes

1 Williams and Harjo, "American Indian Feminism."
2 Starblanket, "Being Indigenous Feminists."
3 Goeman and Denetdale, "Native Feminisms."
4 J. Green, "Taking More Account," 3.
5 LaRocque, "Métis and Feminist," 57.
6 Arvin, Tuck, and Morrill, "Decolonizing Feminism"; J. Green, "Taking More Account"; L. Maracle, *I Am Woman*; LaRocque, "Métis and Feminist"; Scudeler, "Indigenous Feminisms."
7 J. Green, "Taking More Account," 17.
8 Arvin, Tuck, and Morrill, "Decolonizing Feminism"; J. Green, "Taking More Account"; LaRocque, "Métis and Feminist"; Ross, "From the 'F' Word"; Smith and Kauanui, "Native Feminisms Engage American Studies"; Starblanket, "Being Indigenous Feminists"; St. Denis, "Feminism Is for Everybody."
9 J. Green, "Taking More Account"; J. Green, *Making Space for Indigenous Feminism.*
10 Forsythe, "Métis Women."
11 Adese, "Restoring the Balance."
12 Flaminio, Gaudet, and Dorion, "Métis Women Gathering."
13 Gaudet, "Keeoukaywin."
14 Farrell Racette, "Sewing Ourselves Together."
15 J. Green, "Taking More Account"; LaRocque, "Métis and Feminist"; Starblanket, "Being Indigenous Feminists."
16 Arvin, Tuck, and Morrill, "Decolonizing Feminism"; J. Green, "Taking More Account"; LaRocque, "Métis and Feminist"; Maracle, *I Am Woman*; Million, "Felt Theory"; Starblanket, "Being Indigenous Feminists."
17 Arvin, Tuck, and Morrill, "Decolonizing Feminism"; J. Green, "Taking More Account."
18 Lajimodiere, "American Indian Females"; Ross, "From the 'F' Word"; A. Smith, "Native American Feminism"; A. Smith, "Dismantling"; Starblanket, "Being Indigenous Feminists."
19 Roscoe, *Changing Ones.*
20 Arvin, Tuck, and Morrill, "Decolonizing Feminism," 8.
21 LaRocque, "Métis and Feminist"; Freire, *Pedagogy*; hooks, *Feminist Theory.*
22 Canada, Indian Act.
23 Arvin, Tuck, and Morrill, "Decolonizing Feminism"; Kauanui, "Native Hawaiian Decolonization"; J. Green, "Taking More Account."
24 J. Green, "Taking More Account"; LaRocque, "Métis and Feminist."
25 Starblanket, "Being Indigenous Feminists"; Kermoal, "Métis Women's."
26 Arvin, Tuck, and Morrill, "Decolonizing Feminism." Note that this has been retroactively changed for numerous women with the passing of Bill C-31 governing band membership.
27 J. Green, "Taking More Account"; Lajimodiere, "American Indian Females"; Smiley, "Not Sacred."
28 R. Green, "The Pocahontas Perplex"; Lajimodiere, "American Indian Females"; Smiley, "Not Sacred."

29 LaRocque, "Métis and Feminist"; National Inquiry into Missing and Murdered Indigenous Women and Girls, *Reclaiming Power and Place,* Vol. 1a; National Inquiry into Missing and Murdered Indigenous Women and Girls, *Reclaiming Power and Place,* Vol. 1b; Desmarais, "Spare a Thought"; Lajimodiere, "American Indian Females"; Maracle, *I Am Woman*; Smiley, "Not Sacred"; Hunt, "Embodying Self-Determination"; Arvin, Tuck, and Morrill, "Decolonizing Feminism"; J. Green, "Taking More Account"; Hunt, "Everyday Decolonization"; Kermoal, "Métis Women's"; Meyer, "Indigenous and Authentic"; Starblanket, "Being Indigenous Feminists"; Anderson and Lawrence, *Strong Women Stories*; Monchalin, Smylie, and Bourgeois, "It's Not Like"; Monchalin, Smylie, and Nowgesic, "'I Guess'"; Smylie and Firestone, "Back to the Basics"; Clark, Barkaskas, and Davey, *Thanks for Listening*; McIvor, "Aboriginal Women Unmasked."

30 Nickel, "I Am Not a Women's Libber"; K. Anderson, *Life Stages*; K. Anderson, "Multi-Generational Indigenous Feminisms"; J. Green, "Constitutionalising the Patriarchy"; J. Green, *Making Space*; J. Green, "Taking More Account"; Ouellette, *The Fourth World*; St. Denis, "Feminism Is for Everybody."

31 Denetdale, "Securing"; Ross, "From the 'F' Word"; Lajimodiere, "American Indian Females"; A. Smith, "Native American Feminism"; A. Smith, "Dismantling."

32 K. Anderson, "Multi-Generational Indigenous Feminisms"; J. Green, "Taking More Account"; LaRocque, "Métis and Feminist"; Maracle, *I Am Woman*; Starblanket, "Being Indigenous Feminists."

33 Starblanket, "Being Indigenous Feminists."

34 Coulthard, *Red Skin, White Masks*; Alfred and Corntassel, "Being Indigenous"; Hunt, "Violence, Law"; Hunt, "Everyday Decolonization"; Kermoal, "Métis Women's"; Simpson, "Indigenous Resurgence."

35 Meyer, "Indigenous and Authentic."

36 Kermoal, "Métis Women's."

37 Goeman, "(Re)Mapping Indigenous Presence."

38 National Inquiry into Missing and Murdered Indigenous Women and Girls, *Reclaiming Power and Place,* Vol. 1a; National Inquiry into Missing and Murdered Indigenous Women and Girls, *Reclaiming Power and Place,* Vol. 1b.

39 Drawson, Toombs, and Mushquash, "Indigenous Research Methods"; The First Nations Information Governance Centre, *Ownership, Control*; L. Smith, *Decolonizing Methodologies*; J. Green, "Towards a Détente"; Silva, *Aloha Betrayed*; Thobani, *Exalted Subjects.*

40 Hungry Wolf, *The Ways of My Grandmothers.*

41 LaRocque, "Métis and Feminist."

42 Lajimodiere, "American Indian Females," 105.

43 Emberly, *Thresholds of Difference*, 56.

44 Adese, "Restoring the Balance"; Bonvillain, "Gender Relations"; Bell, "Gender in Native America."

45 Amott and Matthaei, *Race, Gender*; Bell, "Gender in Native America"; Bonvillain, "Gender Relations"; Medicine, "Professionalization"; Mihesuah, *Indigenous American Women*; A. Smith *Conquest.*

46 Emberly, *Thresholds of Difference.*

47 Carter, *Capturing Women.*

48 Starblanket, "Being Indigenous Feminists."

49 Donovan, *Feminist Theory*; LaRocque, "Métis and Feminist"; Starblanket, "Being Indigenous Feminists"; Adese, "Restoring the Balance."
50 Donovan, *Feminist Theory*.
51 Starblanket, "Being Indigenous Feminists."
52 Ibid.
53 LaRocque, "Métis and Feminist."
54 Desmarais, "Spare a Thought"; Dhamoon, *Identity-Difference Politics*.
55 Van Kirk, *Many Tender Ties*; St-Onge, *Saint-Laurent, Manitoba*: Iseke-Barnes, "Grandmothers of the Métis Nation."
56 Desmarais, "Spare a Thought."
57 Ibid.
58 Desmarais, "Spare a Thought"; Turpel-Lafond, *In Plain Sight*.
59 LaRocque, "Métis and Feminist," 139.
60 Reading, "Introduction."
61 Desmarais, "Spare a Thought."
62 LaRocque, "Métis and Feminist."
63 Desmarais, "Spare a Thought."
64 Adese, "Restoring the Balance"; Campbell, "Foreword"; Troupe, "Métis Women."
65 Adese, "Restoring the Balance"; Macdougall, *One of the Family*; Campbell, "Foreword."
66 Van Kirk, *Many Tender Ties*; Troupe, "Métis Women"; Farrell Racette, "Sewing Ourselves Together."
67 Campbell, "Foreword."
68 Adese, "Restoring the Balance."
69 Ibid.
70 Troupe, "Métis Women."
71 Adese, "Restoring the Balance."
72 Dyck, "Social Determinants."
73 Desmarais, "Spare a Thought."
74 Ibid.
75 National Inquiry into Missing and Murdered Indigenous Women and Girls, *Reclaiming Power and Place*, Vol. 1a; National Inquiry into Missing and Murdered Indigenous Women and Girls, *Reclaiming Power and Place*, Vol. 1b.
76 Desmarais, "Spare a Thought"; Government of Canada, *Working Guide*; Smylie and Firestone, "Back to the Basics."
77 Clark, Barkaskas, and Davey, *Thanks for Listening*; Truth and Reconciliation Commission, *Final Report*; Truth and Reconciliation Commission, *Calls to Action*.
78 Clark, Barkaskas, and Davey, *Thanks for Listening*.
79 Hunt, "Violence, Law."
80 LaRocque, "Métis and Feminist"; hooks, "Feminism"; Arvin, Tuck, and Morrill, "Decolonizing Feminism"; Starblanket, "Being Indigenous Feminists."
81 Starblanket, "Being Indigenous Feminists," 39.
82 Ibid.
83 Starblanket, "Being Indigenous Feminists."
84 Dyck, "Social Determinants."

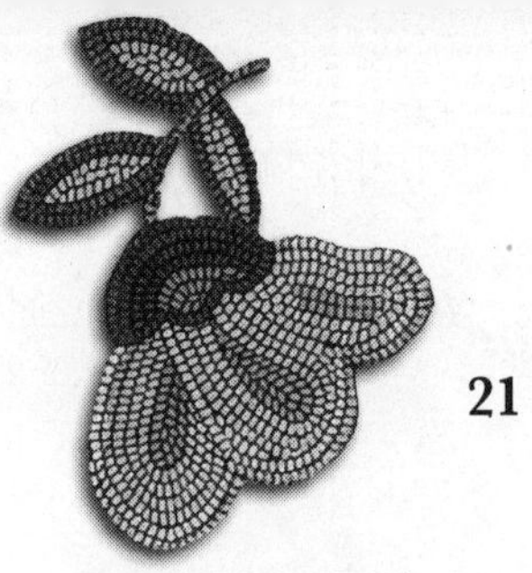

21

Celebrating the Wisdom of Our Métis Matriarchs:

Sewing Our Wellness All Together—Kood Toot Aansamb

Leah Dorion, Janice Cindy Gaudet, and Hannah Bouvier

Research specific to knowledge created by and with Métis is emerging, yet remains sparse. The growing scholarship about Métis women's health and wellness is increasingly making visible Métis women's historical and contemporary knowledge, stories, and resilience.[1] The invisibility of our Métis women's stories and lives in Canada's colonial history has had a direct effect on the quality of our lives as Michif People. Renée Monchalin and Lisa Monchalin speak to how ignoring Métis women's voices and narratives has also impacted "Métis identity in Canada."[2] Brenda Macdougall, a Métis scholar, contextualizes Métis health and well-being as directly linked to our extensive kinship networks, values, and ways of being in relationship: "In short, people were expected to be good relatives by looking out and caring for one another. This understanding of the world ensured the health and wellbeing of communities through its emphasis on shared responsibility."[3] These values informed an identity and a way of life that valued and relied upon Métis women's social, political, economic, and cultural contributions.

The purpose of our research was primarily to learn from Métis women located in a specific South Saskatchewan region originally settled by Métis families. We contribute to place-based knowledge (the gifts of place) that centres, with the highest respect and esteem, on Métis women's wisdom and traditions. Through the knowledge and stories, as shared in this article by the eight Métis Matriarchs we interviewed, we invest in centring Métis women's innovative and creative sewing practices informed by their values, connection, and kinship-caring ways. In doing so, we remember that "Métis women are still contributing to our national development, and we have a proud tradition of sharing, caring and kindness to celebrate with others. It is time to draw inspiration and strength from the courage and lives of our historical Métis grandmothers so that we can restore this power to our contemporary women to ensure that future generations of children can learn to respect the land, honour women's connection to the land, and know about our special Métis way of life."[4] The visibility of Métis women's creative work is important for multiple reasons: a) strengthening women's kinship connections; b) regenerating old/new ways of living and being well; c) qualifying the role of gender in caring and sustaining social and economic life; and d) decolonizing dominant forms of knowledge production.

Centring Métis Women's Cultural Knowledge Production

We draw on Métis-specific research to further Métis women's cultural knowledge production through artistic practices such as the culture of sewing. The historical research of Métis scholars Dr. Sherry Farrell Racette and Dr. Cheryl Troupe highlights Métis women's identity in cultural and creative expression. With their research, we begin to understand the complex social, spiritual, and economic nature of Métis women's sewing practices.[5] Their research demonstrates the multifaceted practice of sewing as a means of communicating territory, family belonging, social and economic context, and Métis identity as a creative and visual social group. Their research examines material culture; techniques, uses, and purpose; the fur-trade economy; and lifestyle from the early nineteenth century to the mid-twentieth century. Farrell Racette and Troupe's research speaks of specific Métis styles that were extensions of visually represented Métis cultural identifiers. Farrell Racette tells us that most of the Métis material collections in museums can be tied to specific Métis and Half Breed families and communities, and they are functional and decorative items made for a household.[6]

Farrell Racette and Troupe show the fine quality of material that Métis women purchased from local suppliers from neighbouring communities, often forming long-standing relationships. Their historical research makes visible Métis women's unique and diverse social and economic relationships with Europeans and with their extended kinship: "The requirements of clothing production for both trade and survival brought European men and local women together, and through their shared activity, created an interactive zone where sewing techniques and materials were exchanged."[7] Dress and the creation of clothing brought people together in forms of collaboration. Relationships and the environment in which they lived influenced styles and how garments could be made and adapted. Dr. Troupe's research on the late nineteenth century points to how "Métis women's fashions were never static. In addition to the clothing they made themselves, Métis women enjoyed purchasing the latest styles, if they could afford them."[8] Her research further demonstrates how Métis women's artistic expression was present in a wide range of items: blankets, coats, leggings, moccasins, mittens and gauntlets, pad saddles, firebags, cradleboards, and a wide array of practical accessories, including household accessories.[9] The tools and materials they worked with were also extensive. The sophisticated skills required to create beautiful objects using diverse materials, such as beaver, furs, hides, horsehair, porcupine quills, beads, leather, silk, recycled fabric, and burlap potato or grain sacks, were passed down from generation to generation. Métis cultural aesthetics played a significant role in ensuring the centrality of relationality and resiliency in Métis life. It is apparent through historical research that Métis women were at the forefront of fashion sense. Knowledge of how to dress was not isolated from social, spiritual, and economic life.

Our research builds on the continuity of sewing culture in Métis women's families and communities. Our discussions with Métis Matriarchs helped guide ways of thinking about a future that is economically, spiritually, and socially sustainable.

Community-Engaged Methodology

Our research contributes to the continuity of historical and contemporary research on Métis women's creative expression and identity. Our place-based focus draws on the relationship between Métis women in a specific South Saskatchewan region, St. Louis, and our own relations. A community-engaged research methodology was an important approach in our broader Métis women's wellness research project. Our wellness activities were a way of being in relation with the community and creating a supportive space within which to visit and gather as

Métis women.[10] With our kinship responsibilities at heart, we reached out to Métis women we already knew in an effort to learn together, and to strengthen community-building with community leadership. This way of being sparked the creation of a Métis women's sewing studio, and extended to conversational interviews and visits with eight Métis Matriarchs, to whom we are deeply indebted for their stories and the relationships formed with them and their daughters.

> Margaret Sophie McDougall is the daughter of Mary Leona McDougall and Robert James Boyer, and was born on 22 December 1928 in her mother's family home in St. Louis, Saskatchewan.
>
> Marlene Vandale was born in 1949 in St. Louis, Saskatchewan. She is a descendent of Métis families from the region, including the Richard and Lafontaine families.
>
> Vivian Meabry was born in 1936 in the Lindsay District near McDowell, Saskatchewan. She is from the Pocha family, a large Métis family from the Duck Lake and McDowell region.
>
> Elsie Sanderson was born in 1941 in the community of Cumberland House, Saskatchewan. She was raised in an intergenerational home with her grandfather, sisters, aunties, and her many siblings and cousins.
>
> Ann Lepine was born in 1948 in the Prince Albert, Saskatchewan, hospital. She is the daughter of Lillian May Williamson and James Elford Short.
>
> Claudette Lavergne was born in St. Louis, Saskatchewan, in 1955. Her mom was Jeanne Boucher from St. Louis, born in 1914. Claudette is also the daughter of Edward Vandale.
>
> Norma Gaudet is the daughter of Auxile Lepine and Norman Morrison. She was born on 18 November 1936 at the family homestead in Hoey, Saskatchewan.
>
> Ruth Bird was born on 5 February 1939. Her father, Rich Corrigal, was from Winnipeg. Ruth has resided in St. Louis since 1972, and as a child, stayed with her grandmother, Magabelle Corrigal.

Putting Our Methodology into Action

We worked within an existing Métis cultural centre and within our existing relationships to create a designated Métis women's sewing studio in the growing River Road Centre (St. Louis, Saskatchewan). The principal researcher worked with the Métis designer and entrepreneur of the River Road Centre, Christine Tournier-Tienkamp, and her mother, Louise (née Boucher) Tournier, both skilled sewers in the community, to identify tools required, the best value sewing machines for beginning sewing, materials, supplies for setting up workstations, irons and other supplies from second-hand stores, and materials to be upcycled, and to set up a designated sewing studio, which has remained as such.

The sewing studio space set-up took place over a few months, and the first sewing workshop offered two basic sewing classes, with Louise Tournier sharing her love and gift of sewing. This provided Métis women with basic sewing skills and, just as important, a gathering space within which to sew together, and to begin a conversation about wellness and their personal relationships with sewing. Some women were already skilled sewers. From this initial workshop came a traditional Métis ribbon skirts workshop. These workshops were followed by weekly skirt-making sessions, and five consecutive Tuesday sewing bees, led again by Louise Tournier, in which we participated. The skirt-making process and the dedicated "interactive" sewing space created a positive climate, in which the community of sewers identified Matriarchs who could teach us more about the significance of family sewing practices and principles.

During the summer months of 2019, we called the Métis Matriarchs, and met and visited in these women's homes when invited in. This required the integrity and trust inherent in a reciprocal, respectful, and relational research approach. As is common with Métis women–led methodologies, the conversational interviews included other family members as well. Some of the daughters were contacted and invited to take part in the interviews, and in order to assure wellness accountability, direction, and approval. These steps and protocols are part of Métis diplomatic relationality. It was also important for the daughters to confirm that their mothers were well enough. Some of the daughters contributed by sharing their own experiences and helping their mothers to remember and affirm their instrumental contributions. These conversational interviews were often shared at the kitchen table over a cup of coffee, visiting, or having a relaxed conversation while contributing to sewing studio knowledge projects. The conversations allowed for us to hear incredible stories of how sewing has contributed to family and community life, and how sewing has been shared within families for generations. After we received both oral and written consent and obtained the University of Alberta ethics review, the interviews were recorded and transcribed. Gifts and honorariums were given to each Matriarch in honour of her time and stories shared.

Honouring the Wisdom Traditions of Our Métis Matriarchs

We chose to identify the Métis women we interviewed as "Matriarchs." By doing so, we reclaim the kinship principles of women's leadership roles that assured balance in our homes, communities, and lands. The older women known as the Matriarchs in land-based societies held spiritual and political power and authority in the household, in the broadest sense, which included economics, life stage knowledge, education, food production and distribution, and continuity of family values and ethics.[11] Matriarchs sustained the continuity of identity, sense of belonging, and values to live by. Genevieve Vaughan explains that matriarch models hold important principles for the future as "they have maintained and sustained themselves without domination, without hierarchies, and without wars."[12] With the women's consent and follow-up verification, we include their names as an important part of our methodology. In this way, we honour their lives and the qualities of creativity, care, love, strength, and self-reliance that they embody.[13] This makes visible the often hidden labour and creative force of the generations of Matriarchs who carved and blazed trails of resistance for us.

Meaning-Making Process

Making meaning of the knowledge shared involved various steps. The interviews were reviewed line by line, and specific stories were identified within broader themes. The overarching themes were shared within a Métis-women-specific celebration that honoured the unique beauty of each of the women's skirts and the completion of the research project. The research team came together to deepen their analysis and narrow down the themes. A fourth analysis was completed individually, then reviewed collectively. The article was reviewed further by three Métis women who participated in the sewing classes, and finally by the remaining five Matriarchs who participated in the research for further review and accuracy of our meaning-making process.

Telling Our Story through Sewing

Métis Women as Providers and Innovators

Sewing together and learning to sew at home were a way of life described by all of the Matriarchs. Many of the women recalled learning the basics from their mothers, aunties, and grandmothers. This acknowledges the traditional value that sewing was education for a lifelong skill at home, with our mothers, aunties, and grandmothers as teachers. Elsie Sanderson shared,

> In my family and the houses my family occupied, the women would get together with the young girls that they were teaching. And I just assumed that's the way it was in other houses; I never really did go and participate in their sewing circles, family sewing circles. But of course you always saw the product of sewing, because they would, if it was a big project, like a parka to embroider . . . then everyone would participate in it. So we would all sit around and do our embroidering or beadwork and then it came to sewing the product together then the more older, more experienced seamstresses would do that job. But that's how it was done.[14]

Sophie McDougall explained that there was not much to do growing up, so she learned to knit at a very young age, and still knits shawls and afghans for her family members and friends of the family. These gifts are deeply treasured by those who received them. For both Sophie and Norma, gifting warmth, care, and comfort is part of their values. "It's about the love," as Sophie reminded us.[15] She also explained how her mother handmade their first baseball out of different pieces of material, as well as a baby swing (li malloo aen Michif) that would sit above or beside her bed. Marlene Vandale also reflected on this when sharing how her mother provided for her children: "My mom [Eva Lafontaine], she was a hard worker."[16] She explained how the way of providing included sewing clothes for the children both with a sewing machine and by hand, gardening and preserving foods, and chopping and sawing wood to keep the house warm.

Métis women's skillful labour and cultural production contributed in many ways to the social and economic wellness of their families. The ability to sew produced not only quality clothing for their families but also a lifelong creative and resourceful skill set that sustained the local gifting economy, including generating income. Vivian Meabry spoke of how her grandmother would sell hooked rugs (made on old gunny sacks) for two dollars. She commented on the extensive labour of cutting the strips and hooking them. Her labour would provide for the purchase of essentials: "Once a month, she would make a trip to town with her rugs, mitts, and socks, and she had enough money to get . . . the essentials."[17] Their creations were part of the economic market and in demand. Elsie shared that her sister (Isabelle Impey) was known for her beautiful parkas. She spoke of how many women in her family contributed to the economy of sewing, sharing their sewing talent through their beadwork, sewing, and mending. Some recalled the economic structure of trade and exchange. Ruth Bird shared, "We would stay with my grandmother during our holidays, and she would be sewing for different people, and she would get maybe a chicken."[18] Ann Lepine also spoke of how the money her mom made would be used to go on trips once a year, such as bus trips that they enjoyed.

The sewing that we learned went beyond the narrow sense of needles and thread. In its broadest sense, sewing included beadwork, embroidery, spinning, knitting, hooking rugs, making wool blankets out of sheep's wool, parka making, quilts, toys, capotes and blankets, and leather crafting and tailoring. The multifaceted labour of sewing is extensive, time-consuming, and, for many, a necessity, yet it also brought great pleasure to many. The work being produced was made visible, often engaged many members of the family, and was worn proudly by family members.

Vivian spoke of being with her grandmother, mom, and cousins while spinning sheep's wool: "I sat days carting wool my mother and grandmother spun, and they did a lot of knitting, mitts and socks and sweaters. All by hand."[19] There was a role for everyone involved. The women's stories stress the chain of continuity, and that learning in the home was how it occurred. Indirect instruction happened through modelling; many of the women we interviewed shared that their mothers and grandmothers had a sewing machine on the kitchen table. The kitchen is a space that connected and took care of many generations.

Métis Women's Kitchen Tables

Sewing was a vital part of Métis women's households. The kitchen was practically, spiritually, and politically women's creative space, which extended into life outside the home. Even today, it is not uncommon to find a sewing machine on a Métis woman's kitchen table. We learn from the Matriarchs how kitchen spaces are connected to respected roles and responsibilities, and to a Métis way of life. Claudette Lavergne recalled,

> Mom [Jeanne Boucher, born in 1914] was always sewing. . . . She had her sewing machine in the kitchen . . . right at the table. She wouldn't be the only one. . . . Dad built her a sewing table and her desk. It was right under the window. Like food and sewing, so she could have stuff on the stove and so she could go and do sewing as well. . . . That was such a big part of her life and her identity. She used to do all the sewing for her siblings and children. She was the sewer of the family. There were thirteen kids.[20]

Ann Lepine remembered that her mother (Liliane) also sewed at the kitchen table. Her home was known as the "sewing house."[21] Loretta Vandale (Marlene's daughter) explained, "When we needed to get something mended or fixed, she was the one that everyone knew."[22] Ann talked about how her dad built a sewing table for her mom: "He built her a sew table or bench, and so she had the kitchen window right there and her desk was right there under the kitchen window."[23] Ruth Bird spoke of how her sewing space was dedicated to the kitchen table: "I worked at the kitchen table. I just had a machine that just sat on the table."[24] Some of the Matriarchs shared how they have, or had, designated sewing spaces built right in their homes. Norma eventually had her own dedicated sewing room added with her house extension, as her sewing skill was an economic contribution to the family. She sewed her children's clothing for years, and also sewed her own clothes. Her fond memories included the ways in which her mother was there to show her and help her when she needed it.

The value of sewing was, and for many of the women's families continues to be, a significant element of a healthy and prosperous household; some have sewing studios in their homes today. Sophie recalled that her mom would invite women from the Anglican church, who lived on the north side of the Saskatchewan River, to her home for regular sewing bees. Her gramma was Anglican and was confined to the house because she had physical challenges. The women would come to her and do their quilting at her house. Sewing brought women together from different Métis communities, with different religions and ways of life, to visit, create, and gather as a way of caring for themselves and their families. Though they had different religions—Catholic and Anglican—they still had good relationships with one another because, for Sophie, Métis women stuck together regardless of religious differences. For Sophie, it was about enjoying each other's company and supporting each other during difficult times. She said that "being considerate of others is part of Métis women's values, because it is about quality of sharing in each other's lives, and simply, we love to share."[25]

Métis Women's Entrepreneurship: Being Resourceful

Métis women had to be resourceful to access sewing supplies. When they could not purchase material through the catalogues, purchasing fabric outside the home was a big undertaking. Travel was costly and rare. Claudette explained that her family would take two weeks off in the summer to go down to the United States, and an important part of these excursions was purchasing material. For Norma, this was often a two-day outing that would include a family excursion of camping and picnicking. The fabric stores were located outside their communities, requiring major excursions and planning to purchase supplies. These investments in tools, materials, and intergenerational skill-sharing supported families and communities both economically and socially. Claudette's mom did alterations to bring in extra income for her family. She had a high skill level, and the community relied on her skill despite her having left the community and returning later. She was known, and was not forgotten, for the meaningful ways she was of service.

Ann talked about her great-grandmother, Catherine Isbister, who was a well-known dressmaker and had a shop in Prince Albert, Saskatchewan. Her mom, Lillian, was also a skilled seamstress. The women spoke of sewing not only for people but also for animal relatives.

"She [Lillian] made everything from wedding and bridesmaid dresses to horse blankets, and everything in between."[26] Square dancing was also part of Ann's family life. She explained how square dancing outfits showcased Métis women's sewing and design skills. Her mom made square dancing dresses as well as clothes for special events, such as the Midnight Mass. Patching, repairing, modifying, and hemming existing clothes were also common topics in the conversations.

Vivian talked about mending being her first teaching, and about learning how to stitch by hand. Norma recalled appreciating the creative choices of colours and styles when making new clothes. Her mom instilled in her pride in her own accomplishments: "Well, Mom helped me. Whenever I needed something, she'd say 'Okay, well let's go, and you're gonna pay for it this time, pay for your material.' So then we'd go to buy material, and she'd be there to help me sew. We were proud to get the material we could afford, because the price was high, so we'd buy what we could, and from there we were proud."[27]

Although making clothes for their children was expressed as a necessity, it was also seen as a way of life, asserting values, dignity, resilience, and life skills. Sewing was not viewed as being necessary due to a lack of material goods. To the contrary, the women felt a sense of pride in their creative work and in their capacity to be self-reliant and self-sustaining. As Vivian commented, "You get a great deal of satisfaction about completing a project, sewing or even patching something."[28] The art of sewing was a way to provide and care for themselves and their families, and was a unique and creative means of Métis expression. We learned from Claudette Lavergne that her mother made wedding dresses and veils. She beaded and sewed everything, and even made a mink flower bouquet for Queen Elizabeth and a beaded hide jacket for Prince Philip. Her exquisite creations were gifted to the royals during the 1970 Manitoba Centennial in The Pas.

Economic Sensibility:
Valuing Remnants—Turning Old into New

Being resourceful also included timing. The generations of the Matriarchs' mothers and grandmothers did not have the luxury of electricity until the 1950s. They would sew on their treadle machines during the day's light or with an oil lamp at night. The women learned and still remember and describe the practice of transforming raw materials into usable and practical products. Old scrap material and new material never went to waste, whether that was for skirts or toys and dolls for the children. These "extra" pieces of material were often used in quilts and blankets, as the Matriarchs explained. Vivian spoke of how leftovers from an old blouse or any piece of clothing, such as zippers and buttons, were "taken off and reused."[29] Gunny sacks were used for patchwork. Marlene talked about how her mom would keep all the scraps: "They wouldn't get rid of it. They would keep it and do quilts."[30]

We learned from the Matriarchs that sewing was a practical skill for keeping families properly and beautifully (fashionably) clothed. Modifying and tailoring clothes to fit other family members and creating new pieces from old fabrics were also important. Nothing was wasted. The women remembered keeping all the remnants to make quilts, blankets, dresses, and even toys to bring their children joy. Handmade toys included "stuffed horses" and knitted dolls. The women spoke of how these toys were durable: "Everything last longer if its homemade."[31] Creating doll clothes was a common practice, as was the welcoming of new babies with handmade blankets. Ann spoke of her mother (Liliane) making "scrap quilts" from old pieces of fabric, and rag rugs from old canvas sacks. Recycling buttons and zippers and refurbishing old fabric were part of a conscious effort to make use of everything. Basic mending was a family skill.

Patchwork was part of the upcycling of materials: "Everything was recycled. Patches were made of anything you can lay your hands on. Sometimes flour sacks with the backing" would be used for patching.[32] Purchasing of new clothing was rare for these women and their mothers. Vivian recounted, "I can remember my mother sitting at the sewing machine and making clothes."[33] Despite its necessity, for many of the Matriarchs sewing was an activity they respected. Ann talked about her mom's commitment, explaining that "sewing was her passion. When she was depressed, she sewed. When she was happy, she sewed."[34] Ruth Bird talked about her grandmother moving in after her mother passed at an early age. Her grandma would teach her to sew, "then take my mother's shirt and made one for me."[35] She also took Ruth's mother's coat and made it into a coat for Ruth's first son.

Turning old materials into new was a high-quality skill. The process of transforming old into new implied resourcefulness as a value and a way of life: "Grandma would go to the Salvation Army to buy a bunch of old coats and old clothes and give them to Mom. Mom would turn them over and make new jackets, coats, and dresses. Dresses, new everything. Well, they were new with old clothes."[36] Claudette shared how her mom made practical, functioning clothes. She expanded her sewing skills, working with a sewing collective in Manitoba, learning to work with fur, with northern designs like duffle coats, and with wool. Ann's mom would take an old men's coat and turn it inside out to make new jackets. The women did not use patterns. As Elsie explained, "They would just take the material and size you up, and cut it out like that and sew it up."[37] They would often make their own patterns. Sewing was perceived as an expression of their creativity and identity. Claudette shared that her mother experimented through colour combination but also through different mediums such as fur and hide.

Métis Women's Expression of Creativity, Kinship, Love, and Care

Through the women's sharing, we learned how sewing was an expression of Métis women's creativity, care, and love for their kin. Claudette remembers the sewing sound: "The sound of the sewing machine. That was my comfort."[38] Vivian shared, "I can remember my mother sitting at the sewing machine and making clothes and patching, so we wouldn't have to go to school with a hole in our jeans."[39] Elsie spoke of how her Godmother would make her clothes, including clothing for special occasions: "My Godmother would make mine when I needed something special."[40] Laurie Paul, Ruth's daughter, shared the special pieces made by her mother. She recalled, "Whenever we needed something, Mom would—like my sister and I, whenever we went to any weddings or anniversaries—Mom would always make us dresses. She would sew us dresses. She would make us our nightgowns, little baby dolls to go to bed in."[41] Ruth also shared about a special sewing project, a dress she started at age seventeen. At one point, she got frustrated with the project and put it away. She fondly recalled her grandmother coming to finish it for her. For Ruth, patience was one of the values that sewing taught her. Vivian also reflected on this: "You learn a lot of patience, and when you're talking to someone while doing it, you're visiting."[42] Some of the women spoke about how their mothers used sewing to move through periods of stress and illness.

Preserving their mothers' sewing machines, for example, treadle machines, sewing items, and other material culture, was important to the women. Claudette proudly displays her mother's artistic tools in her home. Their sewing tools not only held memories to be cherished but also held the knowledge and resilience of the women in their families. The daughters who participated in the interviews also shared how they cherished the creations made by their mothers and grandmothers. The material objects passed on from generation to generation allowed them to feel a connection, and to know that even though their relative had passed to the spirit world, they were still being cared for through the items, especially blankets made just for them. Norma shared how important it was for her to have her mom's (Auxile Lepine) handmade afghan on her bed: "On dirait que Maamaa est laa laa avec moi. [It's like Mom is right here with me.]"[43] Loretta Vandale (Marlene's daughter) also spoke proudly of a family heirloom in her possession. Ruth Bird, who lost her mother, talked about how her mother lives on through the repurposed items. The story of family belonging and kinship care lives in the clothing. Elsie spoke of the value of doing things well and right, and the time and patience it takes: "One of Mom's teachings—if it's worth doing, do it right, or else don't bother. It was a teaching translated in Cree. If you hate to do something for somebody else, don't do it."[44]

Community programming came later, in the 1970s and 1980s, through the 3HO Club and Métis Nation programs. In school, some of the women explained, sewing was taught as part of home economics, and not in the flexible visiting tradition, in the ways of their mothers and grandmothers. The Matriarchs shared the different ways in which they had learned. Most learned from their mothers, while some also took courses in the community for skill development purposes. Their mothers' generation would have been self-taught; they learned from their women kin. "My grandmother got sick, so Mom had to quit school and help at home," recalled Claudette.[45] Métis women leaving school to help their mothers care for their families was a common topic in the stories of our Matriarchs. Norma Gaudet left school in grade eight to help her mom with the care of her younger twin sisters. Education remained rooted in the home, and was taught within the family and community. Claudette's mom and older sister taught sewing classes in the former St. Louis Métis Hall. Vivian talked about each step in this learning: "Start here, go there."[46] Métis women valued sewing, and often hired women they knew and had relationships with. This community-based economic system assured that resources remained within the community and supported the community, in this case, the women and their households. This way of conceiving and supporting the economy ensured that family was an integral part of community wellness. The Matriarchs can help us expand our understanding of wellness to include kinship care, learning with one another, caring for one another, being creative and proud of one's accomplishments, and fostering values from generation to generation as part of our resourceful, talented, and resilient mindset.

In Discussion with Our Matriarchs

The Métis Matriarchs we interviewed have a sewing legacy in the region, telling their story of entrepreneurship, kin, strength, creativity, wellness, and love. Inheriting their moms' and grandmothers' items as family heirlooms—material cultural items such as family blankets—shows how valuable their creations were, and still are. The relationship of gift, maker, and receiver functions as a means of communication and expression of relationality and the spiritual process of alchemy. For some, these items are given a place of honour in the home, as they hold the vibrancy and currency of loved ones.

The multi-genre activity that we classify as "sewing" was broad. There is a need to more deeply examine sewing through the gender-critical lens of Indigenous women's sovereignty and relationality, as demonstrated by the Matriarchs. A critical lens offers a perspective on sewing within its context of social and economic wellness. Wellness can then be contextualized within the multifaceted expression of sewing that embodies long-standing kinship care. To help provide additional context, Dr. Sherry Farrell Racette's presentation at the 2018 Congress in Regina, Saskatchewan, spoke of how Métis women "dressed and blessed" the bodies of horses during Métis buffalo hunting brigades.[47] She shared pictures of an exquisitely beaded horse blanket, referring to each bead as a woman's prayer, beads of protection sewed together. In our research, we learned that Ann Lepine's mom made horse blankets in the community, and some still survive due to their high quality, made with care and commitment. In addition to their being highly respected and skilled in creative and complex design, we are reminded through the interviews of the diverse ways in which the Métis Matriarchs "dressed and blessed" their children, families, communities, and relatives, both human and non-human. Sewing is a connector to our grandmothers, Godmothers, mothers, sisters, and aunties, rooted in prayers of protection, belonging, beauty, and love.

The uninterrupted artistic practice of sewing was shared, remembered, and lived in three, and sometimes four, kinship generations of Métis women. Claudette proudly shared stories of her grandmother, mother, sisters, and herself, and how they also taught sewing in the community. The generations include kinship relations among Métis women that upheld mutual care and love. The ability to care for one another, in addition to hand-sewing and beading skills, remains important to these women despite the modernization of sewing technology. Pride, dignity, and sovereignty were evident as the women shared solutions for ensuring the continuity of sewing, and discussed the importance of a dedicated Métis women's sewing studio. The capacity to purchase sewing items, as their grandmothers did, was seen as important to ensure a balanced economy. The Matriarchs' sewing income was often redistributed toward family outings and within the community.

Reaffirming the value of sewing can help to address the emergence of a "throw-away" society, and to relearn and show respect for a value system based on resourcefulness, leading to what Vaughan calls "an economy of balance." Vaughan critiques the tensions of a patriarchal economic system and examines closely the radical differences upheld within "matriarchal societies grounded in an economic system of reciprocity."[48] Vivian talked about how "handmade items last longer."[49] This reaffirms a return to such values as defined, governed, and shared by the women: a work ethic, knowledge sharing, visiting, resourcefulness, and an economic system through which women provided and sustained intergenerational wellness. By using the sewing knowledge that many women had learned being with their mothers and grandmothers, Claudette felt, sewing could still serve as an economy for women with limited income. Norma said that it was important to ensure that women are sewing because they are interested in it, and that it is not imposed on them.

Sewing knowledge and skills remain pertinent in a contemporary context, and can become effective ways to regenerate mutually beneficial economic systems that include ways of learning. Some Matriarchs spoke of the expenses involved in sewing today, and pointed out that clothes can be purchased cheaply, minimizing the art of sewing. Many women do not know how to sew, and therefore Métis cultural knowledge, values, and teachings are not being passed down. In discussing the value of a dedicated Métis women's sewing studio, Matriarchs reminded us of the importance of interactive family and community sewing spaces.

Within these spaces, the Matriarchs promote a learning-by-doing model and a mentorship model rooted in kinship-caring practices. Many younger women do not have the skill set, so step-by-step instructions are needed to support continuity. The kitchen table as a symbol of women's authority has changed. Vivian suggested visiting and sitting with a granny or relative who still sews as a way to learn. We also know that the old ways of visiting have changed.[50] Learning in a non-institutional setting was seen as important because it allows flexibility in pattern-development, colour, and material choices, accessing self-creativity, and gathering together in a way that is meaningful. Learning within one's respective kinship system continues to be seen as a beautiful and caring way of upholding our old ways of being together. Sewing is a form of embodying kinship. As our interviews revealed, the living experiences upheld within family systems speak to how Métis women's material culture has, as Farrell Racette asserts, its own stories to tell.

Conclusion

When we story with and learn from our Métis Matriarchs, our women's social kinship system is strengthened. We increasingly think of one another, exchange with one another, rely on one another, support and help one another, and reflect on how we and our families can live well in the changing future. An interactive sewing/creative space and culture, established within a contemporary context, reinforces the importance of rethinking social and economic wellness through the lens of Métis women's community engagement, community care, and community resourcefulness. In listening and visiting with our Matriarchs, we feel encouraged to be more mindful in the ways we speak (what stories we tell), and how we own ourselves by telling our own stories. What does wellness mean to us? Métis Women Sewing All Together—kood toot aansamb, as expressed to us in Michif by our Michif relative Graham Andrews—is a Michif life philosophy connected to properly putting the pieces together when we do things all together. We, in a collective, inclusive sense, are mending that which, and those who, need to be looked after. It is a spiritual, multi-dimensional approach embodied by Métis women/Lii Faam Michif, together sewing justice, wellness, and healing.

Maarsi to the generations of Métis Matriarchs for guiding the good way of putting the pieces of our life teachings and women's knowledge back together, and helping us to engage with and reflect deeply on the cultural meanings of sewing and mending. You are the leaders we need to turn toward to regenerate toot aansamb a just and kind Nation for our kin today, and for those to come.

Acknowledgements

We are grateful to the Matriarchs for sharing their stories, time, and commitment to keeping our family and communities healthy and happy. We also are appreciative of the research assistance provided by Hannah Bouvier, a University of Alberta Métis student.

We acknowledge the funding support provided by the Canadian Institutes of Health Research Catalyst Grant, advancing Indigenous approaches to wellness research.

Notes

1 Adese, "Spirit Gifting"; K. Anderson, *Life Stages*; Carrière and Richardson, *Calling*; Dorion, "Opikinawasowin"; Fiola, *Rekindling*; Flaminio, "Kiyokewin"; Flaminio, Gaudet, and Dorion, "Métis Women Gathering"; Hodgson-Smith and Kermoal, "Community-Based Research"; Kermoal, "Métis Women's"; Macdougall, *One of the Family*; Macdougall, "Land, Family and Identity"; Monchalin and Monchalin, "Closing"; Payment, *The Free People*; St-Onge, "Memories of Métis Women"; Troupe, *Expressing Our Heritage*.

2 Monchalin and Monchalin, "Closing," 2.

3 Macdougall, "Land, Family and Identity," 10.

4 Dorion, *Country Wives*.

5 Farrell Racette, "Beads"; Farrell Racette, "Sewing"; Troupe, *Expressing Our Heritage*.

6 Farrell Racette, "Sewing."

7 Ibid., 69.

8 Troupe, *Expressing Our Heritage*, 10.

9 Ibid.

10 See Flaminio, Gaudet, and Dorion, "Métis Women Gathering."

11 K. Anderson, *Life Stages*.

12 Vaughan, *Women and the Gift Economy*, 104.
13 Kovach, "Conversational Method"; Kovach, "Emerging from the Margins"; Kovach, *Indigenous Methodologies*.
14 Elsie Sanderson, personal communication, 2019.
15 Sophie McDougall, personal communication, 2019.
16 Marlene Vandale, personal communication, 2019.
17 Vivian Meabry, personal communication, 2019.
18 Ruth Bird, personal communication, 2019.
19 Vivian Meabry, personal communication, 2019.
20 Claudette Lavergne, personal communication, 2019.
21 Ann Lepine, personal communication, 2019.
22 Loretta Vandale, personal communication, 2019.
23 Ann Lepine, personal communication, 2019.
24 Ruth Bird, personal communication, 2019.
25 Sophie McDougall, personal communication, 2020.
26 Ann Lepine, personal communication, 2019.
27 Norma Gaudet, personal communication, 2019.
28 Vivian Meabry, personal communication, 2019.
29 Ibid.
30 Marlene Vandale, personal communication, 2019.
31 Vivian Meabry, personal communication, 2019.
32 Ibid.
33 Ibid.
34 Ann Lepine, personal communication, 2019.
35 Ruth Bird, personal communication, 2019.
36 Claudette Lavergne, personal communication, 2019.
37 Elsie Sanderson, personal communication, 2019.
38 Claudette Lavergne, personal communication, 2019.
39 Vivian Meabry, personal communication, 2019.
40 Elsie Sanderson, personal communication, 2019.
41 Laurie Paul, personal communication, 2019.
42 Vivian Meabry, personal communication, 2019.
43 Norma Gaudet, personal communication, 2019.
44 Elsie Sanderson, personal communication, 2019.
45 Claudette Lavergne, personal communication, 2019.
46 Vivian Meabry, personal communication, 2019.
47 Farrell Racette, "Kitchen Table Theory."
48 Vaughan, *Women and the Gift Economy*, 101.
49 Vivian Meabry, personal communication, 2019.
50 Flaminio, Gaudet, and Dorion, "Métis Women Gathering."

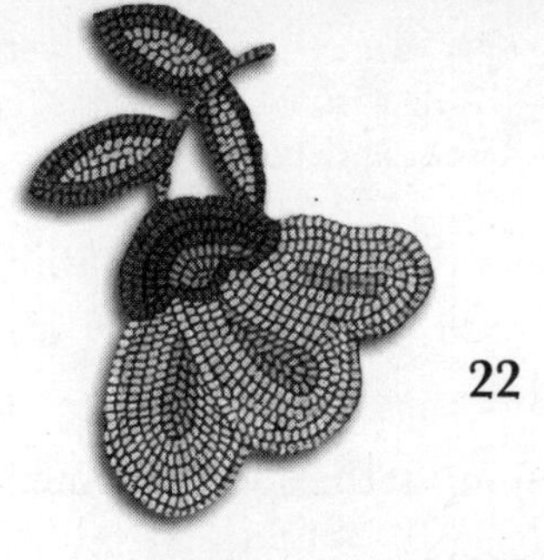

22

if the land could speak

Rita Bouvier

"if the land could speak" was initially prepared for a panel address on "Body, Memory, Language" at Indigenous Intervention into the "Indigenous Narrative" conference held at the Institute of Indigenous American Arts, Santa Fe, New Mexico, in 2016.

> *"Listen, there are words almost everywhere. I realized that in a chance moment. Words are in the air, in our blood, words were always there. . . . Words are in the snow, trees, leaves, wind, birds, beaver, the sound of ice cracking; words are in fish and mongrels, where they've been since we came to this place with the animals."*
>
> —Kimberley Blaser, quoting from Gerald Vizenor, *Landfill Meditation*, 8

Introduction

sometimes I find myself weeping at the oddest moment[1]

sometimes
I find myself
weeping
at the oddest moment.

an unexpected voice
mônôk Andre
calling Christmas day
wishing me
a Merry Christmas.

and I am
that little girl
walking across the lake
with her grandfather
to check on the snares
and traps he has set
in this frost
exploding moon
on surrounding islands.

the frost is biting
and he motions I walk
in the shade
of his warm body.

soon, he claims
we will be
in the thick of brush
and we will make a fire
to warm our bodies
drink li tî muskeg.

Sometimes, the weight of the world weighs heavy on my shoulders. The words of my late grandfather haunt me. I am leaving my home community for the first time to attend high school in the south, and he is worried I will forget my mother tongue; I will forget the ways of knowing, seeing, and being they have passed on to me; and worse, I will think myself better than the people of my community. It also springs from an implied ethical responsibility and relationship with learners implicit in my profession in the education system, and implied in the polysynthetic[2] word *okiskinohamâkêw*—one who shows the way with future generations in mind, and to my creative practice as a poet.

Sometimes, breaking through the "brick wall"[3]—the universalizing western thought and tradition of the "education system" I have been immersed in—to imagine and create is nothing short of monumental. In an embattled lingering colonial state, *words* have/are often used to demonize and dehumanize our experiences.[4] But we also know from our storytelling traditions that *words* are transformative and can be used to weave a human story of purpose and survival—one that acknowledges culturally diverse ways of knowing and being in the world to address the frailties of human existence in a living, dynamic universe that we do not control. Knowing this, how does one give expression to one's existence and make whole one's aliveness in the world, here and now? Poetry as an artistic/creative and cultural expression of a lived life in a messed-up world can provide beauty and insight on how to reconcile the transgressions on our sacred bodies and lands, by creating anew our relationships and by remembering to live in this place with grace, humility, love, and joy. However, *words* are only one aspect of language; languages also encompass a worldview and culturally significant performative measures that can be utilized to give perspective and meaning on the page and in oral recitation. Like all ancient cultures, Indigenous peoples worldwide are rich in the traditions of storytelling, enriched by languages to explain the origin, purpose, and meaning of life, to posit significant questions on the purposefulness of being.[5]

This paper is a creative exploration of how I apply and use my mother tongue in my own artistic practice to shape my own consciousness and imagination, to transcend and navigate the oppressive conditions that have rendered our intellectual traditions as lacking depth and/or as obsolete. Is the meaning embedded in my first language lost in translation? Perhaps, but like many other Indigenous writers, I am conscious of staying the course and legacy of my ancestors, persisting in defining my community and myself by bringing my first language to work and to play for me.[6]

Sometimes, I apply my first language strategically without translation or with translation in juxtaposition, knowing full well that its meaning is not equivalent in the absence of a shared worldview. Other times, it is used resourcefully and creatively, drawing on its sound and/or meaning. In this case, only the Michif-Cree speaker and perhaps a discernable listener would catch the subtlety or double entendre. The use of the sonic mnemonic sound of seagulls, "kiyâs, kiyâs, kiyâs" in "under the cover of rain" in *nakamowin'sa for the seasons*[7] is an example. It also contains an aspect of a phrase for someone who is a liar. Or, simply, the poem is a translation from my mother tongue into English. In hindsight, I think I could have served such poems better by sticking to my first language, such as in "a Cree soliloquy" in *papîyâhtak*[8] and "Just Another Barroom Conversation" in *Blueberry Clouds*.[9] The latter is hilarious in my first language.

My first language is applied in the context of remembering knowledge passed down to me, by dreaming, by gathering strength—resisting and reconciling what has happened and is happening to our communities and to the natural environment, and by rejoicing in the one life gifted to me. More often, I find myself returning to "place"[10]—to the sounding of *the music of our mother's movement and voice*—as an important source of knowing and being human.

ikiskisiyan—I am remembering

As I stir in my bed for a comfortable spot, I can hear *nimoshôm* rattling pots by the blackened woodstove. He doesn't like to drink his tea at sunrise alone, and so he seizes the opportunity to entice me out of bed on this occasion.

nimoshôm and I[11]

caw! caw! caw!
the crows are calling
nitanis wanisca! my daughter wake up!
it is time to begin the day.
we will be home
when the sun is straight over our heads
and I will fry fresh l'dôrrî wall-eyed pike
over the open fire
and nitanis
the tastiest part will be for you.

the sun is just peeking
over Big Island
mist rising off the lake
when nimoshôm and I set out. my grandfather
there is a perfect spot
over there, he points
a slight movement
of his lips and chin.

we stop to set our net.
I guide the canoe towards the mainland,
church steeple my guide.
it is the same journey we take
after the nets are cleaned
dried and mended.
it is reassuring to know

what is asked of me.
it is reassuring to hear
my grandfather's voice—

êkosi *ekwa nitânis*	*that's it for now my daughter*
kîwîtak ekwa.	*let's go home now*

I remember our kinship is always relationally stated to life (seen and unseen) around us. However, it isn't only words that reflect and enact this relationship with others and the rest of the world; long silences (as white space on the page) can also accomplish this state of being. I grew up on an island, known to the local people as Ile Bouleau—Birch Island, in my home community of *sakitawak* or Île-à-la-Crosse in Saskatchewan. sakitawak is the physical, emotional, geographical, and spiritual space I connected to first when I came to this world. This is the place where I met my family, became familiar with entities of the natural world (seen and unseen), which gave me a language: a way of seeing, knowing, and being in the world, albeit mixed with the influences of many different cultures and the Catholic Church. Multicultural and multilingual in its heyday,[12] the people speak Michif. Linguistically, the Michif of my home community is Cree-based (y-dialect *borrowed* from the Cree inhabiting the region and with whom we have a strong abiding kinship)[13] with French nouns thrown in for good measure, often combining the grammatical rules of both languages.[14] By the time I was old enough to attend school, the language of instruction at the school, run by the Oblates of Mary Immaculate and the Grey Nuns, was English before I had learned to speak, read, and write in the language.

Despite the challenge of this policy, I loved school (who doesn't love life's purpose of learning), the exception being when my wandering mind would get me into trouble with my teachers. A daydreamer, I hold memories of whacks to the head for not paying attention. During the warmer times of the year, I could hardly wait for school to end. Mimicking our teachers, my cousin Josie and I would start the lessons of the day all over again in a work shed that our grandfather used to dry medicinal herbs on rafters high over our head. The sweet pungent smell still fills my nostrils when I tell the story. Our cousins and siblings didn't seem to mind when Josie and I would take turns reliving the lessons of the day. Cousins and siblings who were not old enough to attend school were welcome in "our school." It was the way we were taught to be. When we got tired, the whole thing would dissipate without much ado, as it is the way with all children. Then, with the whole island as our playground, we would move to a collective game of hide and seek, again inclusive of our younger siblings. As the sun shone and we were *borne up into clouds,*[15] the days seemed endless then.

ipôwâtaman—I am dreaming

All humans are innately curious. *tâpwê!* On the side of a sandstone cliff in south-central Saskatchewan, Canada, are petroglyphs of several symbols—human and animal. After a rain, a time when the petroglyphs appear to show up more clearly, a petroglyph of a stylized human face appears to be crying. I wonder why?

one morning after the rain[16]

her breath a whisper she awakens her brood
wild creatures in first light her offering
a song of songs   only birds can sing.
hillside a light mist clings covering her face.

the early light catches each strand of grass
swaying in the breeze   imitating the flow of life.
the grass dance is sure to begin   but not
until the night hawk on his perch rests.

in glory blood red sky blue grass yellow
dancers will whirl and whirl and whirl a circle
in honour of her beauty.   humbled.
a winged mid-flight embrace of birds is a reminder

they know this place better than anyone. she cries
in relief when rains come knowing all is well.

if the land could speak . . . and it does each and every time the consciousness embedded in Indigenous languages is shared, spoken, and heard. Our languages carry the memories and ethos of place—the mnemonic-sonic sounds of our relatives, and the sacred laws governing life and our relationships. Our active, verb-based languages also remind us everything is alive and changing. When we listen deeply, our mother's movement and voice touch us, shaping our consciousness and imagination. Our languages, then, are an indispensable part of being from this place that we know as Turtle Island, and the etymology—the knowledge gained through study of our languages is a gift that belongs to all of us.

isohkitaman—I am gathering strength

As an educator and a writer, I have many opportunities to weave my cultural story, my Indigenist/feminist concerns, and acts of resistance together, albeit with difficulty on occasion. Retired, I am self-employed, supporting the work of communities and organizations promoting lifelong learning and the holistic well-being of our communities. Challenging the material and imaginative failures of colonial policies resulting in genocide—extermination through residential schools, displacement, depopulation through disease, neglect, and the continuing marginalization of our knowledge systems and languages through an imposed Eurocentric education is difficult work, as is undoing its effects on our communities.[17]

What sustains me in this work and in my own writing is the foundation of love fostered in my early education, naming the world guided by people who loved me, and a language embedded with an ethos of being in relationship—in kinship with all the people and life around me. This is a space/time when squirrels were relatives. This is a space/time when it rained, my grandparents would say: *imatout nitanis—she [they] is [are] crying, my daughter. tapwe!*—this is the truth! And such truths were underscored—a significant performative measure as I have done time and time again. My schooling in the English language challenged every aspect of this learning. Eventually, I learned to navigate and live in this complex and challenging environment but not without loss and a pervading sense of longing. Through "education"—credentialed, self-directed, but mostly through dialogue with others of like mind, heart, and spirit in various national and global movements committed to justice and equality, I learned how entrenched and entangled Eurocentric and hierarchical *thinking* was and is in our lives—in law, economics, science, religion, education, and so-called history reinforced through our public education systems. I have wondered aloud: to what extent are we entangled and complicit in this mess?

Reconciling the complicity of Catholic priests in our struggles to hold on to a land base in the Northwest region of Canada prior to the creation of Manitoba, Saskatchewan, and Alberta as provinces was challenging but important to me, because of the respect and love I had for my grandmother. Her faith in the goodness of humanity was unwavering, especially for those who dedicated their lives to *kisîman'tô*—the kind, loving creator of all. In this poem, I imagine how a priest complicit in the land grab reconciles his own humanity in a letter to a friend. The poem is dedicated to my late grandmother, Flora (Gardiner) Bouvier.

letter to a friend[18]

my dear friend,
as the railway trails its way
                    west
there is unrest among the Indians
                    and the Metis.

Louis Riel has appeared
on the Canadian scene
                    once again
                    a thorn
in the side of government.

the government has nearly
completed its operation
of impounding the Cree,

but Big Bear is no one's fool.

the Indians are in a sad state
throughout *the Northwest*.
living in confined spaces

many are starving
rations, having been withheld.

a blind government
has sent small foolish men
to lord over them.
all the while settlers arrive
on promised land
        splashing upon its valleys
        and washing over its ridges.

what will become of the Indian?
land on which the Metis live
has been surveyed
the Metis fear
their land will be taken
        sub-divided
against their wishes
        once again.
a people can not raise their young
        homeless.
a people can not live on air
        alone.

what will become of the Metis?

the Metis, who have treated us
        like family
now show distrust for us
questioning our loyalty.

the government is not
        without blame
        having ignored
all their petitions to be heard.

on this winter, star lit night
the beauty of kîwîtin shines.   district of the north wind
I pray for you and wish you well.

your friend, Father LaCombe
December 1884

As stated earlier, on more than one occasion, the relationship fostered with a living, dynamic universe in my mother tongue has been my salvation. My grandmother's singsong laments of human frailties to the unseen energies of the universe resonate. Thinking in my mother tongue and applying the foundational values/principles embedded in the language have nurtured my own being, even though my education in my first language ended abruptly when I was thirteen years of age, leaving me with a pervading sense of loss and longing.

Indigenous peoples' intellectual and imaginative engagement worldwide is making a significant dent on the dominant Eurocentric consciousness permeating the globe—a *thinking* based on a hierarchy of being, on racial and gender-bound exclusions as rational to displace people from place—their lands, their languages, and their identities, and then reinforced through history, systems, and institutions.[19] Indigenous narratives—the stories and *thinking* offered by Indigenous scholars and artists are important to the well-being of our communities, and perhaps to the well-being of our planet.

Sadly, the nexus of this predominant western philosophical tradition has been science, sometimes with religion not far behind.[20] This is not to suggest that the knowledge and wisdom that come from the tradition of the sciences and spiritual dimensions of religions have nothing to offer us. My own community and nation, the Metis, were not averse to *borrowing* the best of all the intellectual traditions presenting themselves through kinship and love of the land that gave them life.[21] They embraced the spiritual influences of both the "gratitude rituals/ceremonies" of our Indigenous ancestors and the Catholic Church, and from both informal and formal education processes (where available) for the survival and well-being of their families and communities.[22] I note *sadly* because science—read as a study of "the natural world"—*is* the foundation of the core values and teachings of Indigenous peoples worldwide, and it *is* at the core of Indigenous spirituality. Interdependence is not a wishy-washy idea.

imiyowâtaman—I am rejoicing

We are human and we are but a small part of life. Whatever inner or outer landscapes we find ourselves in, it is easy to make a fool of oneself. I had been immersed in all that is poetry 24–7 for seven days at Banff's Writing with Style program in 2013. I was in a vulnerable state emotionally, having spent time writing and rewriting poetry for a collection I was working on. In our last gathering, Elizabeth Phillips, coordinator of the program (and later, editor for my collection), wished us the best and issued a bit of caution. Half serious and half joking, she shared with us how many a participant had left their job, their family, or moved halfway around the world following such an intense experience.

While waiting to board my flight home at the Calgary airport, I had a glass of wine and reflected on the week—the places I had travelled in my head and in my heart, and all that I was thankful for—an invocation of sorts, albeit with a glass of red wine in my hand. When my flight was called, I gathered my belongings and headed to my gate. A few steps away, I came upon a wall of made-in-China Indigenous goods. It was too much for a full and heavy heart. Inspired by the Irish poet Paul Durcan's imaginative and humorous narrative tradition, I wrote *for sale.*

for sale[23]

thanks for the warning,

the rain of love to ease the coming down

from heights of snow-capped mountains,

soaring solitary eagle flights.

maybe it wasn't a good decision
to have a glass of wine
with my tortilla soup after all;
but I wanted to extend the glow,

the orgy of poetry and mountain air.
recount the gems I collected along the way.
enjambment taking us to . . .
unknown territories.

the ghazal, couplet like
tips of trees rising
out of water.   punctuation . . .
is punctuation. need I say more?

the servitude of emotion
for the poem and only the poem.
and, if the poem isn't working
begin with the last line.

words.   just remember
every   single   last   one
is important.   turn each one
over and over again.

kill the darlings!
erase your footsteps!
get out of the poem!
listen deeply, be still—

dadirri, I whisper to myself,
when the call of a gate change
for passengers heading to Saskatoon
reminds me I am at the Calgary airport.

I rise slowly taking that last sip,
head to gate 50, my brown leather-bound
notebook clutched close to the heart.
the next moment though is unclear

when I suddenly find myself
sobbing at the site
of "authentic" Indigenous goods
for sale, recalling:

every word counts.
it's The Trading Post Rita,
get a fucking grip on yourself
people are watching you

fall apart, unravel
the mystery of your circumstance.
a pretty mukluked brown faced
doll   dream catching,

amidst an abundance of
real stones, gems and turquoise.
moose jerky and token animals
is not the real thing.

the new-aged sounds of nature,
the ancient drum songs

on a hard-pressed disc,
near a reel Indian

head-dressed next to the Inukshuk
are made in China,
for God's sake.
take flight and just remember:

what is not for sale.

Conclusion

Perhaps, the greater work—our greater responsibility in this time of Indigenous renaissance or resurgence lies right in front of us, on the lands from which we sprang and to the sounding—*the music of our mother's movement and voice*, of which our unique and distinctive languages are a part of the whole. Through scholarship and artistic expressions, we can animate our rich and generative cultural legacies as a gift to our communities and the world. *nitanis kimâmitonicikan âpacitâh* echoes in my ear; it is my grandfather, the late Joseph Bouvier, speaking to me in relationship, reminding me to use the power of my mind and imagination.

maarsi, niwîciwâkanak—thank you my fellow travellers—ones with whom I make a path for listening and hearing my words today!

Notes

1 R. Bouvier, *Blueberry Clouds*.

2 Another term used recently by Neuhaus (*Decolonizing Poetics*) is "holophrase," meaning a one-sentence word or clause.

3 Blair, *Privileging*. Not intended as pejorative but to reinforce that processes of the re/production of knowledge in this system is "lock step," referring specifically to research processes required of students engaged in the completion of a master's and/or doctoral level work, and the primacy of objectivity versus subjectivity.

4 LaRocque, *When the Other*.

5 Hymes, *"In Vain."*
6 McLeod, "Introduction."
7 R. Bouvier, *nakamowin'sa.*
8 R. Bouvier, *papîyâhtak.*
9 R. Bouvier, *Blueberry Clouds.*
10 "Place" defined as multi-dimensional—physical and spiritual, relational, experiential, local, and land-based (Michell et al., *Learning Indigenous Science*).
11 R. Bouvier, *Blueberry Clouds.*
12 Daum Shanks, "Searching for Sakitawak."
13 It is also important to note that sakitawak has a strong kinship with the Dene, who live down the river from us. A few Dene words and expressions are manifest from time to time. My late grandfather lovingly referred to me in front of his friends as "ma'petit fou yazza." I know "yazza" is not a Cree derivative.
14 Bakker, *A Language of Our Own.*
15 R. Bouvier, *nakamowin'sa.*
16 Ibid.
17 Ibid.
18 R. Bouvier, *papîyâhtak,* 61.
19 L. Smith, *Decolonizing Methodologies*; Hoppers and Richards, *Rethinking Thinking.*
20 Deloria, *Evolution.*
21 Daum Shanks, "Searching for Sakitawak."
22 Anuik, "Métis Families."
23 R. Bouvier, *nakamowin'sa.*

BIBLIOGRAPHY

Absolon, Kathleen. *Kaandossiwin: How We Come to Know.* Black Point: Fernwood Publishing, 2011.

Acoose, Janice. *Iskwewak Kah' Ki Yaw Ni Wahkomakanak: Neither Indian Princesses nor Easy Squaws.* Toronto: Women's Press, 1995.

Adams, Howard. *Prison of Grass: Canada from the Native Point of View.* Toronto: General Publishing, 1975.

———. *Prison of Grass: Canada from the Native Point of View.* Rev. ed. Markham: Fifth House, 1989.

———. *A Tortured People: The Politics of Colonization.* Penticton: Theytus Books, 1995.

Adese, Jennifer. "Restoring the Balance: Métis Women and Contemporary Nationalist Political Organizing." In *A People and a Nation: New Directions in Contemporary Métis Studies*, edited by Jennifer Adese and Chris Andersen, 115–45. Vancouver: UBC Press, 2021.

———. "'R' Is for Métis: Contradictions in Scrip and Census in the Construction of a Colonial Métis Identity." *TOPIA: Canadian Journal of Cultural Studies* 25 (September 2011): 203–12.

———. "Spirit Gifting: Ecological Knowing in Métis Life Narratives." *Decolonization: Indigeneity, Educations Society* 3, no. 3 (2014): 48–66.

Adese, Jennifer, and Zoe Todd. "Mediating Métis Identity: An Interview with Jennifer Adese and Zoe Todd." Interview by Shaun Stevenson. *MediaTropes* 7, no. 1 (2017): 1–25. https://mediatropes.com/index.php/Mediatropes/article/view/29157.

Ahmed, Sara. *Complaint!* Durham: Duke University Press, 2021.

Albert, Caroline. "An Exploration of Indigenousness in the Western University Institution." *Canadian Journal of Native Education* 31, no. 1 (2008): 41–55.

Alfred, Taiaiake, and Jeff Corntassel. "Being Indigenous: Resurgences against Contemporary Colonialism." *Government and Opposition* 40, no. 4 (2005): 597–614.

Allen, Peter. "*Geneish: An Indian Girlhood* by Jane Willis, and: *Halfbreed* by Maria Campbell, and: *No Foreign Land: The Biography of a North American Indian* by Wilfred Pelletier and Ted Poole (Review)." *University of Toronto Quarterly* 43, no. 4 (1974): 405–9.

Amott, Teresa, and Julie Matthaei. *Race, Gender and Work: A Multicultural Economic History of Women in the U.S.* 2nd ed. Boston: South End Press, 1999.

———. *The First Métis: A New Nation*. Edmonton: UVISCO Press, 1985.

Andersen, Chris. *"Métis": Race, Recognition, and the Struggle for Indigenous Peoplehood.* Vancouver: UBC Press, 2014.

———. "Urban Aboriginality as a Distinctive Identity, in Twelve Parts." In *Indigenous in the City: Contemporary Identities and Cultural Innovation*, edited by Evelyn Peters and Chris Andersen, 46–68. Vancouver: UBC Press, 2013.

Andersen, Chris, and Jennifer Adese. "Introduction: A New Era of Métis Studies Scholarship." In *A People and a Nation: New Directions in Contemporary Métis Studies*, edited by Jennifer Adese and Chris Andersen, 3–17. Vancouver: UBC Press, 2021.

Anderson, Anne. "Affirmations of an Indigenous Feminist." In *Indigenous Women and Feminism: Politics, Activism, Culture*, edited by Cheryl Suzack, Shari M. Huhndorf, Jeanne Perreault, and Jean Barman, 81–91. Vancouver: UBC Press, 2010.

Anderson, Kim. "Kika'ige Historical Society." *Shekon Neechie*, 21 June 2018. https://shekonneechie.ca/2018/06/21/kikaige-historical-society/.

———. *Life Stages and Native Women: Memory, Teachings, and Story Medicine.* Winnipeg: University of Manitoba Press, 2011.

———. "Multi-Generational Indigenous Feminisms: From F word to what IFs 1." In *Routledge Handbook of Critical Indigenous Studies*, edited by Brendan Hokowhitu, Aileen Moreton-Robinson, Linda Tuhiwai-Smith, and Chris Andersen, 37–51. New York: Routledge, 2020.

———. "On Seasons of an Indigenous Feminism, Kinship, and the Program of Home Management." *Hypatia* 35, no. 1 (2020): 204–13.

———. *A Recognition of Being: Reconstructing Native Womanhood.* 1st ed. Toronto: Sumach Press, 2000.

Anderson, Kim, Maria Campbell, and Christi Belcourt, eds. *Keetsahnak / Our Missing and Murdered Indigenous Sisters.* Edmonton: University of Alberta Press, 2018.

Anderson, Kim, and Bonita Lawrence. *Strong Women Stories: Native Vision and Community Survival.* Toronto: Sumach Press, 2003.

Anderson, Kim, Elena Flores Ruíz, Georgina Tuari Stewart, and Madina Tlostanova. "What Can Indigenous Feminist Knowledge and Practices Bring to 'Indigenizing' the Academy?" *Journal of World Philosophies* 4, no. 1 (2019): 121–55.

Anuik, Jonathon. "Métis Families and Schools: The Decline and Reclamation of Métis Identities in Saskatchewan, 1885–1980." PhD diss., University of Saskatchewan, 2009. https://harvest.usask.ca/handle/10388/etd-03252009-161825.

Archibald, Jo-Ann. *Indigenous Storywork: Educating the Heart, Mind, Body, and Spirit.* Vancouver: UBC Press, 2008.

Arvin, Maile, Eve Tuck, and Angie Morrill. "Decolonizing Feminism: Challenging Connections between Settler Colonialism and Heteropatriarchy." *Feminist Formations* 25, no. 1 (2013): 8–34.

Association of Canadian Deans of Education. "Accord on Indigenous Education." 2010. https://csse-scee.ca/acde/wp-content/uploads/sites/7/2017/08/Accord-on-Indigenous-Education.pdf.

Atalay, Sonya. "Indigenous Archaeology as Decolonizing Practice." *American Indian Quarterly* 30, no. 3/4 (2006): 280–310.

Atter, Heidi. "'It's About Feeling Seen': Métis Collective Hopes to Bring Young People Together Online from across Canada." *CBC News*, 22 April 2019. https://www.cbc.ca/news/canada/saskatchewan/metis-collective-young-people-across-canada-1.5106487.

Bailey, Moya. *Misogynoir Transformed: Black Women's Digital Resistance.* New York: New York University Press, 2021.

Bakker, Peter. *A Language of Our Own: The Genesis of Michif, the Mixed Cree-French Language of the Canadian Métis.* Oxford Studies in Anthropological Linguistics. New York: Oxford University Press, 1997.

Ball, Jessica, and Pauline Janyst. "Enacting Research Ethics in Partnerships with Indigenous Communities in Canada: 'Do It in a Good Way.'" *Journal of Empirical Research on Human Research Ethics* 3, no. 2 (2008): 33–51.

Bang, Megan, Lawence Curley, Adam Kessel, Amanda Marin, Eli S. Sukovich III, and George Strack. "Muskrat Theories, Tobacco in the Streets, and Living Chicago as Indigenous Land." *Environmental Education Research* 20, no. 1 (2014): 37–55.

Bannerji, Himani. *The Dark Side of the Nation: Essays on Multiculturalism, Nationalism, and Gender.* Toronto: Canadian Scholars Press, 2000.

Barkwell, Lawrence. "Audreen Hourie: Cultural Education and Patriot." The Virtual Museum of Métis History and Culture, 27 May 2008. https://www.metismuseum.ca/resource.php/07411.

———. "Maria Campbell." The Virtual Museum of Métis History and Culture, 12 January 2010. https://www.metismuseum.ca/resource.php/11900.

———. "Victoria Anne (Belcourt) Callihoo." The Virtual Museum of Métis History and Culture, 10 October 2013. https://www.metismuseum.ca/resource.php/13921.

Barkwell, Lawrence, Leah Dorion, and Audreen Hourie. *Métis Legacy II: Michif Culture, Heritage, and Folkways.* Saskatoon: Gabriel Dumont Institute of Native Studies and Applied Research, 2006.

Barkwell, Lawrence, Leah Dorion, and Darren Préfontaine. *Métis Legacy: A Métis Historiography and Annotated Bibliography.* Saskatoon: Gabriel Dumont Institute, 2001.

Barkwell, Lawrence, Darren Préfontaine, and Anne Carrière-Acco. "Metis Spirituality." In *Metis Legacy II*, edited by Lawrence Barkwell, Leah Dorion, and Audreen Hourie, 184–99. Saskatoon: Gabriel Dumont Institute of Native Studies and Applied Research, 2006.

Barron, F. Laurie, and James B. Waldram, eds. *1885 and After: Native Society in Transition.* Regina: Canadian Plains Research Center, 1986.

Bastien, Betty. *Blackfoot Ways of Knowing: The Worldview of the Siksikaitsitapi.* Calgary: University of Calgary Press, 2004.

Battiste, Marie Ann. *Decolonizing Education: Nourishing the Learning Spirit.* Saskatoon: Purich Publishing, 2013.

BBC News. "Proud Boys: Canada Labels Far-Right Group a Terrorist Entity." *BBC News*, 3 February 2021. https://www.bbc.com/news/world-us-canada-55923485.

Beals, Ann Marie, and Ciann Wilson. "Mixed-Blood: Indigenous-Black Identity in Colonial Canada." *AlterNative: An International Journal of Indigenous Peoples* 16, no. 1 (2020): 29–37.

Bédard, Renée. "An Anishinaabe-kwe Ideology on Mothering and Motherhood." In *"Until Our Hearts Are On the Ground": Aboriginal Mothering, Oppression, Resistance and Rebirth*, edited by Memee Lavell-Harvard and Jeannette Lavell, 65–75. Toronto: Demeter Press, 2006.

Belanger, Yale D. "Breaching Reserve Boundaries: Canada v. Misquadis and the Legal Creation of the Urban Aboriginal Community." In *Indigenous in the City: Contemporary Identities and Cultural Innovation*, edited by Evelyn Peters and Chris Andersen, 69–87. Vancouver: UBC Press, 2013.

Bell, B. "Gender in Native America." In *A Companion to American Indian History*, edited by Philip J. Deloria and Neal Salisbury, 307–20. New York: John Wiley and Sons, 2002.

Benton-Banai, Edward. *The Mishomis Book: The Voice of the Ojibway*. Hayward: Indian Country Communications, 1988.

Bird-Wilson, Lisa. *Is An Institute of Our Own: A History of the Gabriel Dumont Institute.* Saskatoon: Gabriel Dumont Institute of Native Studies and Applied Research, 2011.

Blair, Nerida. *Privileging Australian Indigenous Knowledge: Sweet Potatoes, Spiders, Waterlilys and Brick Walls.* Urbana-Champaign: Common Ground Publishing, 2015.

Blaser, Kimberly M. *Gerald Vizenor: Writing in the Oral Tradition*. Norman: University of Oklahoma Press, 1996.

Blumlo, Daniel I. "The Creoles of Russian America." In *Contours of a People: Metis Family, Mobility, and History*, edited by Brenda Macdougall, Carolyn Podruchny, and Nicole St-Onge, 368–91. Norman: University of Oklahoma Press, 2012.

Blunt, Marney. "Manitoba Judge Rules Province's Legislation Concerning Legal Parentage Unconstitutional." *Global News*, 9 November 2020. https://globalnews.ca/news/7452487/judge-manitoba-legal-parentage-legislation-unconstitutional/.

Bonvillain, Nancy. "Gender Relations in Native North America." *American Indian Culture and Research Journal* 13, no. 2 (1989): 1–28.

Bouvier, Rita. *Blueberry Clouds*. Saskatoon: Thistledown Press, 1999.

———. *nakamowin'sa for the seasons*. Saskatoon: Thistledown Press, 2015.

———. *papîyâhtak*. Saskatoon: Thistledown Press, 2004.

Bouvier, Victoria. "kaa-waakohtoochik (The Ones Who are Related to Each Other): An Inquiry of Métis Understandings With/In/Through the City." Accessed 8 February 2023. https:www.livingmichif.com.

———. "Ni kaakiihtwaamaan itootamihk waapamishoon aan mii wiichaytoowuk: I Am Practice Reflected in Relationships." *Book 2.0* 9, nos. 1/2 (2019): 31–44.

———. "Restorying Métis Spirit: Honouring Lived Experiences." Master's thesis, University of Calgary, 2016. https://prism.ucalgary.ca/handle/11023/2963.

———. "Truthing: An Ontology of Living an Ethic of *Shakihi* (Love) and *Ikkimmapiipitsin* (Sanctified kindness)." *Canadian Social Studies* 50, no. 2 (2018): 39–44.

Bouvier, Victoria, and Jennifer MacDonald. "Spiritual Exchange: A Methodology for a Living Inquiry with All Our Relations." *International Journal of Qualitative Methods* 18 (2019). https://doi.org/10.1177/1609406919851636.

Brayboy, Duane. "Two-Spirits, One Heart, Five Genders." *Indian Country Today Media Network*, updated 13 September 2018. https://ictnews.org/archive/two-spirits-one-heart-five-genders.

Brown, Jennifer S.H. *Strangers in Blood: Fur Trade Company Families in Indian Country*. Vancouver: UBC Press, 1980.

———. "Woman as Centre and Symbol in the Emergence of Métis Communities." *Canadian Journal of Native Studies* 3, no. 1 (1983): 39–46.

Brubaker, Rogers, and Frederick Cooper. "Beyond 'Identity.'" *Theory and Society* 29, no. 1 (2000): 1–47.

Burley, David V. "Rooster Town: Winnipeg's Lost Métis Suburb, 1900–1960." *Urban History Review* 42, no. 1 (2013): 3–25.

Burley, David V., Gayel A. Horsfall, and John Brandon. *Structural Considerations of Métis Ethnicity: An Archaeological, Architectural, and Historical Study*. Vermillion: University of South Dakota Press, 1992.

Cairnie, Julie. "Writing and Telling Hybridity: Autobiographical and Testimonial Narratives in Maria Campbell's *Halfbreed*." *Journal of Postcolonial Writing* 34, no. 2 (1995): 94–108.

Cajete, Gregory. *Indigenous Community: Rekindling the Teachings of the Seventh Fire*. St. Paul: Living Justice Press, 2015.

Callihoo, Victoria. "Early Life in Lac Ste. Anne and St. Albert in the Eighteen Seventies." *Alberta Historical Review* 1, no. 3 (1953): 21–26.

———. "Iroquois in Alberta." *Alberta Historical Review* 7, no. 2 (1959): 17–18.

———. "Our Buffalo Hunts." *Alberta Historical Review* 8, no. 1 (1960): 24–25.

Campbell, Maria. "Foreword: Charting the Way." In *Contours of a People: Metis Family, Mobility, and History*, edited by Brenda Macdougall, Carolyn Podruchny, and Nicole St-Onge, xiii–xvi. Norman: University of Oklahoma Press, 2012.

———. *Halfbreed*. Toronto: McClelland and Stewart, 1973.

———. *Halfbreed*. Rev. ed. Toronto: McClelland and Stewart, 2019.

———. "Michif." Lecture delivered in the Indigenous Knowledge Public Lecture Series, University of Calgary, Calgary, AB, 13 January 2021.

———. *Stories of the Road Allowance People*. Penticton: Theytus Books, 1995.

———. "We Need to Return to the Principles of Wahkotowin." *Eagle Feather News*, November 2007. https://mgouldhawke.wordpress.com/2019/11/05/we-need-to-return-to-the-principles-of-wahkotowin-maria-campbell-2007/.

Canadian Council on Learning. *Redefining How Success Is Measured in First Nations, Inuit, and Métis Learning*. Canadian Council on Learning, 2007. http://www.afn.ca/uploads/files/education/5._2007_redefining_how_success_is_measured_en.pdf.

Cardinal, Harold, and Walter Hildebrandt. *Treaty Elders of Saskatchewan: Our Dream Is That Our People Will One Day Be Recognized as Nations*. Calgary: University of Calgary Press, 2000.

Carlson, Keith. *The Power of Place, the Problem of Time: Aboriginal Identity and Historical Consciousness in the Cauldron of Colonialism.* Toronto: University of Toronto Press, 2010.

Carrière, Jeannine, and Catherine Richardson, eds. *Calling Our Families Home: Métis Peoples' Experiences with Child Welfare.* Vernon: JC Charlton Publishing, 2017.

Carter, Sarah. *Capturing Women: The Manipulation of Cultural Imagery in Canada's Prairie West.* Montreal and Kingston: McGill-Queen's University Press, 1997.

Cidro, Jaime, Stephanie Sinclair, Sarah Delaronde, and Leona Star. "Restoring Ceremony as the Methodological Approach in Indigenous Research: The Indigenous Doula Project." In *Indigenous Knowledge Systems and Research Methodologies: Local Solutions and Global Opportunities,* edited by Elizabeth Sumida Huaman and Nathan D. Martin, 102–20. Toronto: Canadian Scholars Press, 2020.

Chacaby, Maya Ode'amik. "(The Missing Chapter) On Being Missing: From Indian Problem to Indian Problematic." In *Keetsahnak / Our Missing and Murdered Indigenous Sisters*, edited by Kim Anderson, Maria Campbell, and Christi Belcourt, 138. Edmonton: University of Alberta Press, 2018.

Clark, Natalie, Patricia Barkaskas, and Robline Davey. *Thanks for Listening: Witnessing Métis Women & Girls Experiences of Violence & Pathways to Healing.* Surrey: Métis Nation British Columbia, 2021.

Clarke, John. "Proud Boys Face Canada's Anti-Terror Law." *Spectre Journal*, 8 February 2021. https://spectrejournal.com/proud-boys-face-canadas-anti-terror-law/.

Cook, Katsi. "Women Are the First Environment: An Interview with Mohawk Elder Katsi Cook." Interview by Leslee Goodman. *Moon Magazine*, 31 March 2018. https://medium.com/@MOONmagazineEditor/women-are-the-first-environment-an-interview-with-mohawk-elder-katsi-cook-40ae4151c3c0.

Cook-Lynn, Elizabeth. *Why I Can't Read Wallace Stegner and Other Essays.* Madison: University of Wisconsin Press, 1996.

Corntassel, Jeff. "Re-Envisioning Resurgence: Indigenous Pathways to Decolonization and Sustainable Self-Determination." *Decolonization: Indigeneity, Education and Society* 1, no. 1 (2012): 86–101.

Coulthard, Glen S. *Red Skin, White Masks: Rejecting the Colonial Politics of Recognition.* Minneapolis: University of Minnesota Press, 2014.

Craft, Aimée. "We Are Born into This Land: Birthing Babies and Raising Children as Expressions of Territorial Sovereignty and Women's Jurisdiction." Lecture presented at the Canada Research Chair Speakers Series, University of Winnipeg, Winnipeg, Manitoba, 6 February 2020.

Damm, Kateri. "Dispelling and Telling: Speaking Native Realities in Maria Campbell's *Halfbreed* and Beatrice Culleton's *In Search of April Raintree.*" In *Looking at the Words of Our People*, edited by Jeannette Armstrong, 93–114. Penticton: Theytus Books, 1993.

Daniel, Beverly-Jean. "Teaching While Black: Racial Dynamics, Evaluations, and the Role of White Females in the Canadian Academy in Carrying the Racism Torch." *Race Ethnicity and Education* 22, no. 1 (2019): 21–37.

Daniels v. Canada (Indian Affairs and Northern Development) [2016] 1 S.C.R. 12, 2016 SCC 12. https://scc-csc.lexum.com/scc-csc/scc-csc/en/item/15858/index.do.

Daschuk, James. *Clearing the Plains: Disease, Politics of Starvation, and the Loss of Aboriginal Life*. Regina: University of Regina Press. 2013.

Daum Shanks, Signa A.K. "Searching for Sakitawak: Place and People in Northern Saskatchewan's Île-à-la-Crosse." PhD diss., University of Western Ontario, 2015. https://ir.lib.uwo.ca/etd/3328.

Davis, Angelique M., and Rose Ernst. "Racial Gaslighting." *Politics, Groups, and Identities* 7, no. 4 (2019): 761–74.

Deloria, Vine. *Custer Died for Your Sins: An Indian Manifesto*. Norman: University of Oklahoma Press, 1969.

Deloria, Vine, Jr. *Evolution, Creationism, and Other Modern Myths*. Golden: Fulcrum Publishing, 2002.

Denetdale, Jennifer Nez. "Securing Navajo National Boundaries: War, Patriotism, Tradition and the Dine Marriage Act of 2005." *Wicazo Sa Review* 24, no. 2 (2009): 131–48.

Desmarais, Diedre A. "Spare a Thought for Métis Women Elders." In *Making Space for Indigenous Feminism*. 2nd ed., edited by Joyce Green, 192–212. Halifax: Fernwood Publishing, 2017.

Devine, Heather. "Les Desjarlais: The Development and Dispersion of a Proto-Métis Hunting Band, 1785–1870." In *From Rupert's Land to Canada: Essays in Honour of John E. Foster*, edited by Theodore Binnema, Gerhard J. Ens, and Rod Macleod, 129–58. Edmonton: University of Alberta Press, 2001.

———. *The People Who Own Themselves: Aboriginal Ethnogenesis in a Canadian Family, 1660–1900*. Calgary: University of Calgary Press, 2004.

Dhamoon, Rita Kaur. *Identity-Difference Politics: How Difference Is Produced and Why It Matters*. Vancouver: UBC Press, 2009.

Donovan, Josephine. *Feminist Theory: The Intellectual Traditions of American Feminism*. New York: Continuum, 1990.

Dorion, Leah. *Country Wives and Daughters of the Country: Métis Women of this Land*. Saskatoon: Friends of Batoche and Gabriel Dumont Institute, 2012.

———. "Opikinawasowin: The Life Long Process of Growing Cree and Métis Children." Master's thesis, Athabasca University, 2010. http://dtpr.lib.athabascau.ca/action/download.php?filename=mais/Final%20Paper%20MAIS%20701-5.pdf.

Dorion, Leah, and Darren R. Préfontaine. "Deconstructing Métis Historiography: Giving Voice to the Métis People." In *Métis Legacy: Michif Culture, Heritage, and Folkways*, edited by Lawrence Barkwell, Leah Dorion, and Audreen Hourie, 13–78. Saskatoon: Gabriel Dumont Institute of Native Studies and Applied Research, 2006.

Dorries, Heather, Robert Henry, David Hugill, Tyler McCreary, and Julie Tomiak. *Settler City Limits: Indigenous Resurgence and Colonial Violence in the Urban Prairie West*. Winnipeg: University of Manitoba Press, 2019.

Drawson, Alexandra S., Elaine Toombs, and Christopher J. Mushquash. "Indigenous Research Methods: A Systematic Review." *International Indigenous Policy Journal* 8, no. 2 (2017). https://doi.org/10.18584/iipj.2017.8.2.5.

Dumont, Marilyn. "The Gift." In *Writing the Circle: Native Women of Western Canada—An Anthology*, edited by Jeanne Perreault and Sylvia Vance, 44–46. Edmonton: NeWest Press, 1990.

———. *A Really Good Brown Girl.* London, ON: Brick Books, 1996.

Duran, Eduardo. *Healing the Soul Wound: Counseling with American Indians and Other Native Peoples.* New York: Teachers College Press, 2006.

Duran, Eduardo, and Bonnie Duran. *Native American Postcolonial Psychology.* Albany: State University of New York Press, 1995.

Dyck, Miranda. "Social Determinants of Métis Health." Métis Centre National Aboriginal Health Organization. Accessed 13 March 2013. https://fnim.sehc.com/getmedia/960a0972-2313-4fff-b0dd-f407fc71c94d/Research_SocialDeterminantsofHealth.pdf.aspx?ext=.pdf.

Edwards, Brendan Frederick R. "Maria Campbell's *Halfbreed*: 'Biography with a Purpose.'" Hamilton, ON: McMaster Digital Collections, 2015. http://hpcanpub.mcmaster.ca/hpcanpub/case-study/maria-campbells-halfbreed-biography-purpose.

Eigenbrod, Renate. "The Oral in the Written: A Literature Between Two Cultures." *Canadian Journal of Native Studies* 15, no. 1 (1995): 89–102.

———. *Travelling Knowledges: Positioning the Im/Migrant Reader of Aboriginal Literatures in Canada.* Winnipeg: University of Manitoba Press, 2005.

Emberly, Julia V. *Thresholds of Difference: Feminist Critique, Native Women's Writings, Post-Colonial Theory.* Toronto: University of Toronto Press, 1993.

Fagan, Brian M. *The Adventure of Archaeology.* Washington, DC: National Geographic, 1985.

Fagan, Kristina, Stephanie Danyluk, Bryce Donaldson, Amelia Horsburgh, Robin Moore, and Martin Winquist. "Reading the Reception of Maria Campbell's *Halfbreed*." *Canadian Journal of Native Studies* 29, no. 2 (2009): 257–81.

Farrell Racette, Sherry. "Beads, Silk, and Quills: The Clothing and Decorative Arts of the Métis." In *Métis Legacy: A Métis Historiography and Annotated Bibliography*, edited by Lawrence J. Barkwell, Leah Dorion, and Darren R. Préfontaine, 181–88. Winnipeg: Pemmican Publications, 2000.

———. "Kitchen Table Theory." Lecture at the Sâkêwêwak Artists' Collective Storytellers Festival, Regina, SK, 3 February 2017.

———. "Looking for Stories and Unbroken Threads: Museum Artifacts as Women's History and Culture." In *Restoring the Balance: First Nations Women, Community, and Culture,* edited by Eric Guimond, Gail Guthrie Valaskakis, and Madeleine Dion Stout, 283–312. Winnipeg: University of Manitoba Press, 2009.

———. "Sewing for a Living: The Commodification of Métis Women's Artistic Production." In *Contact Zones: Aboriginal and Settler Women in Canada's Colonial Past,* edited by Myra Rutherdale and Katie Pickles, 17–46. Vancouver: UBC Press, 2005.

———. "Sewing Ourselves Together: Clothing, Decorative Arts and the Expression of Métis and Half Breed Identity." PhD diss., University of Manitoba, 2004. http://hdl.handle.net/1993/3304.

———. "Showing Care: Centring Indigenous Perspectives in Historical Research." Lecture at the NAISA Annual Meeting, May 2021.

Farrell Racette, Sherry, and Cathy Mattes. "Métis Kitchen Table Talk on Methodologies of Making." Lecture hosted by Ociciwan at CKUA, Edmonton, AB, 24 March 2019.

Ferland, Nicki. "Kishkeetamawin li tereen oschi: Urban Land-Based Learning as a Remembering and Reclaiming of Place." In *Walking Together in Indigenous Research,* edited by Laura Forsythe and Jennifer Markides, 45–52. New York: Dio Press, 2020.

———. "Michif: Another Gift for Our Children." *Red Rising Magazine*, 2018.

———. "This is Indigenous Land: An Indigenous Land-Based Approach to Climate Change Education." Case study. Washington, DC: Global Environmental Education Partnership, 2020. https://thegeep.org/learn/case-studies/indigenous-land-indigenous-land-based-approach-climate-change-education.

Ferland, Nicki, Anny Chen, and Gerardo Villagrán Becerra. "Working in Good Ways: A Framework and Resources for Indigenous Community Engagement." Consultation report. Winnipeg: University of Manitoba, 2021. https://umanitoba.ca/sites/default/files/2021-05/framework-guide.pdf.

Ferris, Shawna. "Working from the Violent Centre: Survival Sex Work and Urban Aboriginality in Maria Campbell's *Halfbreed*." *ESC: English Studies in Canada* 34, no. 4 (2008): 123–45.

Fiola, Chantal. "Diaspora, Spirituality, Kinship and Nationhood: A Métis Woman's Perspective." In *Relation and Resistance: Racialized Women, Religion and Diaspora,* edited by Sailaja Krishnamurti and Becky R. Lee, 259–80. Montreal: McGill-Queen's University Press, 2021.

———. "Naawenangweyaabeg Coming In: Intersections of Indigenous Sexuality and Spirituality." In *In Good Relation: History, Gender, and Kinship in Indigenous Feminisms,* edited by Sarah Nickel and Amanda Fehr, 136–53. Winnipeg: University of Manitoba Press, 2020.

———. *Rekindling the Sacred Fire: Métis Ancestry and Anishinaabe Spirituality.* Winnipeg: University of Manitoba Press, 2015.

———. *Returning to Ceremony: Spirituality in Manitoba Métis Communities*. Winnipeg: University of Manitoba Press, 2021.

Fiola, Chantal, and Albert McLeod. "Two-Spirit Resistance and Resurgence in Winnipeg." In *Indigenous Resistance and Institutional Development in Winnipeg: 1960–2000*, edited by Shauna MacKinnon and Kathy Mallett, 197–219. Winnipeg: Arbeiter Ring, 2023.

Fiola, Chantal, and Sharanpal Ruprai. "Two-Spirit and Queer Trans People of Colour: Reflecting on the Call to Conversation Conference (C2C)." *Canadian Journal of Native Studies* 39, no. 1 (2019): 45–64.

First Nations Information Governance Centre. *Ownership, Control, Access and Possession (OCAP™): The Path to First Nations Information Governance*. Ottawa: The First Nations Information Governance Centre, 2014. https://achh.ca/wp-content/uploads/2018/07/OCAP_FNIGC.pdf.

Flaminio, Anna Corrigal. "Kinship-Visiting: Urban Indigenous Deliberative Space." In *Renewing Relationships: Indigenous Peoples and Canada*, edited by Karen Drake and Brenda L. Gunn, 143–67. Saskatoon: Wiyasiwewin Mikiwahp Native Law Centre, 2019.

———. "Kiyokewin: Urban Indigenous Kinship-visiting Methodology and Approach for Urban Indigenous Youth." PhD diss., University of Toronto, 2018.

Flaminio, Anna Corrigal, Janice Cindy Gaudet, and Leah Marie Dorion. "Métis Women Gathering: Visiting Together and Voicing Wellness for Ourselves." *AlterNative: An International Journal of Indigenous Peoples* 16 (2020): 55–63.

Forsythe, Laura. "Métis Women in the Academy." PhD diss., University of Manitoba, 2022.

Freed, Don. "Daughters of the Country" (song). The Virtual Museum of Métis History and Culture, n.d. https://www.metismuseum.ca/resource.php/05242.

Freire, Paulo. *Pedagogy of the Oppressed.* Translated by Myra Bergman Ramos. New York: Herder and Herder, 1970.

Gabriel Dumont Institute. "Oral History and Traditional Stories Collection." Accessed 4 October 2020. http://www.metismuseum.ca/browse/index.php/57.

Gaudet, Janice Cindy. "Keeoukaywin: The Visiting Way—Fostering an Indigenous Research Methodology." *Aboriginal Policy Studies* 7, no. 2 (2018): 47–64.

Gaudet, Janice Cindy, and Diane Caron-Bourbonnais. "It's in Our Blood: Indigenous Women's Knowledge as a Critical Path to Women's Well-Being." *AlterNative: An International Journal of Indigenous Peoples* 11, no. 2 (2015): 164–76.

Gaudet, Janice Cindy, Leah Marie Dorion, and Anna Corrigal Flaminio. "Exploring the Effectiveness of Métis Women's Research Methodology and Methods: Promising Wellness Research Practices." *First Peoples Child and Family Review* 15, no. 1 (2020): 12–26.

Gaudry, Adam. "Communing with the Dead: The 'New Métis,' Métis Identity Appropriation, and the Displacement of the Living Métis Culture." *The American Indian Quarterly* 42, no. 2 (2018): 162–90.

———. "Insurgent Research." *Wicazo Sa Review* 26, no. 1 (2011): 113–36.

———. "Métis in Canada: History, Identity, Law, and Politics." *Aboriginal Policy Studies* 3, no. 1–2 (2014): 231–37.

———. "The Métis-ization of Canada: The Process of Claiming Louis Riel, Métissage, and the Métis People as Canada's Mythical Origin." *Aboriginal Policy Studies* 2, no. 2 (2013): 64–87.

Gaudry, Adam, and Chris Andersen. "*Daniels v. Canada*: Racialized Legacies, Settler Self-Indigenization and the Denial of Indigenous Peoplehood." *TOPIA: Canadian Journal of Cultural Studies* 36 (Fall 2016): 19–30.

Gaudry, Adam, and Robert Hancock. "Decolonizing Métis Pedagogies in Post-Secondary Settings." *Canadian Journal of Native Education* 35, no. 1 (2012): 7–22.

Gaudry, Adam, and Darryl Leroux. "White Settler Revisionism and Making Métis Everywhere: The Evocation of Métissage in Quebec and Nova Scotia." *Critical Ethnic Studies* 3, no. 2 (2017): 116–42.

George, Corrine. "'If I Didn't Do Something, My Spirit Would Die . . .': Grassroots Activism of Aboriginal Women in Calgary and Edmonton, 1951–1985." Master's thesis, University of Calgary, 2007.

Ghostkeeper, Elmer. *Spirit Gifting: The Concept of Spiritual Exchange.* 2nd ed. Raymond: Writing on Stone Press, 2007.

Goeman, Mishuana. "(Re)Mapping Indigenous Presence on the Land in Native Women's Literature." *American Quarterly* 60, no. 2 (2008): 295–302.

Goeman, Mishuana, and Jennifer Nez Denetdale. "Native Feminisms: Legacies, Interventions, and Indigenous Sovereignties." *Wicazo Sa Review* 24, no. 2 (2009): 9–13.

Goulet, Linda, and Keith Goulet. *Teaching Each Other: Nehinuw Concepts and Indigenous Pedagogies*. Vancouver: UBC Press, 2014.

Government of Canada. Indian Act.1985. https://www.canlii.org/en/ca/laws/stat/rsc-1985-c-i-5/latest/rsc-1985-c-i-5.html.

———. *Working Guide on Gender Analysis*. Indigenous and Northern Affairs Canada, 2013. https://www.sac-isc.gc.ca/eng/1660053791440/1660053808557.

Graveline, Fyre. *Circle Works: Transforming Eurocentric Consciousness*. Black Point: Fernwood, 1998.

Green, Joyce. "Constitutionalising the Patriarchy: Aboriginal Women and Aboriginal Government." *Constitutional Forum constitutionnel* 4 (1992): 110.

———. *Making Space for Indigenous Feminism*. Black Point: Fernwood Publishing, 2007.

———. "Taking More Account of Indigenous Feminism: An Introduction." In *Making Space for Indigenous Feminism*. 2nd ed., edited by Joyce Green, 1–20. Halifax: Fernwood Publishing, 2017.

———. "Towards a Détente with History: Confronting Canada's Colonial Legacy." *International Journal of Canadian Studies* 12 (1995): 85–105.

Green, Rayna. "The Pocahontas Perplex: The Image of Indian Women in American Culture." *The Massachusetts Review* 16, no. 4 (1975): 698–714.

Gubrium, Aline. "Digital Storytelling: An Emergent Method for Health Promotion Research and Practice." *Health Promotion Practice* 10, no. 2 (2009): 186–91.

Guillemin, Marilys, and Lynn Gillam. "Ethics, Reflexivity and 'Ethically Important Moments' in Research." *Qualitative Inquiry* 10, no. 2 (2004): 261–80.

Hancock, Robert L.A. "The Power of Peoplehood: Reimagining Metis Relationships, Research and Responsibilities." In *A People and a Nation: New Directions in Contemporary Métis Studies*, edited by Jennifer Adese and Chris Andersen, 40–66. Vancouver: UBC Press, 2021.

Harrison, Julia D. *Métis: People Between Two Worlds*. Calgary: Glenbow-Alberta Institute and Douglas and McIntyre, 1985.

Hart, Michael. "Indigenous Worldviews, Knowledge, and Research: The Development of an Indigenous Research Paradigm." *Journal of Indigenous Voices in Social Work* 1, no. 1 (2010): 1–16. https://journalhosting.ucalgary.ca/index.php/jisd/article/view/63043.

Haskins, Victoria K. "Beyond Complicity: Questions and Issues for White Women in Aboriginal History." *Australian Humanities Review* 39–40 (September 2006). http://australianhumanitiesreview.org/2006/09/01/beyond-complicity-questions-and-issues-for-white-women-in-aboriginal-history/.

Henry, Frances, Carl James, Peter S. Li, Audrey Kobayashi, Malinda Sharon Smith, Howard Ramos, and Dua Enakshi. *The Equity Myth: Racialization and Indigeneity at Canadian Universities*. Vancouver: UBC Press, 2017.

Henry, Robert, Caroline Tait, and STR8 UP. "Creating Ethical Research Partnerships—Relational Accountability in Action." *Engaged Scholar Journal* 2, no. 1 (2016): 183–204.

Hildebrandt, Walter. "The Battle of Batoche." In *The Western Métis: Profile of a People*, edited by Patrick C. Douaud, 213–60. Regina: Canadian Plains Research Center, 2007.

Hodgson-Smith, Kathy, and Nathalie Kermoal. "Community-Based Research and Métis Women's Knowledge in Northwestern Saskatchewan." In *Living on the Land: Indigenous Women's Understanding of Place*, edited by Nathalie Kermoal and Isabel Altamirano-Jiménez, 139–67. Edmonton: Athabasca University Press, 2016.

Hokowhitu, Brendan. "Producing Indigeneity." In *Indigenous in the City: Contemporary Identities and Cultural Innovation*, edited by Evelyn Peters and Chris Andersen, 354–76. Vancouver: UBC Press, 2013.

hooks, bell. "Feminism: Crying for Our Souls." *Women and Therapy* 17, no. 1–2 (1995): 265–71.

———. *Feminist Theory: From Margins to Center*. Boston: South End Press, 1984.

———. "Sisterhood: Political Solidarity between Women." *Feminist Review* 23, no. 1 (1986): 125–38.

Hoppers, Catherine Odora, and Howard Richards. *Rethinking Thinking: Modernity's "Other" and the Transformation of the University*. Pretoria: University of South Africa, 2012.

Horn-Miller, Kahente. "Distortion and Healing: Finding Balance and a 'Good Mind' Through the Rearticulation of Sky Woman's Journey." In *Living on the Land: Indigenous Women's Understanding of Place*, edited by Nathalie Kermoal and Isabel Altamirano-Jiménez, 19–38. Edmonton: Athabasca University Press, 2016.

Hourie, Audreen, and Anne Carrière-Acco. "Métis Families." In *Metis Legacy II: Michif Culture, Heritage and Folkways,* edited by Lawrence Barkwell, Leah Dorion, and Audreen Hourie, 56–63. Saskatoon: Gabriel Dumont Institute, 2006.

Howard-Bobiwash, Heather. "Women's Class Strategies as Activism in Native Community Building in Toronto: 1950–1975." *American Indian Quarterly* 27, no. 3/4 (2003): 566–82.

Hoy, Helen. *How Should I Read These? Native Women Writers in Canada.* Toronto: University of Toronto Press, 2001.

Hubbard, Tasha, Joi T. Arcand, Zoey Roy, Darian Lonechild, and Marie Sanderson. "'It Just Piles On, and Piles On, and Piles On': Young Indigenous Women and the Colonial Imagination." In *In Good Relation: History, Gender, and Kinship in Indigenous Feminisms,* 66–81. Winnipeg: University of Manitoba Press, 2020.

Hungry Wolf, Beverly. *The Ways of My Grandmothers*. New York: William Morrow Paperbacks, 1998.

Hunt, Sarah. "Embodying Self-Determination: Beyond the Gender Binary." In *Determinants of Indigenous Peoples' Health*. 2nd ed., edited by Margo Greenwood, Sarah de Leeuw, and Nicole Marie Lindsay, 22–39. Toronto: Canadian Scholars Press, 2018.

———. "Everyday Decolonization: Living a Decolonizing Queer Politics." *Journal of Lesbian Studies* 19, no. 2 (2015): 154–72.

———. "Violence, Law and the Everyday Politics of Recognition: Comments on Glenn Coulthard's *Red Skin, White Masks*." Paper presented at the Native American and Indigenous Studies Association (NAISA), Washington, DC, 3–6 June 2015.

Hymes, Dell. *"In Vain I Tried to Tell You": Essays in Native American Ethnopoetics*. Lincoln: University of Nebraska Press, 2004.

Innes, Robert. *Elder Brother and the Law of the People: Contemporary Kinship and Cowessess First Nation*. Winnipeg: University of Manitoba Press, 2013.

Institute for the Advancement of Aboriginal Women. "About Us." Accessed 26 March 2021. https://iaaw.ca/about-us.

Isaac, Thomas. *A Matter of National and Constitutional Import: Report of the Minister's Special Representative on Reconciliation with Métis: Section 35 Métis Rights and the Manitoba Métis Federation Decision*. Ottawa: Indigenous and Northern Affairs Canada, 2016. https://publications.gc.ca/collections/collection_2016/aanc-inac/R5-123-2016-eng.pdf.

Iseke, Judith M. "Indigenous Digital Storytelling in Video: Witnessing with Alma Desjarlais." *Equity and Excellence in Education* 44, no. 3 (2011): 311–29.

———. "Indigenous Storytelling as Research." *International Review of Qualitative Research* 6, no. 4 (2013): 559–77.

Iseke, Judith, and Leisa A. Desmoulins. "The Life and Work of the Honourable Thelma Chalifoux, White Standing Buffalo." *Canadian Journal of Native Studies* 33, no. 2 (2013): 29–54.

Iseke, Judith, and Sylvia Moore. "Community-Based Indigenous Digital Storytelling with Elders and Youth." *American Indian Culture and Research Journal* 35, no. 4 (2011): 19–38.

Iseke-Barnes, Judith. "Grandmothers of the Métis Nation: A Living History with Dorothy Chartrand." *Native Studies Review* 18, no. 2 (2008): 25–60.

Janovicek, Nancy. "'Assisting Our Own': Urban Migration, Self-Governance, and Native Women's Organizing in Thunder Bay, Ontario, 1972–1989." *American Indian Quarterly* 27, nos. 3–4 (2003): 548–65.

Jobin, Shalene. "Double Consciousness and Nehiyawak (Cree) Perspectives." In *Living on the Land: Indigenous Women's Understanding of Place*, edited by Nathalie Kermoal and Isabel Altamirano-Jiménez, 39–58. Edmonton: Athabasca University Press, 2016.

Jobin, Shalene, Kirsten Lindquist, and Avery Letendre. "Indigenous Governance Programming in Academia: Reflections on Community-Responsive Philosophy & Practice." *Aboriginal Policy Studies* 10, no. 1 (2022): 3–32. https://doi.org/10.5663/aps.v10i1.29389.

———. *Métis Nation of Alberta: Governance Framework Review January 2016–January 2017*. Edmonton: University of Alberta. Unpublished report, 2017.

Johnson, Paul. "The Post-Colonial Hangover." *New Statesman*, 1 July 1963.

Kauanui, J. Kēhaulani. "Native Hawaiian Decolonization and the Politics of Gender." *American Quarterly* 60, no. 2 (2008): 281–87.

Kearns, Laura-Lee. "(Re)claiming Métis Women Identities: Three Stories and the Storyteller." In *Métis in Canada: History, Identity, Law and Politics*, edited by C. Adams, G. Dahl, and I. Peach, 59–92. Edmonton: University of Alberta Press, 2013.

Kenny, Carolyn. *Leadership: Native Narratives on Building Strong Communities*. Vancouver: UBC Press, 2012.

Kermoal, Nathalie. "Métis Women's Environmental Knowledge and the Recognition of Métis Rights." In *Living on the Land: Indigenous Women's Understanding of Place*, edited by Nathalie Kermoal and Isabel Altamirano-Jiménez, 107–38. Edmonton: Athabasca University Press, 2016.

Kermoal, Nathalie, and Isabel Altamirano-Jiménez, eds. *Living on the Land: Indigenous Women's Understanding of Place.* Edmonton: Athabasca University Press, 2016.

Kimmerer, Robin Wall. *Braiding Sweetgrass: Indigenous Wisdom, Scientific Knowledge and the Teachings of Plants.* Minneapolis: Milkweed Editions, 2013.

King, Thomas. "Introduction." *All My Relations: An Anthology of Contemporary Canadian Native Fiction,* edited by Thomas King, ix–xvi. Toronto: McClelland and Stewart, 1990.

———. *The Truth about Stories: A Native Narrative.* Toronto: House of Anansi, 2003.

Kirkness, Verna, and Ray Barnhardt. "First Nations and Higher Education: The Four R's—Respect, Relevance, Reciprocity, Responsibility." *Journal of American Indian Education* 30, no. 3 (1991): 1–15.

Konsmo, Erin, and Karyn Recollet. "Afterword: Meeting the Land(s) Where They Are At: A Conversation between Erin Marie Konsmo (Métis) and Karyn Recollet (Urban Cree)." In *Indigenous and Decolonizing Studies in Education: Mapping the Long View*, edited by Linda Tuhiwai Smith, Eve Tuck, and K. Wayne Yang, 238–51. New York: Routledge, 2018.

Kovach, Margaret. "Conversational Method in Indigenous Research." *First Peoples Child and Family Review* 4 (2010): 40–48.

———. "Emerging from the Margins: Indigenous Methodologies." In *Research as Resistance: Critical, Indigenous, and Anti-oppressive Approaches*, edited by Leslie Brown and Susan Strega, 19–36. Toronto: Canadian Scholars Press, 2005.

———. *Indigenous Methodologies: Characteristics, Conversations, and Contexts.* Toronto: University of Toronto Press, 2009.

Krouse, Susan Applegate, and Heather A. Howard, eds. *Keeping the Campfires Going: Native Women's Activism in Urban Communities.* Lincoln: University of Nebraska Press, 2009.

Lajimodiere, Denise K. "American Indian Females and Stereotypes: Warriors, Leaders, Healers, Feminists; Not Drudges, Princesses, Prostitutes." *Multicultural Perspectives* 15, no. 2 (2013): 104–9.

Laliberte, Ron. "Being Métis: Exploring the Construction, Retention, and Maintenance of Urban Métis Identity." In *Indigenous in the City: Contemporary Identities and Cultural Innovation*, edited by Evelyn Peters and Chris Andersen, 110–31. Vancouver: UBC Press, 2013.

Lambert, Joe. *Digital Storytelling Cookbook.* Berkeley: Digital Diner Press, 2010. https://www.storycenter.org/inventory/digital-storytelling-cookbook.

Lambert, Joe, and Brooke Hessler. *Digital Storytelling: Capturing Lives, Creating Community.* New York: Routledge, 2018.

Lampert, Joanne. "The Alabaster Academy: Being a Non-Indigenous Academic in Indigenous Studies." *Australian Journal of Teacher Education* 22, no. 3 (2003): 23–26.

Landry, Andrea. "Colonialism Has Motherhood All Wrong." Facebook, 27 December 2020. https://www.facebook.com/andrea.landry.7/posts/10158887692187380.

———. "Why I Carried My Baby in a Tikinagan." *Today's Parent,* 30 April 2020. https://www.todaysparent.com/family/parenting/why-i-carried-my-baby-in-a-tikinagan/.

LaRocque, Emma. "The Colonization of a Native Woman Scholar." In *Women of the First Nations: Power, Wisdom, and Strength,* edited by Cheryl Miller and Patricia Chuchryk, 11–18. Winnipeg: University of Manitoba Press, 1996.

———. "Contemporary Metis Literature: Roots, Resistance, Innovation." In *The Oxford Handbook of Canadian Literature,* edited by Cynthia Sugars, 129–49. New York: Oxford University Press, 2015.

———. "Conversations on Métis Identity." *Prairie Fire* 7, no. 1 (1986): 19–24.

———. *Defeathering the Indian.* Toronto: The Book Society of Canada, 1975.

———. "Foreword: Resist no Longer: Reflections on Resistance Writing and Teaching." In *More Will Sing their Way to Freedom: Indigenous Resistance and Resurgence*, edited by Elaine Coburn, 5–23. Black Point: Fernwood, 2015.

———. "From the Land to the Classroom: Broadening Aboriginal Epistemology." In *Pushing the Margins: Native and Northern Studies,* edited by Jill Oakes, Roderick R. Riewe, Marilyn Bennett, and Brenda Chisolm, 12–14. Winnipeg: University of Manitoba, 2000.

———. "Métis and Feminist: Ethical Reflections on Feminism, Human Rights and Decolonization." In *Making Space for Indigenous Feminism,* edited by Joyce Green, 20–32. Black Point: Fernwood Publishing, 2007.

———. "The Metis in English Canadian Literature." *Canadian Journal of Native Studies* 3, no. 1 (1983): 85–94.

———. "Native Identity and the Métis: Otehpayimsuak Peoples." In *A Passion for Identity: Canadian Studies for the 21st Century,* edited by Beverly Jean Rasporich and David Taras, 381–400. Toronto: Nelson Thomson Learning, 2001.

———. "Racism Runs through Canadian Society." In *Racism in Canada,* edited by O. McKague, 73–76. Markham: Fifth House Publishers, 1991.

———. "Reflections on Cultural Continuity Through Aboriginal Women's Writings." In *Restoring the Balance: First Nations Women, Community and Culture*, edited by Gail Gutherie Valaskakis, Madeleine Dion Stout, and Eric Guimond, 149–74. Winnipeg: University of Manitoba Press, 2009.

———. "Three Conventional Approaches to Native People in Society and in Literature." In *Survival of the Imagination: The Mary Donaldson Memorial Lectures*, edited by Brett Balon and Peter Resch. Saskatoon: Coteau Books, 1993.

———. "The Uniform of the Dispossessed." In *Writing the Circle: Native Women of Western Canada*, edited by Jeanne Perrault and Sylvia Vance, 153–54. Edmonton: NeWest Press, 1990.

———. "Violence in Aboriginal Communities." In *The Path to Healing: Report of the National Round Table on Aboriginal Health and Social Issues*, 72–89. Ottawa: Canada Communication Group, 1993. https://data2.archives.ca/rcap/pdf/rcap-451.pdf.

———. *When the Other Is Me: Native Resistance Discourse 1850–1990.* Winnipeg: University of Manitoba Press, 2010.

———. "When the 'Wild West' Is Me: Re-Viewing Cowboys and Indians." In *Challenging Frontiers: The Canadian West*, edited by Lorry Felske and Beverly Jean Rasporich, 136–53. Calgary: University of Calgary Press, 2004.

Laurence, Margaret. *The Diviners*. Toronto: McClelland and Stewart, 1974.

LaVallee, Amanda. "Converging Methods and Tools: A Métis Group Model Building Project on Tuberculosis." PhD diss., University of Saskatchewan, 2014. https://harvest.usask.ca/handle/10388/ETD-2014-04-1535.

LaVallee, Amanda, Cheryl Troupe, and Tara Turner. "Negotiating and Exploring Relationships in Métis Community-Based Research." *Engaged Scholar Journal* 2, no. 1 (2017): 167–82.

Lavallee, Lynn F. "Is Decolonization Possible in the Academy?" In *Decolonizing and Indigenizing Education in Canada*, edited by Sheila Cote Meek and Taima Moeke-Pickering, 117–33. Toronto: Canadian Scholars Press, 2020.

Leclair, Carole, and Sandi Warren. "Portals and Potlatch." In *Information Technology and Indigenous People*, edited by Laurel Evelyn Dyson, Max Hendriks, and Stephen Grant, 1–13. Hershey: Information Science Publishing, 2007.

Leclair, Carole, Lynn Nicholson, and Elize Hartley. "From the Stories that Women Tell: The Métis Women's Circle." In *Strong Women Stories: Native Vision and Community Survival*, edited by Kim Anderson and Bonita Lawrence, 55–69. Toronto: Sumach Press, 2003.

Lefebvre, Henri. *Rhythmanalysis: Space, Time, and Everyday Life*. Translated by Stuart Elden and Gerald Moore. London: Bloomsbury, 2013.

Leo, Geoff. "Indigenous or Pretender? Some Colleagues Say a Leading Health Scientist Is Faking Indigenous Ancestry." *CBC News*, 27 October 2021. https://www.cbc.ca/newsinteractives/features/carrie-bourassa-indigenous.

Lezard, Percy, Joanne Aandeg DiNova, and Lynn F. Lavallee. "Misogyny kʷil Misogyny-Miskwaa: Misogyny within the Indigenous Community." Stoop Talk Speaker Series, Toronto Metropolitan University. 30 September 2022. YouTube Video, 1:31:30. https://youtu.be/eNrwmZCwEEQ.

Lischke, Ute, and David T. McNab, eds. *The Long Journey of a Forgotten People: Métis Identities and Family Histories*. Waterloo: Wilfrid Laurier University Press, 2007.

Little Bear, Leroy. "Jagged Worlds Colliding." In *Reclaiming Indigenous Voice and Vision*, edited by Marie Battiste, 77–85. Vancouver: UBC Press, 2009.

Locke, John. *Two Treatises of Government*. London, UK: Awnsham Churchill, 1689.

Logan, Tricia. "Settler Colonialism in Canada and the Métis." *Journal of Genocide Research* 17, no. 4 (2015): 433–52.

———. "We Were Outsiders: The Métis and Residential Schools." Master's thesis, University of Manitoba, 2007.

Louie, Dustin W. "Aligning Universities' Recruitment of Indigenous Academics with the Tools Used to Evaluate Scholarly Performance and Grant Tenure and Promotion." *Canadian Journal of Education* 42, no. 3 (2019): 791–815.

Louis Riel Institute. "Buffalo Hunt." Accessed 1 June 2021. https://www.louisrielinstitute.com/buffalo-hunt-php/.

———. "Why Choose Us?" Accessed 11 February 2023. https://www.louisrielinstitute.com/why-choose-us/.

Lundgren, Jodi. "'Being a Half-Breed': Discourses of Race and Cultural Syncreticity in the Works of Three Métis Women Writers." *Canadian Literature* 144 (1995): 62–77.

Lutz, Hartmut, Murray Hamilton, and Donna Hembecker, eds. *Howard Adams: Otapawy! The Life of a Métis Leader in His Own Words and in Those of His Contemporaries*. Saskatoon: Gabriel Dumont Institute, 2005.

Macdougall, Brenda. "Land, Family and Identity: Contextualizing Métis Health and Well-Being." Prince George: National Collaborating Centre for Aboriginal Health, 2017. https://www.ccnsa-nccah.ca/docs/context/RPT-ContextualizingMetisHealth-Macdougall-EN.pdf.

———. "The Myth of Métis Cultural Ambivalence." In *Contours of a People: Metis Family, Mobility, and History*, edited by Brenda Macdougall, Carolyn Podruchny, and Nicole St-Onge, 422–64. Norman: University of Oklahoma Press, 2012.

———. *One of the Family: Métis Culture in Nineteenth-Century Northwestern Saskatchewan*. Vancouver: UBC Press, 2010.

———. "Speaking of Métis: Reading Family Life into Colonial Records." *Ethnohistory* 61, no.1 (2014): 27–56.

Macdougall, Brenda, Carolyn Podruchny, and Nicole St-Onge, eds. *Contours of a People: Métis Family, Mobility, and History*. Norman: University of Oklahoma Press, 2012.

Macdougall, Brenda, and Nicole St-Onge. "Rooted in Mobility: Métis Buffalo-Hunting Brigades." *Manitoba History* 71 (2013): 21–33.

MacEwan, Grant. *Mighty Women: Stories of Western Canadian Pioneers*. Vancouver: Greystone Books, 2009.

Mackenzie, Ian R. "Racial Harassment in the Workplace: Evolving Approaches." *Canadian Labour and Employment Law Journal* 3 (1994): 287–312.

MacKinnon, Doris Jeanne. *Metis Pioneers: Marie Rose Delorme Smith and Isabella Clark Hardisty Lougheed*. Edmonton: University of Alberta Press, 2018.

Makokis, Leona, Ralph Bodor, Stephanie Tyler, Amanda McLellan, Ariel Veldhuisen, Kristina Kopp, Suzanne McLeod, and Sharon Goulet. "iyiniw tapwewin ekwa kiskeyihtamowin." In *ohpikinâwasowin: Growing a Child*, edited by Leona Makokis, Ralph Bodor, Avery Calhoun, and Stephanie Tyler. Black Point: Fernwood, 2020. https://canadiancoursereadings.ca/product/iyiniw-tpw-win-kwa-kiskeyihtamowin/.

Makokis, Leona, Marilyn Shirt, Sherri Chisan, Anne Mageau, and Diana Steinhauer. *mâmawi-nehiyaw iyinikahiwewin*. St. Paul: Blue Quills First Nation College, 2010.

Mamawi Project Collective. *Kîyokêwin* [Zine]. Edited by Justin Weibe and Lucy Fowler. 2019.

Manitoba Métis Federation v. Canada [2013] 1 S.C.R. 623, 2013 SCC 14. https://decisions.scc-csc.ca/scc-csc/scc-csc/en/item/12888/index.do.

Maracle, Lee. *I Am Woman: A Native Perspective on Sociology and Feminism*. Vancouver: Press Gang Publishers, 1996.

———. *Memory Serves*. Edmonton: NeWest, 2015.

Maracle, Sylvia. "The Eagle Has Landed: Native Women, Leadership, and Community Development." In *Strong Women Stories: Native Vision and Community Survival*, edited by Kim Anderson and Bonita Lawrence, 70–80. Toronto: Sumach Press, 2003.

Markides, Jennifer. "Being Indigenous in the Indigenous Education Classroom: A Critical Self-Study of Teaching in an Impossible and Imperative Assignment." In *Fostering a Relational Pedagogy: Self-Study as Transformative Praxis,* edited by Ellen Lyle, 35–44. Leiden: Brill, 2018.

———. "Examining the Ethical Implications and Emotional Entailments of Teaching Indigenous Education: An Indigenous Educator's Self-Study." In *Self-Study and Diversity III,* edited by Julian Kitchen, Linda Fitzgerald, and Deborah Tidwell, 103–21. Leiden: Brill, 2021.

Martel, Karine. "*Daniels v. Canada:* The Supreme Court's Racialized Understanding of the Métis and Section 91 (24)." In *Looking Back and Living Forward: Indigenous Research Rising Up,* edited by Jennifer Markides and Laura Forsythe, 145–54. Leiden: Brill, 2018.

Mazur, Derek, dir. *Places Not Our Own*. Ottawa: National Film Board of Canada, 1986. http://www.nfb.ca/film/places_not_our_own.

McCall, Sophie. "Diaspora and Nation in Métis Writing." In *Cultural Grammars of Nation, Diaspora, and Indigeneity in Canada,* edited by Christine Kim, Sophie McCall and Melinda Baum Singer, 21–41. Waterloo: Wilfrid Laurier University Press, 2013.

McCauley, Beth. "Students on Hopi Partitioned Land Learn in Spite of Stress." *Indian Country Today*, 24 February 1997.

McGill, Jena. "An Institutional Suicide Machine: Discrimination against Federally Sentenced Aboriginal Women in Canada." *Race/Ethnicity: Multidisciplinary Global Contexts* 2, no. 1 (2008): 89–119.

McIvor, Sharon Donna. "Aboriginal Women Unmasked: Using Equality Litigation to Advance Women's Rights." *Canadian Journal of Women and the Law* 16 (2004): 106–36.

McLeod, Neal. "Exploring Cree Narrative Memory." PhD diss., University of Regina, 2005. http://hdl.handle.net/10294/14133.

———. "Introduction." In *Indigenous Poetics in Canada*, edited by Neil McLeod, 1–15. Waterloo: Wilfrid Laurier University Press, 2015.

McNiven, Ian J. "Theoretical Challenges of Indigenous Archaeology: Setting an Agenda." *American Antiquity* 81, no. 1 (2016): 27–41.

Medicine, Beatrice. "Professionalization of Native American Women: Towards a Research Agenda." *Wicazo Sa Review* 4 (1988): 31–42.

Métis Centre of the National Aboriginal Health Organization. "Paucity of Métis-Specific Health and Well-Being Data and Information: Underlying Factors." Ottawa: National Collaborating Centre for Indigenous Health, 2011.

Métis Crossing. "About Métis Crossing." Accessed 26 May 2021. https://metiscrossing.com/about-metis-crossing/.

Métis in Space. "Back 2 the Land." *Briarpatch*, 3 September 2020. https://briarpatchmagazine.com/articles/view/back-2-the-land-2land-2furious.

Métis Nation of Alberta. "Governance." Accessed 12 March 2023. https://albertametis.com/governance/.

Métis National Council. *Métis Education Report: A Special Report on Métis Education Prepared by the Métis National Council for the Summit on Aboriginal Education.* Saskatoon: Gabriel Dumont Institute and Métis National Council, 2006.

Meyer, Manulani Aluli. "Acultural Assumptions of Empiricism: A Native Hawaiian Critique." *Canadian Journal of Native Education* 25 (2001): 188–98.

———. "Hoea Ea: Land Education and Food Sovereignty in Hawaii." *Environmental Education Research* 20 (2014): 98–101.

———. "Indigenous and Authentic: Hawaiian Epistemology and the Triangulation of Meaning." In *Handbook of Critical and Indigenous Methodologies*, edited by Norman K. Denzin, Yvonna S. Lincoln, and Linda Tuhiwai Smith, 217–32. Thousand Oaks: Sage Publications, 2008.

———. "The War on Academic Women: Reflections on Postfeminism in the Neoliberal Academy." *Journal of Communication Inquiry* 37, no. 4 (2013): 274–83.

Michell, Herman, Yvonne Vizina, Camie Augustus, and Jason Sawyer. *Learning Indigenous Science from Place: Research Study Examining Indigenous-Based Science Perspectives in Saskatchewan First Nations and Métis Community Contexts.* Executive Summary. Saskatoon: University of Saskatchewan Aboriginal Education Research Centre, 2008. https://aerc.usask.ca/downloads/Learning-Indigenous-Science-From-Place.pdf.

Mihesuah, Devon Abbott. "American Indians, Anthropologists, Pothunters, and Repatriation: Ethical, Religious, and Political Differences." *American Indian Quarterly* 20, no. 2 (1996): 229–37.

———. *Indigenous American Women: Decolonization, Empowerment, Activism.* Lincoln: University of Nebraska Press, 2003.

Miller, Susan A., and James Riding In, eds. *Native Historians Write Back: Decolonizing American Indian History.* Lubbock: Texas Tech University Press, 2011.

Million, Dian. "Felt Theory." *American Quarterly* 60, no. 2 (2008): 267–72.

———. *Therapeutic Nations: Healing in an Age of Indigenous Human Rights.* Tucson: University of Arizona Press, 2013.

Monchalin, Renée, and Lisa Monchalin. "Closing the Health Service Gap: Métis Women and Solutions for Culturally-Safe Health Services." *Journal of Indigenous Wellbeing* 3, no. 1 (2018): 18–29.

Monchalin, Renée, Janet Smylie, and Cheryllee Bourgeois. "'It's Not Like I'm More Indigenous There and I'm Less Indigenous Here': Urban Métis Women's Identity and Access to Health and Social Services in Toronto, Canada." *AlterNative: An International Journal of Indigenous Peoples* 16, no. 4 (2020): 323–31.

Monchalin, Renée, Janet Smylie, and Earl Nowgesic. "'I Guess I Shouldn't Come Back Here': Racism and Discrimination as a Barrier to Accessing Health and Social Services for Urban Métis Women in Toronto, Canada." *Journal of Racial and Ethnic Health Disparities* 7, no. 2 (2020): 251–61.

Moreton-Robinson, Aileen. *Talkin' up to the White Woman: Aboriginal Women and Feminism.* Brisbane: University of Queensland Press, 2000.

Murphy, Lucy Eldersveld. "Public Mothers: Native American and Métis Women as Creole Mediators in the Nineteenth-Century Midwest." *Journal of Women's History* 14, no. 4 (2003): 142–66.

Murphy, Paul P., Katelyn Polantz, Marshall Cohen, and Evan Perez. "At Least 150 People Charged by Justice Department in U.S. Capitol Riot." *CNN Digital*, 26 January 2021. https://www.ctvnews.ca/world/at-least-150-people-charged-by-justice-department-in-u-s-capitol-riot-1.5282887.

Murry, Adam Thomas, Cheryl Barnabe, Sharon Foster, Aisha S. Taylor, Elaine J. Atay, Rita Henderson, and Lindsay Crowshoe. "Indigenous Mentorship in the Health Sciences: Actions and Approaches of Mentors." *Teaching and Learning in Medicine* 34, no. 3 (2021): 266–76.

Muzyka, Kyle. "What's Métis Scrip? North America's 'Largest Land Swindle,' Says Indigenous Lawyer." *CBC News*, 25 *April 2019*. https://www.cbc.ca/radio/unreserved/from-scrip-to-road-allowances-canada-s-complicated-history-with-the-m%C3%A9tis-1.5100375/what-s-m%C3%A9tis-scrip-north-america-s-largest-land-swindle-says-indigenous-lawyer-1.5100507.

National Inquiry into Missing and Murdered Indigenous Women and Girls. *Reclaiming Power and Place. The Final Report of the National Inquiry into Missing and Murdered Indigenous Women and Girls*. Volume 1a. Vancouver: National Inquiry into Missing and Murdered Indigenous Women and Girls, 2019. https://www.mmiwg-ffada.ca/wp-content/uploads/2019/06/Final_Report_Vol_1a-1.pdf.

———. *Reclaiming Power and Place. The Final Report of the National Inquiry into Missing and Murdered Indigenous Women and Girls*. Volume 1b. Vancouver: National Inquiry into Missing and Murdered Indigenous Women and Girls, 2019. https://www.mmiwg-ffada.ca/wp-content/uploads/2019/06/Final_Report_Vol_1b.pdf.

Neuhaus, Mareike. *Decolonizing Poetics of Indigenous Literatures*. Regina: University of Regina Press, 2015.

Nicholas, George P., and Thomas D. Andrews. "Indigenous Archaeology in the Post-Modern World." In *At a Crossroads: Archaeology and First Peoples in Canada*, edited by George P. Nicholas and Thomas D. Andrews, 1–18. Burnaby: SFU Press, 1997.

Nickel, Sarah A. "'I Am Not a Women's Libber Although Sometimes I Sound Like One': Indigenous Feminism and Politicized Motherhood." *American Indian Quarterly* 41, no. 4 (2017): 299–335.

Norris, Mary Jane, Stewart Clatworthy, and Evelyn Peters. "The Urbanization of Aboriginal Populations in Canada: A Half Century in Review." In *Indigenous in the City: Contemporary Identities and Cultural Innovation*, edited by Evelyn Peters and Chris Andersen, 29–45. Vancouver: UBC Press, 2013.

Oberholtzer, Cath. "'A Womb with A View': Cree Moss Bags and Cradleboards." In *Papers of the Twenty-Eighth Algonquian Conference*, edited by David Pentland, 258–73. Winnipeg: University of Manitoba, 1997.

O'Reilly-Scanlon, Kathleen, Christine Crowe, and Angelina Weenie. "Pathways to Understanding: 'Wahkohtowin' as a Research Methodology." *McGill Journal of Education/Revue des sciences de l'éducation de McGill* 39, no. 1 (2004): 29–44.

Oster, Bailey, and Marilyn Lizee, eds. *Stories of Métis Women: Tales My Kookum Told Me*. Calgary: Durvile and UpRoute Books, 2021.

Ouellette, Grace. *The Fourth World: An Indigenous Perspective on Feminism and Aboriginal Women's Activism*. Halifax: Fernwood Publishing, 2002.

Paci, Chris. *Research on Effective Practices to Support Métis Learners' Achievement and Self-Identification Project. Final Report*. Ottawa: Métis Nation of Ontario, 2011.

Pannekoek, Frits. "Métis Studies: The Development of a Field and New Directions." In *From Rupert's Land to Canada: Essays in Honour of John E. Foster*, edited by Theodore Binnema, Gerhard J. Ens, and Rod Macleod, 111–28. Edmonton: University of Alberta Press, 2001.

Parsons, Elizabeth, and Vincenza Priola. "Agents for Change and Changed Agents: The Micro-Politics of Change and Feminism in the Academy." *Gender, Work and Organization* 20, no. 5 (2013): 580–98.

Paulson, Jennifer, Yvonne Poitras Pratt, and Guido Contreras. *Métis Education in Alberta: K-12 Policy Discussion Paper.* Edmonton: Rupertsland Institute, 2015. https://www.rupertsland.org/wp-content/uploads/2017/08/metis-education-k-12-final-march-13-2015.pdf.

Payment, Diane. *The Free People—Li Gens Libres: A History of the Métis Community of Batoche, Saskatchewan.* Calgary: University of Calgary Press, 2009.

———. "*Une femme en vaut deux*—'Strong Like Two People': Marie Fisher Gaudet of Fort Good Hope, Northwest Territories." In *Contours of a People: Metis Family, Mobility, and History*, edited by Brenda Macdougall, Carolyn Podruchny, and Nicole St-Onge, 265–99. Norman: University of Oklahoma Press, 2012.

———. "'La Vie en Rose?' Métis Women at Batoche, 1870–1920." In *Women of the First Nations: Power, Wisdom, and Strength*, edited by Christine Miller and Patricia Chuchryk, 19–38. Winnipeg: University of Manitoba Press, 1996.

Peters, Evelyn, and Chris Andersen, eds. *Indigenous in the City: Contemporary Identities and Cultural Innovation*. Vancouver: UBC Press 2013.

Peters, Evelyn, Matthew Stock, and Adrian Werner. *Rooster Town: The History of an Urban Métis Community, 1901–1961.* Winnipeg: University of Manitoba Press, 2018.

Peterson, Jacqueline. "Red River Redux: Métis Ethnogenesis and the Great Lakes Region." In *Contours of a People: Metis Family, Mobility, and History*, edited by Brenda Macdougall, Carolyn Podruchny, and Nicole St-Onge, 22–58. Norman: University of Oklahoma Press, 2012.

Peterson, Jacqueline, and Jennifer S.H. Brown, eds. *The New Peoples: Being and Becoming Métis in North America*. Winnipeg: University of Manitoba Press, 1985.

Pettipas, Katherine. *Severing the Ties that Bind: Government Repression of Indigenous Religious Ceremonies on the Prairies*. Winnipeg: University of Manitoba Press, 1994.

Podruchny, Carolyn, and Nicole St-Onge. "Scuttling Along a Spider's Web: Mobility and Kinship in Métis Ethnogenesis." In *Contours of a People: Metis Family, Mobility, and History,* edited by Brenda Macdougall, Carolyn Podruchny, and Nicole St-Onge, 59–92. Norman: University of Oklahoma Press, 2012.

Poitras Pratt, Yvonne. *Digital Storytelling in Indigenous Education: A Decolonizing Journey for a Métis Community*. New York: Routledge, 2020.

———. "A Family of Learners: Métis People in Canada and Their Educational Lifeworlds." In *Adult Education and Lifelong Learning in Canada: Advancing a Critical Legacy,* edited by Susan M. Brigham, Robert McGray, and Kaela Jubas, 15–25. Toronto: Thompson, 2020.

Poitras Pratt, Yvonne, and Sulyn Bodnaresko, eds. *Truth and Reconciliation through Education: Stories of Decolonizing Practices*. Edmonton: Brush Education, 2023.

Poitras Pratt, Yvonne, and Lyn Daniels. "Metis Remembrances of Education: Bridging History with Memory." In *Proceedings of the IDEAS: Rising to Challenge Conference,* edited by Paulino Preciado Babb, 179–87. Calgary: Werklund School of Education, University of Calgary, 2014.

Poitras Pratt, Yvonne, and Solange Lalonde. "The Alberta Métis Education Council: Realizing Self-Determination in Education." In *Knowing the Past, Facing the Future: Indigenous Education in Canada,* edited by Sheila Carr-Stewart, 265–87. Saskatoon: Purich, 2019.

Pratyush, Dayal. "Carrie Bourassa's Suspension 'Bittersweet,' Says Métis Professor Who Brought Complaint to U of S." *CBC News*, 2 November 2021. https://www.cbc.ca/news/community-members-say-they-are-displeased-at-carrie-bourassa-1.6234213.

Préfontaine, Darren R. "Métis Writers." The Virtual Museum of Métis History and Culture, 30 May 2003. https://www.metismuseum.ca/resource.php/00733.

Ramirez, Renya. *Native Hubs: Culture, Community, and Belonging in Silicon Valley and Beyond.* Durham: Duke University Press, 2007.

Reading, Charlotte. "Introduction: Rethinking Determinants of Aboriginal Peoples' Health." In *Determinants of Indigenous Peoples' Health*, edited by Margo Greenwood, Sarah de Leeuw, Nicole Marie Lindsay, and Charlotte Reading, 3–17. Toronto: Canadian Scholars Press, 2015.

Reder, Deanna, and Alix Shield. "'I Write This for All of You'": Recovering the Unpublished RCMP 'Incident' in Maria Campbell's *Halfbreed* (1973)." *Canadian Literature* 237 (2019): 13–24.

Richmond, Chantelle, Debbie Martin, Libby Dean, Heather Castleden, and Namaste Marsden. *Transformative Networks: How ACADRE/NEAHR Support for Graduate Students Has Impacted Aboriginal Health Research in Canada.* Victoria: Aboriginal Health Research Networks Secretariat, 2013. http://hdl.handle.net/1828/5419.

Riddle, Emily. "Mâmawiwikowin: Shared First Nation and Métis Jurisdiction on the Prairies." *Briarpatch* 49, no. 5 (2020): 22–24.

Rivard, Étienne. "Le Fond De L'Ouest: Territoriality, Oral Geographies, and the Métis in the Nineteenth-Century Northwest." In *Contours of a People: Metis Family, Mobility, and History,* edited by Brenda Macdougall, Carolyn Podruchny, and Nicole St-Onge, 143–68. Norman: University of Oklahoma Press, 2012.

Robertson, Carmen, and Sherry Farrell Racette. *Clearing a Path: New Ways of Seeing Traditional Indigenous Art.* Regina: Canadian Plains Research Center, University of Regina, 2009.

Robinson, Shanneen. "The Sundance Ceremony, Part 1." *APTN*, 14 August 2013. https://www.aptnnews.ca/featured/the-sun-dance-ceremony/.

Roscoe, W. *Changing Ones: Third and Fourth Genders in Native North America.* New York: St. Martin's Press, 1998.

Ross, Luana. "From the 'F' Word to Indigenous/Feminisms." *Wicazo Sa Review* 24, no. 2 (2009): 39–52.

Ruest, Agnes M. "A Pictorial History of the Métis and Non-Status in Saskatchewan." The Virtual Museum of Métis History and Culture, December 1976. https://www.metismuseum.ca/resource.php/12301.

R. v. Powley [2003] 2 S.C.R. 207, 2003 SCC 43. https://scc-csc.lexum.com/scc-csc/scc-csc/en/item/2076/index.do.

Santilli, Mara. "Here's How Lactation Experts Are Working to Redefine and Decolonize Breastfeeding." *Well+Good*, 7 December 2020. https://www.wellandgood.com/decolonizing-breastfeeding/.

Saunders, Kelly, and Janique Dubois. *Métis Politics and Governance in Canada*. Vancouver: UBC Press, 2019.

Sawchuk, Joe, Patricia Sawchuk, Terry Ferguson, and Métis Association of Alberta. *Metis Land Rights in Alberta: A Political History*. Edmonton: Métis Association of Alberta, 1981.

Scofield, Gregory. *I Knew Two Métis Women*. Victoria: Polestar Book Publishers, 1999.

———. *Thunder Through My Veins: Memories of a Métis Childhood*. Toronto: HarperCollins, 1999.

Scott, Bryanna. "Métis Women's Experiences in Higher Education." *Genealogy* 5, no. 2 (2021): 49. https://doi.org/10.3390/genealogy5020049.

Scott, Duncan C. *Annual Report of the Department of Indian Affairs: Superintendent of Indian Education*. Ottawa: Dominion of Canada, 1910.

Scott, James C. *Seeing Like a State: How Certain Schemes to Improve the Human Condition Have Failed*. New Haven: Yale University Press, 1998.

Scudeler, June. "Indigenous Feminisms." *Canadian Literature* 220 (2014): 138–39.

Sealey, D. Bruce, and Antoine S. Lussier. *The Métis: Canada's Forgotten People*. Winnipeg: Manitoba Métis Federation Press, 1975.

Shore, Frederick J. *Threads in the Sash: The Story of the Métis People*. Winnipeg: Pemmican Publications, 2017.

Silva, Noenoe K. *Aloha Betrayed: Native Hawaiian Resistance to American Colonialism*. Durham: Duke University Press, 2014.

Simpson, Leanne. *As We Have Always Done: Indigenous Freedom through Radical Resistance*. Minneapolis: University of Minnesota Press, 2017.

———. "Birthing an Indigenous Resurgence: Decolonizing Our Pregnancy and Birthing Ceremonies." In *"Until Our Hearts Are On the Ground": Aboriginal Mothering, Oppression, Resistance and Rebirth*, edited by Memee Lavell-Harvard and Jeannette Lavell, 25–33. Toronto: Demeter Press, 2006.

———. "Indigenous Resurgence and Co-Resistance." *Critical Ethnic Studies* 2, no. 2 (2016): 19–34.

Smiley, Cherry. "Not Sacred, Not Squaws: Indigenous Feminism Redefined." PhD diss., Concordia University, 2022.

Smith, Andrea, *Conquest: Sexual Violence and American Indian Genocide*. Cambridge, MA: South End Press, 2005.

———. "Dismantling the Master's Tool with the Master's House: Native Feminist Liberation Theologies." *Journal of Feminist Studies in Religion* 22 (2006): 85–97.

———. "Native American Feminism, Sovereignty, and Social Change." *Feminist Studies* 31, no. 1 (2005): 116–32.

Smith, Andrea, and J. Kēhaulani Kauanui. "Native Feminisms Engage American Studies." *American Quarterly* 60, no. 2 (2008): 241–49.

Smith, Linda Tuhiwai, *Decolonizing Methodologies: Research and Indigenous Peoples*. London, UK: Zed Books, 1999.

Smylie, Janet, and Michelle Firestone. "Back to the Basics: Identifying and Addressing Underlying Challenges in Achieving High Quality and Relevant Health Statistics for Indigenous Populations in Canada." *Statistical Journal of the IAOS* 31, no. 1 (2015): 67–87.

Spaulding, Tom. "Métis Receive Song." *Métis Voyageur: The Official Publication of the Métis Nation of Ontario*, September and October 2004. https://www.metisnation.org/wp-content/uploads/2020/02/mv04_michif_song.pdf.

Spear, Andrew D. "Gaslighting, Confabulation, and Epistemic Innocence." *Topoi* 39, no. 1 (2020): 229–41.

Spillett-Sumner, Tasha. "Gender, Land, and Place: Considering Gender within Land-Based and Place-Based Learning." *Journal for the Study of Religion, Nature and Culture* 15, no. 1 (2021): 11–31.

———. "Pandemic Parenthood." *Raising the Revolution* (blog). 7 December 2020. https://tashaspillett.com/pandemic-parenthood/.

———. "Raising the Revolution." *Canadian Art Magazine*, 3 December 2020. https://canadianart.ca/features/raising-the-revolution/.

Sprague, Douglas N. "Asserting Canadian Authority over Assiniboia." In *Canada and the Métis, 1869–1885*, 33–54. Waterloo: Wilfrid Laurier University Press, 1988.

Spry, Irene M. "The Métis and Mixed Bloods of Rupert's Land Before 1870." In *The New Peoples: Being and Becoming Métis in North America*, edited by Jacqueline Peterson and Jennifer S.H. Brown, 95–118. St. Paul: Minnesota Historical Society Press, 1985.

Starblanket, Gina. "Being Indigenous Feminists: Resurgences against Contemporary Patriarchy." In *Making Space for Indigenous Feminism*. 2nd ed., edited by Joyce Green, 21–41. Halifax: Fernwood Publishing, 2017.

Statistics Canada. "The Daily: Aboriginal Peoples in Canada: Key Results from the 2016 Census." 25 October 2017. https://www150.statcan.gc.ca/n1/daily-quotidien/171025/dq171025a-eng.htm.

St. Denis, Verna. "Feminism Is for Everybody: Aboriginal Women, Feminism, and Diversity." In *Making Space for Indigenous Feminism*. 2nd ed., edited by Joyce Green, 42–62. Halifax: Fernwood Publishing, 2017.

Stevenson, Allyson, and Cheryl Troupe. "From Kitchen Tables to Formal Organizations: Indigenous Women's Social and Political Activism in Saskatchewan to 1980." In *Compelled to Act: Histories of Women's Activism in Western Canada*, edited by Sarah Carter and Nanci Langford, 218–52. Winnipeg: University of Manitoba Press, 2020.

Stieb, Joseph. "Drawing the Line at Taking down Confederate Monuments." *Raleigh News and Observer*, 31 August 2017. https://www.newsobserver.com/opinion/op-ed/article170585572.html.

St-Onge, Nicole. "Memories of Métis Women of Saint-Eustache, Manitoba: 1910–1980." *Native Studies Review* 17, no. 2 (2008): 45–68.

———. *Saint-Laurent, Manitoba: Evolving Métis Identities, 1850–1914*. Regina: University of Regina Press, 2004.

St-Onge, Nicole, Carolyn Podruchny, and Brenda Macdougall, eds. *Contours of a People: Metis Family, Mobility, and History*. Norman: University of Oklahoma Press, 2012.

Styres, Sandra. "Literacies of Land: Decolonizing Narratives, Storying, and Literature." In *Indigenous and Decolonizing Studies in Education: Mapping the Long View*, edited by Linda Tuhiwai Smith, Eve Tuck, and K. Wayne Yang, 24–37. New York: Routledge, 2019.

Styres, Sandra, Celia Haig-Brown, and Melissa Blimkie. "Toward a Pedagogy of Land: The Urban Context." *Canadian Journal of Education* 36, no. 2 (2013): 188–221.

Supernant, Kisha. "Archaeology of the Métis." In *Historical Archaeology Oxford Handbook Online*, edited by Stephen Silliman. Oxford: Oxford University Press, 2018.

———. "From Haunted to Haunting: Métis Ghosts in the Past and Present." In *Blurring Timescapes, Subverting Erasure: Remembering Ghost on the Margins of History*, edited by Sarah Surface-Evans, Amanda E. Garrison, and Kisha Supernant, 85–104. New York: Berghahn Books, 2020.

———. "Reconciling the Past for the Future: The Next 50 Years of Canadian Archaeology in the Post-TRC Era." *Canadian Journal of Archaeology* 42, no. 1 (2018): 144–53.

Sweet, Paige L. "The Sociology of Gaslighting." *American Sociological Review* 84, no. 5 (2019): 851–75.

Tait, Caroline, Maria Campbell, Kate Gillis, and Autumn LaRose-Smith. "Pretendians and Their Impact on Metis Identity." Virtual Round Table from the University of Regina, 9 December 2021. https://youtu.be/GojYBpiMXdM.

Teillet, Jean. *The North-West Is Our Mother: The Story of Louis Riel's People, the Métis Nation*. Toronto: HarperCollins, 2019.

Thistle, Jesse. *From the Ashes: My Story of Being Métis, Homeless, and Finding My Way Back*. Toronto: Simon and Schuster, 2019.

———. "The Puzzle of the Morrissette-Arcand Clan: A History of Métis Historic and Intergenerational Trauma." Master's thesis, University of Waterloo, 2016. https://uwspace.uwaterloo.ca/handle/10012/10872.

Thobani, Sunera. *Exalted Subjects: Studies in the Making of Race and Nation in Canada*. Toronto: University of Toronto Press, 2007.

Thompson, Charles Duncan. *Red Sun: Gabriel Dumont, the Folk Hero*. Saskatoon: Gabriel Dumont Institute, 2017.

Thrush, Coll. *Native Seattle: Histories from the Crossing-Over Place*. Seattle: University of Washington Press, 2007.

Todd, Zoe. "Honouring our Great-Grandmothers: An Ode to Caroline LaFramboise, Twentieth-Century Métis Matriarch." In *In Good Relation: History, Gender, and Kinship in Indigenous Feminisms*, edited by Sarah Nickel and Amanda Fehr, 171–81. Winnipeg: University of Manitoba Press, 2020.

Tough, Frank. *"As Their Natural Resources Fail": Native People and the Economic History of Northern Manitoba, 1870–1930*. Vancouver: UBC Press, 1996.

Troupe, Cheryl. *Expressing Our Heritage: Métis Artistic Designs*. Saskatoon: Gabriel Dumont Institute, 2002.

———. "Mapping Métis Stories: Land Use, Gender and Kinship in the Qu'Appelle Valley, 1850–1950." PhD diss., University of Saskatchewan, 2019. https://harvest.usask.ca/handle/10388/12122.

———. "Métis Women: Social Structure, Urbanization and Political Activism, 1850–1980." Master's thesis, University of Saskatchewan, 2009. https://harvest.usask.ca/handle/10388/etd-12112009-150223.

———. "Women's Agency Is in Their Kitchen as They Own Their Property." Lecture. Gabriel Dumont Institute Culture Conference, Saskatoon, SK, 6 February 2020.

Truth and Reconciliation Commission of Canada. *Calls to Action*. Truth and Reconciliation Commission of Canada, 2015. https://publications.gc.ca/collections/collection_2015/trc/IR4-8-2015-eng.pdf.

———. *Final Report of the Truth and Reconciliation Commission of Canada (Volume One: Summary): Honouring the Truth, Reconciling for the Future*. Toronto: Lorimer and Company, 2015.

Turpel-Lafond, Mary Ellen. *In Plain Sight: Addressing Indigenous-Specific Racism and Discrimination in B.C. Health Care: Summary Report*. https://engage.gov.bc.ca/app/uploads/sites/613/2020/11/In-Plain-Sight-Summary-Report.pdf.

Underwood, Jody Beck. "Nurse Experiences: Caring for Clients from Cultures which Are Different than the Nurse's Culture of Origin." Master's thesis, Gonzaga University, 1997. ProQuest (AAT 1384659).

United Nations General Assembly. Declaration on the Rights of Indigenous Peoples, A/RES/61/295 (13 September 2007). https://social.desa.un.org/issues/indigenous-peoples/united-nations-declaration-on-the-rights-of-indigenous-peoples.

University of Saskatchewan. "Educational Foundations: Land-Based Indigenous Focus." Department of Education. Accessed 23 June 2018. https://education.usask.ca/departments/efdt.php.

Valaskakis, Gail Gutherie, Madeleine Dion Stout, and Eric Guimond, eds. *Restoring the Balance: First Nations Women, Community, and Culture*. Winnipeg: University of Manitoba Press, 2009.

Van Kirk, Sylvia. *Many Tender Ties: Women in Fur-Trade Society, 1670–1870*. Norman: University of Oklahoma Press, 1983.

Vaughan, Genevieve. *Women and the Gift Economy: A Radically Different Worldview Is Possible*. Toronto: Inanna Publications, 2007.

Voth, Daniel. "'Descendants of the Original Lords of the Soil': Indignation, Disobedience, and Women Who Jig on Sundays." *Native American and Indigenous Studies* 7, no. 2 (2020): 87–113.

———. "Her Majesty's Justice Be Done: Métis Legal Mobilization and the Pitfalls to Indigenous Political Movement Building." *Canadian Journal of Political Science* 49, no. 2 (2016): 243–66.

———. "The Race Question in Canada and the Politics of Racial Mixing." In *A People and a Nation: New Directions in Contemporary Métis Studies*, edited by Jennifer Adese and Chris Andersen, 67–91. Vancouver: UBC Press, 2021.

Vowel, Chelsea. "Giving My Children Cree Names Is a Powerful Act of Reclamation." *CBC News*, 4 November 2018. https://www.cbc.ca/news/indigenous/opinion-cree-names-reclamation-chelsea-vowel-1.4887604.

Voyageur, Cora J. *My Heroes Have Always Been Indians: A Century of Great Indigenous Albertans*. Edmonton: Brush Education, 2018.

Vrooman, Nicholas. "Many Eagle Set Thirsty Dance (Sun Dance) Song: The Metis Receive Sun Dance Song." In *Metis Legacy II*, edited by Lawrence Barkwell, Leah

Dorion, and Audreen Hourie, 187–91. Saskatoon: Gabriel Dumont Institute, 2006.

Wadsworth, William T.D., Kisha Supernant, and Vadim A. Kravchinsky. "An Integrated Remote Sensing Approach to Métis Archaeology in the Canadian Prairies." *Archaeological Prospection* 28, no. 3 (2021): 321–37.

Wang, Caroline, and Mary Ann Burris. "Photovoice: Concept, Methodology, and Use for Participatory Needs Assessment." *Health Education and Behaviour* 24, no. 3 (1997): 369–87.

Watkins, Joe. "Through Wary Eyes: Indigenous Perspectives on Archaeology." *Annual Review of Anthropology* 34 (2005): 429–49.

Watts, Vanessa. "Indigenous Place-Thought and Agency Amongst Humans and Non-Humans (First Woman and Sky Woman Go on a European World Tour!)." *Decolonization: Indigeneity, Education and Society* 2, no. 1 (2013): 20–34.

Weber-Pillwax, Cora. "Indigenous Researchers and Indigenous Research Methods: Cultural Influences or Cultural Determinants of Research Methods." *Pimatisiwin: A Journal of Aboriginal and Indigenous Community Health* 2, no.1 (2004): 77–90.

Welsh, Christine. "Voices of the Grandmothers: Reclaiming a Métis Heritage." *Canadian Literature* 131 (1991): 15–24.

Wetzler, Scott. "Living with the Passive-Aggressive Man." *Cosmopolitan*, October 1992, 238–41.

Whelshula, Martina Marie. "Healing through Decolonization: A Study in the Deconstruction of the Western Scientific Paradigm and the Process of Retribalizing among Native Americans." PhD diss., California Institute of Integral Studies, 1999. ProQuest (AAT 9940039).

Wildcat, Matthew. "Wahkohtowin in Action." *Constitutional Forum* 27, no. 1 (2018): 13–24.

Williams, Susan M., and Joy Harjo. "American Indian Feminism." In *The Reader's Companion to U.S. Women's History,* edited by Wilma Mankiller, Gwendolyn Mink, Marysa Navarro, Barbara Smith, and Gloria Steinem, 30–41. Boston: Houghton Mifflin, 1998.

Willox, Ashlee, Sherilee Harper, Victoria Edge, "My Word" Storytelling and Digital Media Lab, and Rigoulet Inuit Community Government. "Storytelling in a Digital Age: Digital Storytelling as an Emerging Narrative Method for Preserving and Promoting Indigenous Oral Wisdom." *Qualitative Research* 13, no. 1 (2012): 127–47.

Wilson, Alex. "Becoming Intimate with the Land." *Briarpatch* 49, no. 5 (2020): 30–33.

———. "N'tacimowin inna nah': Our Coming in Stories." *Canadian Woman Studies* 26, nos. 3–4 (2008): 193–99.

———. "Our Coming-In Stories: Cree Identity, Body Sovereignty and Gender Self-Determination." *Journal of Global Indigeneity* 1, no. 1 (2015). https://ro.uow.edu.au/cgi/viewcontent.cgi?article=1011&context=jgi.

———. "Queering Land-Based Education during Covid19." *Journal of Global Indigeneity* 5, no. 1 (2021): 1–10. https://www.journalofglobalindigeneity.com/article/19438-queering-land-based-education-during-covid19.

———. "Skirting the Issues: Indigenous Myths, Misses, and Misogyny." In *Keetsahnak / Our Missing and Murdered Indigenous Sisters*, edited by Kim Anderson, Maria

Campbell, and Christi Belcourt, 161–74. Edmonton: University of Alberta Press, 2018.

Wilson, Alex, and Marie Laing. "Queering Indigenous Education." In *Indigenous and Decolonizing Studies in Education: Mapping the Long View*, edited by Linda Tuhiwai Smith, Eve Tuck, and K. Wayne Yang, 131–45. New York: Routledge, 2019.

Wilson, Alex, and Jaylene Murray. "Queering Indigenous Land-Based Education." In *Queer Ecopedagogies: Explorations in Nature, Sexuality, and Education*, edited by Joshua Russell, 219–31. New York: Springer, 2021.

Wilson, Shawn. *Research Is Ceremony: Indigenous Research Methodologies.* Black Point: Fernwood, 2008.

Wilson, Waziyatawin Angela. *Remember This! Dakota Decolonization and the Eli Taylor Narratives.* Translated by Wahpetunwin Carolyn Schommer. Lincoln: University of Nebraska Press, 2005.

Women's Legal Education and Action Fund. "IAAW: An Outstanding Community Partner." Media Release. Accessed 26 March 2021. https://www.leaf.ca/news/iaaw-an-outstanding-community-partner/.

CONTRIBUTORS

Jennifer Adese (she/her) is otipemisiwak/Métis and was born in British Columbia and raised in southern Ontario. Her otipemisiwak/Métis family are the Lenny family from Duffield, Alberta, a family connected to (among other places) Lac Ste. Anne, St. Albert, and Edmonton (Alberta). Dr. Adese is the current Canada Research Chair in Métis Women, Politics, and Community and an Associate Professor in the Department of Sociology at University of Toronto Mississauga. She was previously Associate Professor and Program Coordinator of Indigenous Studies in the School of Indigenous and Canadian Studies at Carleton University. Dr. Adese has worked with Métis organizations in areas related to Métis Nation history, identity, housing, early learning and childcare, and violence against Métis women, girls, and 2SLGBTQQIA+ people. She is also the author of *Aboriginal™: The Cultural & Economic Politics of Recognition* (University of Manitoba Press, 2022) and co-editor of *A People and a Nation: New Directions in Contemporary Métis Studies* (with Chris Andersen, UBC Press, 2021). Her work has been published in *Studies in American Indian Literatures, TOPIA, Decolonization: Indigeneity, Education & Society, American Indian Quarterly, MediaTropes, Public*, and *University of Toronto Quarterly*.

Christi Belcourt (apihtâwikosisâniskwêw / mânitow sâkahikanihk) is a visual artist, designer, community organizer, environmentalist, social justice advocate, and avid land-based arts and language learner. Christi is a visual artist with a deep respect for the traditions and knowledge of her people. Like generations of Indigenous artists before her, she celebrates the beauty of the natural world while exploring nature's symbolic properties. Her paintings are found within many public and permanent collections across North America including the National Gallery of Canada, the Art Gallery of Ontario, the Gabriel Dumont Museum, the Thunder Bay Art Gallery, and the Minneapolis Institute of Art, among others. She was named Aboriginal Arts Laureate for 2014 by the Ontario Arts Council. In 2016 she received both the Premier's Arts Award and a Governor General's Award for Innovation. In 2023 she received an Honorary Doctorate in Visual Arts from Algoma University (Sault Ste. Marie, Ontario) and Honorary Doctor of Letters, Wilfrid Laurier University (Waterloo, Ontario). Christi has also organized several large, national, community-based projects of note including Walking with Our Sisters, the Willisville Mountain Project, Nimkii Aazhibikong, and various works done with Onaman Collective. Christi donates the proceeds from her collaborations and awards to Nimkii Aazhibikong, the year-round Indigenous language and traditional arts camp that she, along with a small group of people, started in 2017. The camp is committed to the revitalization of Anishinaabemowin language along with providing opportunities for Elders and youth to come together in a land-based learning environment.

Hannah Bouvier, BA, is a Métis Juris Doctor candidate. Raised in southeastern Alberta, Hannah has been able to maintain strong kinship ties to her family's home community of San Clara, Manitoba. These kinship connections extend into Boggy Creek, Roblin, and to the historic Métis communities surrounding the Red River. Hannah's own research focuses on traditional plants and medicines in relation to wellness. Additionally, she has been able to work on various projects that further Métis women's wellness.

Rita Bouvier, MEd, is a Metis writer, editor (structural/substantive), and "retired" educator. Her fourth collection of poetry, *a beautiful rebellion,* was released April 2023 by Thistledown Press. Rita's poetry has appeared in literary anthologies and journals—print and online—musicals, and television productions, and has been translated into Spanish, German, and Cree-Michif of her home community of sakitawak—Île-à-la-Crosse, Saskatchewan, Canada—which is situated on the historic trading and meeting grounds of Cree and Dene people (Treaty 10). Rita's maternal kinship ties include Bouvier, Gardiner, Daigneault, Jordain, Lafleur, and Morin lines. Her ancestors worked for the Hudson's Bay Company and Réveillon Frere. Rita has contributed as a speaker, researcher, editor, and author to essays, reports, and books on education, highlighting the experiences of Indigenous people. Rita is honoured to have received recognition for service to the teaching profession and leadership in public education (K–12 and post-secondary), specifically addressing Indigenous education—locally, nationally, and internationally, and for her artistic practice. When called upon, Rita continues to work with communities and public institutions in their responses to the Truth and Reconciliation Commission's Calls to Action. She currently serves as a volunteer with the Saskatchewan Ânskohk Writers Circle Inc. and the Indigenous Editors Association.

Vicki Bouvier, PhD, is a proud and strong Michif woman. Her relatives come from the historic St. Francois Xavier community of the Red River as well as Boggy Creek, Manitoba, where her father was born and raised. Dr. Bouvier grew up in Calgary, Alberta, and has been closely connected to the Métis Nation of Alberta Region 3 her entire life. Her father, the late Ephram Bouvier, served as both Vice-President and President of the Métis Nation of Alberta Region 3 during his lifetime. His legacy has a meaningful impact on Bouvier's passion, research endeavours, and advocacy contributions. Both her master's and PhD research focused on Métis knowledge, experience, and strength. Moreover, Bouvier explores Indigenous oral systems as both pedagogy and knowledge assessment while centring those philosophies and practices in her post-secondary teaching. Dr. Bouvier is currently an Assistant Professor at Mount Royal University, Calgary, teaching in Indigenous Studies.

Robline Davey is a citizen of Métis Nation British Columbia, a PhD candidate at Simon Fraser University in the Educational Technology and Learning Design program, and an Indigenous Experiential Learning Coordinator at Thompson Rivers University. Her funded research, through a Network Environments for Indigenous Health Research Doctoral Scholarship and a Social Sciences and Humanities Research Council Doctoral Fellowship, examines Métis feminisms, Métis methodologies, women's intersectionality, intergenerational trauma, experiences with marginalization, and how resulting self-concepts have shaped access to and engagement with post-secondary education and resulting career paths. Her initiatives create opportunities for Indigenous students, strengthening relationships with community organizations to create pathways for employment. Her maternal grandparents are from St. Norbert, St. Vital, St. Boniface, and St. Pierre Jolys (Manitoba), migrating to British Columbia for economic opportunity in the 1950s with their children. Her settler roots are from her father, whose English ancestors settled in Saskatchewan and Manitoba. Having grown up in British Columbia, Robline is engaged in an ongoing pursuit to rebuild cultural traditions with connections to kin, scholarship, and through volunteer work as an elected board member supporting her local Métis community. Her Métis family names include Charette, Roy, Nault, Gaudry, Lagimodiere, Rochelau, Landry, Morand, Delorme, Lalonde, Gosselin, Lafreniere, and Dease, with scrip records, river lots, and connections to the Red River settlement.

Leah Marie Dorion is an interdisciplinary Metis artist raised in Prince Albert, Saskatchewan. A teacher, painter, filmmaker, and published writer, Leah views her Metis heritage as providing her with a unique bridge for knowledge between all people. Leah holds Bachelor of Education, Bachelor of Arts, and Master of Arts degrees. She has numerous creative projects to her credit, including academic papers for the Royal Commission on Aboriginal Peoples, books for children, gallery showings of her artworks, and numerous video documentaries that showcase Metis culture and history. Leah's paintings honour the spiritual strength of Aboriginal women and the sacred feminine. Leah believes that women play a key role in passing on vital knowledge for all of humanity, a concept that is deeply reflected in her artistic practice. She believes women are the first teachers to the next generation.

Marilyn Dumont is a Metis poet, writer, and professor who teaches for the faculties of Arts and Native Studies at the University of Alberta. Her four collections of poetry have won provincial or national awards: *A Really Good Brown Girl* (1996); *green girl dreams Mountains* (2001); *that tongued belonging* (2007); and *The Pemmican Eaters* (2015). She was awarded the 2018 Lifetime Membership from the League of Canadian Poets for her contributions to poetry in Canada. In 2019, she was awarded the University of Alberta Distinguished Alumni Award and the Alberta Lieutenant Governor's Distinguished Artist Award. Her kinship ties include Boudreau, Vaness, and Dufresne. The Dumonts have been in Alberta since 1790 as suppliers of furs and pemmican, while the Vaness and Dufresne families were language interpreters on the Onion Lake First Nation.

Nicki Ferland, PhD student, is a two-spirit Métis who lives with her wife and daughter in Winnipeg. Her mother and father are both descended from scrip-bearing Métis families with ancestral roots in St. Vital and St. Boniface (Winnipeg), and Lorette, Manitoba. She is the descendent of Sarah Goulet, who, along with her husband, Elzéar Lagimodière, established a permanent community in Lorette, and Marguerite Poitras, a recognized matriarch of the Métis Nation, whose father-in-law was André Beauchemin, MLA for St. Vital in the 1869 provisional government and first Manitoba legislature (1870 to 1874). She also has cousins among the Grants, Ducharmes, Harrisons, and Fishers. Nicki has a Master of Education degree with a concentration in Indigenous land-based education from the University of Saskatchewan. Her research explores Métis relationships with Winnipeg and other prairie cities. She is a land-based educator with the Community Engaged Learning department at the University of Manitoba, and is vice-chair of the Two-Spirit Michif Local.

Chantal Fiola is Michif (Red River Métis) with family from St. Laurent, St. Vital, Ste. Anne, and Ste. Geneviève, Manitoba. Her ancestors Pierre "Bostonnais" Pangman Jr. and Marie Wewejikabawik were among four Michif families who established the historic Métis community of St. Laurent. Chantal is a registered citizen of the Manitoba Métis Federation (MMF). Dr. Fiola is the award-winning author of two books, including *Returning to Ceremony: Spirituality in Manitoba Métis Communities*. Currently, with funding from the Social Sciences and Humanities Research Council of Canada and the Manitoba Research Alliance, she is Project Director on a research study titled "Expressions of Métis Spirituality and Religion Across the Homeland." Dr. Fiola is Interim Associate Vice-President, Indigenous Engagement, at the University of Winnipeg, where she is also the Distinguished Indigenous Scholar's Chair and an Associate Professor. She is a founding member of the Two-Spirit Michif Local of the MMF and is on the Board of Directors for Two-Spirit

Manitoba, which hosted the first-ever Two-Spirit Sundance in 2023. Chantal lives in Winnipeg with her wife and their daughter.

Laura Forsythe, PhD, is a Michif Assistant Professor at the University of Winnipeg in the Faculty of Education. Forsythe's research focuses on Métis-specific contributions to the academy, Métis inclusion efforts, Métis research methodologies, and educational sovereignty. She is also the elected Bison Local Chairperson of the Manitoba Métis Federation, the official democratic and self-governing political representation of the Red River Métis. Her kinship ties include the Huppe, Ward, Berard, Morin, Lavallee, and Cyr lines. Her ancestors worked for the Northwest and Hudson's Bay companies, fought in the Victory of Frog Plain, and owned Lot 31, the site of a contemporary Métis space called Pakan Town.

Lucy Fowler, PhD, is a Two-Spirit Métis woman, born and raised in Winnipeg, Manitoba, and an active member of the Two-Spirit Michif Local of the Manitoba Métis Federation. Her family were Sinclairs, Cummings, Prudens, some of whom took scrip in St. Andrews and St. Johns, and she also has other family and ancestors from Red River, Oxford House, Norway House, and Sioux Valley Dakota Nation, and settler family from Ireland and the Orkney Islands. Lucy is a community organizer and co-founder of the Mamawi Project, a grassroots Métis collective dedicated to virtual knowledge mobilization and creating kinship-building opportunities for Métis young people across the diaspora. Lucy is an Assistant Professor in the Faculty of Education at the University of Manitoba, with a research and teaching focus on Métis youth identity, Indigenous education, queer theory, hip-hop pedagogies, and youth cultures.

Chelsea Gabel, PhD, is a card-carrying member of the Manitoba Métis Federation, Canada Research Chair in Indigenous Well-Being, Community-Engagement & Innovation, and an Associate Professor in the Department of Health, Aging and Society and the Indigenous Studies Department at McMaster University. Chelsea is the lead of the Indigenous Mentorship Network of Ontario and a co-lead of the Network Environments for Indigenous Health Research National Coordinating Centre. Chelsea's current research focuses on Métis health and well-being, arts-based research, and the importance of intergenerational relationships.

Dr. Janice Cindy Gaudet is a daughter, grand-daughter, niece, sister, auntie, and kokum. She belongs to a strong lineage of Métis women's families along the South Saskatchewan River and farming communities near Bellevue, Batoche, St. Laurent, St. Louis, and One Arrow First Nation in what is now the province of Saskatchewan. She has ties to the French-Canadian relations through her father's family. She is an Associate Professor at Campus Saint-Jean, University of Alberta, and Canada Research Chair in Métis Kinship and Land-Based Learning. Métis women's expression of sovereignty is at the forefront of her health and well-being research.

Emily Haines is a Métis and Polish-Canadian woman originally from Winnipeg, Manitoba. She has been living and working in Mistahi Sâkâhikan (St. Albert, Alberta) and Amiskwacîwâskahikan (Edmonton, Alberta) since 2001 and is a citizen of the Métis Nation of Alberta. Her relational network includes the Malaterre, Larocque, Berard, Adam, McIvor, and Fleury families, among many others. While having lived widely across the Métis Homeland over centuries, her relatives have particularly deep roots in the White Horse Plains and the area surrounding Carman, Manitoba, along with strong ties to southern Manitoba and Saskatchewan, and northern North Dakota and Montana more broadly. She is currently pursuing a Master of Arts through the Institute of Prairie and Indigenous Archaeology at the University of Alberta with a specialization in Indigenous Archaeologies. Her research focuses on Métis relationality, resilience, resurgence, and the ongoing ramifications of Métis entanglements with colonialism. She is passionate about supporting the sovereignty, rights, and vitality of all Indigenous nations and understanding the contours of Métis identity and history.

Dr. Shalene Jobin is the founder and first Director of the Indigenous Governance program, and she holds a Canada Research Chair in Indigenous Governance at the Faculty of Native Studies, University of Alberta. Shalene is Cree from her mother (Wuttunee families) and Métis from her father (Jobin and Chalifoux families) and is a member of Red Pheasant Cree First Nation (Treaty 6). Shalene's 2023 book with UBC Press is titled *Nehiyawak Narratives: Upholding Indigenous Economic Relationships*. Jobin has published extensively in edited collections, journals, and community research reports. She has founded and led two large Indigenous research and teaching programs involving multiple faculty partnerships, and is involved in numerous community-led research projects.

Dr. Emma LaRocque is a scholar, author, poet, and professor in the Department of Indigenous Studies at the University of Manitoba, where she has been teaching since 1976. LaRocque is originally from a Cree/Michif-speaking and land-based Metis family and community from northeastern Alberta. Her family's history, culture, and genealogy are rooted in the Red River Metis. She has maintained her family connections and has strongly advocated for gender equality and Metis land, resource, and human rights. Believing in the social purpose of knowledge, Dr. LaRocque has taught and published in the hopes of transforming mainstream Canadian perceptions and policies about Indigenous peoples. Her work has appeared in two books, *Defeathering the Indian* (1975) and *When the Other Is Me: Native Resistance Discourse 1950–1990* (2010), and in a variety of journals and anthologies.

Amanda LaVallee, PhD, is a Red River Metis woman born in Edmonton, Alberta, who grew up in Saskatchewan in the Village of Speers, North Battleford, and Saskatoon. Amanda spent much of her childhood keenly attuned to the prairie landscape through the activities of hunting, trapping, fishing, gathering, and gardening. Her kinship ties include the Branconnier, Beauchamp, Courchene, Delorme, Poitras, Normand, Pilon, Pepin, and Vandale lines. Amanda is an Assistant Professor at the University of Victoria in the School of Social Work, and her research focus is on the health and well-being of Métis people, specifically on their engagement within social systems and their impact on relationships. LaVallee's current research projects focus on intergenerational understandings of Metis identity and Indigenous-specific racism in the academy.

Lynn Lavallee, PhD (she/her), is a citizen of the Métis Nation of Ontario with maternal grandfather ties to Red River (Godon, McIvor,

Swain, Lillie) and paternal ties to the Red River (Taylor), and Metis historic community of Temiscaming (Lavallee, Gauthier, Taylor, Pepin). Lynn has a BA in Kinesiology, BA in Psychology, MSc in Community Health, and PhD in Social Work. Lynn is a full professor and strategic lead, Indigenous Resurgence, in the Faculty of Community Services at Toronto Metropolitan University (TMU). Lynn has fulfilled various administrative roles at the university, all with the focus of advancing Indigenous knowledge in the academy. In 2017, she left TMU and was the University of Manitoba's first Vice Provost Indigenous Engagement. When it became apparent that her and the communities' vision did not align with senior administration's expectations, she resigned and returned to TMU. Lynn's research focus is in the area of Indigenous health, traditional healing and ceremonial practices, mental health and addictions, Indigenous research ethics, and Indigenous research methodologies.

Avery Letendre is a Euro-Canadian settler who works at the Faculty of Native Studies (University of Alberta) as the Continuing Education and Online Project Manager. She holds a Master of Arts (Native Studies) and Bachelor of Commerce from the University of Alberta. Her family names are Berg and Omli (Norway), Fisher (England), Brooks (Germany and Ireland), Till (Hungary), and Chomlack (Ukraine). Avery's partner, Jarod Letendre, and their children are citizens of the Métis Nation of Alberta with Métis family connections from Lac Ste. Anne, Alberta, that include the family names of Belcourt, Gladu, and Gray. Outside of work, Avery serves on the Board of Governors at the Bissell Centre, an organization that works towards poverty elimination in amiskwaciwâskahikan (Edmonton). Avery is committed to working toward decolonization in Canada and is keen to build bridges, interconnections, stronger relationships, and knowledge toward those ends.

Kirsten Lindquist (she/her and they/them) is a PhD student in Indigenous Studies at the Faculty of Native Studies, University of Alberta. They are a citizen of the Métis Nation of Alberta. Kirsten is Cree/Métis from her father (Jenkins, Dion, and Blandion families) and white Euro-settler from her mother. Kirsten's PhD research focuses on connecting arts and performance-based storytelling practices with

Indigenous and research-creation methodologies to explore decolonial sexualities, embodied sovereignties, and diverse kinship relations.

Jennifer Markides, PhD, is a card-carrying member of the Métis Nation of Alberta, SSHRC Tier II Canada Research Chair in Indigenous Youth Wellbeing and Education, and an Assistant Professor in both the Werklund School of Education and the Faculty of Social Work at the University of Calgary. Her research and teaching focus on the holistic well-being of youth and Indigenous education. Critical pedagogy, arts creation, and ethical engagement are at the heart of her practices. She values relationship building and prioritizes listening in community-led projects, allowing her to be responsive to the immediate goals and long-term visions of Indigenous community partners. Jennifer was raised in unceded Wet'suwet'en territory in northern British Columbia and now resides in Treaty 7 territory in southern Alberta. Her Métis family names are McKay, Favel, Ballenden/Ballendine, Linklater, and McDermott/MacDermott, including scrip records and connections to Red River. Like many Métis whose families migrated west, she engages in ongoing processes of learning, relationship building, and honouring commitments of service to Métis people, communities, and organizations, through her academic work and personal life.

Yvonne Poitras Pratt, PhD (citizen of the Métis Nation of Alberta), is Associate Professor at the Werklund School of Education, University of Calgary. Her family roots trace back to Red River with both of her parents from the Fishing Lake Métis Settlement in northern Alberta. Some of the more prominent Métis names in her family tree include Poitras, Parenteau, Fayant, and Calliou, where her great-great grandfather Pierre Poitras served on the 1869 Provisional Government. Dr. Poitras Pratt has long been active in the realm of Métis education, serving as the first-ever Associate Director, Métis Education at the Rupertsland Institute, a Métis Centre of Excellence in 2012–13. She was recruited to the Werklund School of Education in 2013 and continues to serve the Métis community through her academic role at the Rupertsland Centre for Métis Research (University of Alberta). Her 2020 book, *Digital Storytelling in Indigenous Education: A Decolonizing Journey for a Metis Community*, has sold 300 copies globally. As an award-winning educator and researcher, she has published work on reconciliatory and decolonizing pedagogy, critical service-learning, academic integrity from an Indigenous perspective, and the integration of arts in education. Yvonne earned the national Alan Blizzard Award for Collaborative Teaching in 2021.

Angela Rancourt is a Michif educator in St. Louis, Saskatchewan. She was raised in the village of St. Louis along the South Saskatchewan River, where she completed high school and then pursued her dreams of becoming a teacher and attended the Saskatchewan Urban Native Teacher Education Program (SUNTEP) in Saskatoon. Angela graduated from SUNTEP with a BEd in 2009 and a MEd in 2019 from the Gabriel Dumont Institute and University of Regina. She is a mother and an auntie. Her current role is the Michif Early Learning Program Coordinator for the school in her hometown of St. Louis. Angela is a part of the River Women Collective, and is committed to the wellness of families, communities, the land, and the rivers. Her work is guided by the Grandmothers and shared with the youth.

Lisa Shepherd is a celebrated artist and highly respected cultural ambassador and knowledge carrier for the Métis Nation, evidenced by the growth of her artist business, vast number of communities she has empowered through workshop facilitation, number of youth she has mentored, and by the acquisition of her culturally inspired art displayed across the nation and internationally. Lisa has employed her skill in interpreting contemporary Métis perspectives and ancestral histories into artistic works to create space for Indigenous and non-Indigenous communities to learn about Métis culture. In doing so, she has revitalized culture and increased the visibility of Métis people in British Columbia (BC) and across the homeland. Originally from Treaty 6 Territory and within the Métis homelands and Métis Nation of Alberta Region 4, Lisa now resides on the unceded traditional territory of Katzie and Kwantlen First Nations, in BC. Her kinship ties include Campion, Dumont, Grant, Gladue, Lussier, and Chartrand lines. Her ancestors fought in the Victory of Frog Plain, founded the Laboucan Settlement (now Duhamel), and created beadwork that are identity pieces, containing stories that are cherished today.

Allyson Stevenson is a Métis historian and adoptee whose family is from Kinistino, Saskatchewan, and was raised in Regina. She joined the Indigenous Studies Department at the University of Saskatchewan as the Gabriel Dumont Research Chair in Métis Studies in July 2020. She obtained her PhD in history from the University of Saskatchewan in 2015. Her award-winning book, *Intimate Integration: The Sixties Scoop and the Colonization of Indigenous Kinship*, was published with the University of Toronto Press in December 2020. Her current research specializes in histories of Indigenous women's political organizing, the Sixties Scoop, and Cree-Métis histories of the Saskatchewan River. She works closely with the community of Cumberland House, Saskatchewan, to support their efforts to develop a local museum and is undertaking oral histories of women's relationship to water. Allyson Stevenson's paternal Anglo-Métis family line includes the Fidlers, who resided in Headingley, Manitoba, the Isbister Settlement (now Prince Albert, Saskatchewan), Flett's Springs, and Kinistino, Saskatchewan; the Sayeses, who resided in Glen Mary/Pahonan and Cumberland House; the Swains; the Isbister/Bears; the Saunders; and countless other unnamed Indigenous women ancestors. As an adoptee who was raised in a non-Indigenous family in Regina, Stevenson reconnected with her family of origin in 1996.

Dr. Kisha Supernant (she/her) is a citizen of the Métis Nation of Alberta and a Professor of Anthropology at the University of Alberta. She is the Director of the Institute of Prairie and Indigenous Archaeology. Kisha is Métis through her father's side of her family, with roots in the Red River settlement (Knott and Linklater) and connections to many Métis, Cree, and Mohawk families in Alberta (Pelltier/Campbell, Gauthier, Gladu, Blandion/Dion, Desjarlais, Calihoo/Kwarakante, Grey, Cardinal, and Nipissing). Her mother's family are settlers from southwest England. She leads the Exploring Métis Identity Through Archaeology project, a collaborative research project that takes a relational approach to exploring the material past of the Métis. Her research on Métis material heritage, specifically archaeology, explores how the belongings of the ancestors can help support contemporary Métis communities. She uses technology to map how these belongings pattern through space and time, demonstrating Métis presence throughout the homeland. She also uses remote sensing to locate unmarked burials of Indigenous peoples who died at Indian residential schools or other institutions at the request of Indigenous communities.

Dr. Caroline Tait grew up on a farm along the river road between St. Louis and MacDowall, Saskatchewan. She spends much of her time working from her home in Elk Ridge, Saskatchewan, and is mother to her son, Skender. As a Métis scholar and member of the Métis Nation–Saskatchewan, Caroline is a nominated Tier 1 Canada Research Chair in Indigenous Health Equity and Inclusion, at the University of Calgary, where she also holds a joint appointment as a Full Professor in the Faculty of Social Work and the Cumming School of Medicine. Caroline has a BA and PhD in Anthropology from McGill University and a MA in Medical Anthropology from the University of California, Berkeley. She also completed a Post-Doctoral Fellowship in Social and Transcultural Psychiatry at McGill University and the Aboriginal Healing Foundation and was a Fulbright Visiting Fellow in Anthropology at Harvard University. Caroline is the founder of the Saskatchewan First Nations and Métis Organ Donation and Transplantation Network and the International Indigenous Organ Donation and Transplantation (ODT) Network. Her work addresses inequities experienced by Indigenous peoples in ODT treatment and care, and promotes and supports their inclusion in ODT decision-making, research, and knowledge mobilization. She is also the lead author of the *Saskatchewan Métis Research and Data Sovereignty Guidelines*. Caroline's yard is adorned by many beautiful rocks.

Angie Tucker is a member of the Manitoba Métis Federation (Bison Local) and the Métis Nation of Alberta (Local 87). Her family is from the St. Andrews and Poplar Point area of Manitoba, consisting of the Parenteau, Spence, Hallett, and Norquay families. She continues to hold relationships with the Métis Settlements in northern Alberta in addition to local relationships with Métis Nation Region 3, Les Femmes Michif Otipemisiwak, and Indigenous communities living in the traditional territories of the Niitsitapi and Treaty 7 region. With an MA in social anthropology from the University of Calgary, her fieldwork uncovered how residents of Buffalo Lake Métis Settlement in Alberta continue to articulate contemporary forms of Métis belonging. She examined both the complex role of "locality" and the category of "community" as vital components in the transmission and continuation of cultural knowledge. She is a current PhD candidate in Native Studies at the University of Alberta; her work centres on the importance of community-based research that privileges Indigenous women's knowledge.

Dawn Wambold is a member of the Métis Nation of Alberta and a PhD student at the University of Alberta. Born and raised between the Bow and Red Deer rivers, and within sight of the Rocky Mountains, Dawn continues to live in the same lands that her ancestors were intimately connected to. Her Métis and Cree family names include Piche (aka Peechee or Ermineskin), Dumont, Blandion, Boudreau, and many others. Her Irish and English settler family names include Hagerty, Walton, Ward, and Chapman. As a scholar at the Institute of Prairie and Indigenous Archaeology, she is honoured to be able to tell the stories of her ancestors using archaeology. Her research focuses on the lives of the Métis in southern Alberta and Saskatchewan during the latter half of the nineteenth century.